Approaches to the
Twentieth-Century Novel

APPROACHES TO THE TWENTIETH-CENTURY NOVEL

Edited and with an introduction
by JOHN UNTERECKER

THOMAS Y. CROWELL COMPANY

New York / Established 1834

Contents

Contents

Introduction

JOHN UNTERECKER

I THINK there is no such thing as "the modern novel," or if there is, it is something that was practiced by Laurence Sterne and Jane Austen, by Dickens and by Melville—something that was anticipated by Chaucer and by Cervantes, by Dante and by Homer. As even the most "experimental" modern novelist knows —Joyce, for instance, or Beckett—there is no progress in art. There is only contemporary variation on ancient form. What is modern about the modern novel is the copyright date.

There is really nothing at all to say about "the modern novel."

Yet if one cannot make grand statements about the modern novel, there are a good many interesting things that can be said about individual novelists—and about some of the overlapping characteristics which they share. With only a little ingenuity, one can find patterns—"aspects"—that run through the work of a good percentage of our most important contemporary writers.

One of these patterns is, of course, pattern itself. For many of the writers of modern fiction—particularly writers who reached artistic maturity in the 1920's—have been caught up in that great surge of analytical "structuring" that until very recently dominated all of the arts and that is still probably the single most potent force of the recent past, a force against which, needless to say, numerous very young writers, painters, musicians—and even critics—are rebelling.

The great patterned novels of Joyce, Virginia Woolf, Gide, Mann, Faulkner, and Proust come first to mind—novels like Virginia Woolf's *To the Lighthouse*. That novel makes a three-decker sandwich out of time, its major structural elements—time-past and time-present—enclosing a world of time-passing, a world of flux, death, disintegration, and disorder against which the artist must pit all of his strength.

The patterns made by various kinds of time are probably, in fact, those most frequently encountered by the attentive reader —and though not all of them are quite so neat as those in Mrs. Woolf's novel, they show up in book after book. It is the twenty-four hours of June 16, 1904, which tick off Homeric parallels in Joyce's *Ulysses*, just as it is an arrangement of slabs of time which shapes Faulkner's *The Sound and the Fury* and which makes possible its investigation of the complex tensions of the modern world. It is the elastic "lost" time of Proust's *Remembrance of Things Past*, a time that gains meaning only in retrospect, which dominates that huge book and which is controlled by the evocative power of significant remembered objects.

Designs of time hold together some books and designs of significant objects help recapture time in others. In still others, "leitmotifs" of all sorts—everything from physical gesture in Thomas Mann's *Magic Mountain* to a pattern of vowel sounds in Joyce's *Finnegans Wake*—offer the novelist machinery for constructing the ordered world of a book. When these recurring things seem significant enough, we label them *symbols* and sometimes fret about their "meanings." Since symbols—by their very nature—mean different things to different people, we should not be surprised to find them variously interpreted, not only by readers of books but by characters in them. The wind-blown sky writing in Virginia Woolf's *Mrs. Dalloway* that "spells" something different to everyone who looks at it is a good illustration of this sort of symbol. The "sucking stones" in Beckett's *Malone Dies* might be a good illustration of a different kind of symbol—one a little closer to allegory—were it not possible that they are deliberately meaningless. Beckett, after all, ended one of his novels with the sentence: "No symbols where none intended."

But intended or unintended, symbols help authors give form to their works, and almost always help make meaningful otherwise chaotic reality. I must say "almost always," for one quickly thinks of all those metamorphosed objects and actions in Kafka which, ominously, madden both central character and reader. Like the hard edges which outline cloud castles and which give way while we watch to evolve nebulous new structures, Kafka's "symbols" seem always to be dissolving into one another. In his slippery world of shape-changers, design exists in a flow of misinterpreted symbols, a "right" interpretation carefully withheld.

Kafka's symbols, like many of the symbols in Lawrence and Conrad, remind us of reality—but it is more often than not the reality of dream, that special part of our lives in which we can have our cake and eat it too. Though authors knew about and drew on dream imagery long before the birth of Freud or Jung —such imagery runs rampant, for example, in writers as different as Keats, Blake, and Shakespeare—it is certainly true that the investigations of modern psychoanalysis have encouraged many novelists to transplant the vivid material of night to the nightmare world of their fiction. In this world, obsessed characters climb magic mountains, find church arches transforming themselves into pagan rainbows, or enter—as in E. M. Forster's *Passage to India*—caves more destructive and more terrifying than holes in the ground have any right to be. Now that we are all conscious of the unconscious (its symbolic manipulations of our daytime reality having become common knowledge), we are perhaps properly prepared to feel the power of that sea which isolates, unnerves, destroys, yet sometimes capriciously supports many of Conrad's characters, and we can appreciate, as his contemporaries could not, the psychological justice of Captain Ahab's destruction by Melville's Moby Dick.

Of course other patterns than those of echoing theme and symbol weave through the patterned novels of our time. A design of observation holds together many important novels, particularly some of the strongest by André Gide, Lawrence Durrell, Ford Madox Ford, and William Faulkner.

Realizing that no two persons can ever see precisely the same event, these novelists show how false the notion of "objective truth" can be. *The Counterfeiters, The Alexandria Quartet, The Good Soldier,* and *Absalom, Absalom!* are each built on reports of mutually examining characters who, needless to say, report mutually contradictory versions of the events in which they participate. Of these novels, Gide's is probably the most carefully worked out, the layers and layers of reporting and re-examination showing us something of the density and diversity of that reality we so glibly assume everyone else to share. Durrell, finding support for his approach to fiction both in psychoanalysis and in nuclear physics, first works out his ideas in literary criticism, then makes of *The Alexandria Quartet* an elaborate metaphor for "the space-time continuum." Ford and Faulkner, more casually, allow naïve observers conversations with other naïve observers. From their conflicting versions of shared days, the intangibility of truth emerges—and something of the human dilemma: man caught in an unending and unsuccessful struggle to understand the persons and events which touch him. Finally, indeed, like the other men about them, Ford's observers, and Faulkner's also, are revealed to be incognito figures hidden behind a set of shifting disguises, their "true selves" as elusive to them as they are to those curious judges who spend their lives classifying, reclassifying, and always misclassifying them.

Of course not all modern fiction has the sort of formal designs I have been discussing. As I have already suggested, a number of young writers—struck by the lies art imposes on the world —have tried to find a way to represent *natural* (and therefore chaotic) life. To some extent they were anticipated by D. H. Lawrence, a man who believed in natural form but who was so pressed by his own nature that he frequently intruded into his fiction outbursts of private feeling; by Gertrude Stein, some of whose novels record conversation so faithfully as to approximate conversation's aimlessness; and by that arch formalist André Gide who—in spite of a most ordering mind—insisted on the possibility of the *gratuitous act,* the reckless and pointless display of will that in human affairs is the moral equivalent of mathematical chance—and that, like mathematical chance, may never really

occur. Among younger writers, Robbe-Grillet—studiously recording a close-up world of objects—is in the long run perhaps as anti-
formal as Jack Kerouac, who attempts self-consciously unrevised
"spontaneous" novels, or Marc Saporta, that do-it-yourself novelist whose boxed *Composition No. 1*, printed on separate sheets of
paper, can be shuffled like a deck of cards to produce, at each
perusal, a new sequence of events. So long as we have readers,
however, form will undoubtedly triumph over chaos. For man
—that ordering animal who discovers a zodiac of bears, snakes,
and heroes in the star-spattered heavens—imposes, will it or not,
pattern on everything he looks at.

And that brings me to the pattern of this book, a book intended to supplement half a dozen important works by half a
dozen major twentieth-century novelists. These novelists, selected
from the dozens who might have been drawn on, have in common three things: that they are strongly individualistic, that they
are dead, and that had they not lived, contemporary fiction would
be vastly different than it now is.

Because this is a book about very different sorts of books, it
will be most useful for the reader if it is read not as a patterned
thing but if it is read piecemeal—if it is read not even as a set of
"introductions" to the novels but rather, section by section, *after*
each of the novels has been read. And since every essay in this
book was independently written, there is little point in reading
them in the sequence in which they are printed. They are not deliberately related one to the other, and their authors subscribe to
no agreed-on critical approaches. When these critics were asked
to contribute essays they were asked, as a matter of fact, to do
only one thing: to set down what for them were the most significant aspects of the work to be considered. At this point editorial
supervision ceased. The essays that resulted will succeed, I think,
in accomplishing all any criticism can accomplish as they lure
readers into serious thought—perhaps even a second reading of
the books under discussion.

The patterns that emerge from this unpatterned book are,
therefore, likely to show up—if at all—only in retrospect. Yet

some of them seem inevitable: particularly a recurring picture of modern man hopelessly lost in his homemade mechanical universe. Undoubtedly every age has seen itself as the most disordered in history, but certain ages—the seventeenth century and the twentieth—have spent a great deal more time than others talking about their disorders. In *Light in August,* in *A Portrait of the Artist as a Young Man,* and in *Women in Love* there is persistent reference to a past—not necessarily better than the present—which in its heavily structured design helps account for present restlessness. For in apposition to that more coherent world, ours seems meaningless. The contrasted heroic past—whether of the Civil War or of the Trojan War—gives Faulkner and, as Evert Sprinchorn convincingly argues, Joyce opportunities to examine the special neuroses of a present in which only spiritual heroism seems possible. Lawrence—less interested in heroism than in whole men—finds even spiritual heroism repellent. For he is sickened by a world that pulls away both from Christian and from Platonic love and that in the place of those generous, ordering affections sets up in the name of one and in defiance of the other the nineteenth- and twentieth-century dog-eat-dog world of greedy individualism. Conrad, Gide, and Kafka—content to look directly at that which is before them—make no effort to discover a better past or, for that matter, a worse one, the dominant image in *Nostromo,* in *The Counterfeiters,* and in *The Trial* being that of an apparently ordered world which is in fact so shot through with corruption that its order is at best superficial and at worst a screen of middle-class righteousness behind which moral counterfeiters cheerfully corrupt the innocent.

Perhaps because corruption seems so omnipresent to all six of these authors, several of them have gone out of their way to locate characters innocent enough or wise enough or disillusioned enough to endure. And if not every author can discover a Lena Grove, or even a Mrs. Gould, figures like Gide's Edouard and Joyce's Stephen suggest that one way to control the disorder of life is to be a recorder of its shifting patterns.

These two portrayed artists, of course, are only representatives of a large group of fictive writers—Mann's Aschenbach, for instance, in *Death in Venice*—who, in some ways resembling their creators, are just different enough from the men who made them to tease us into long discussions on the relationship between biography and art. That these are not pointless discussions—that they are, indeed, necessary discussions if we are to understand anything at all about the creative process—is amply demonstrated in the following essays.

For a writer's material is always drawn from his double world—that macrocosm in which he is born, walks, talks, eats, makes love, and ultimately dies, and that other world, the distorting microcosm of his mind, in which, in daydream and dream, he improves on the exterior world; in nightmare, is attacked by it; in "rational" moments, attempts to discover meaning in so very much walking, talking, and loving. If he is talented enough, if he is a great writer, he may manage to disguise some of the mirrors into which he now and then glances, mirrors that reflect not just the face of a man but beyond him the serried windows that open out onto the world. But no writer is so great as finally to eliminate himself completely from his book. Joyce's Stephen Dedalus thought he might become such a writer; but Joyce himself went on to scatter distorted portraits of his friends and acquaintances through *Ulysses* and dismembered elements of himself through *Finnegans Wake*.

The great achievement of the great writer, however, is not so much the disguised or undisguised self-portrait but the transfer of one or more of his portraits onto our faces. When we go beyond "understanding" Stephen or Edouard or K. or even Decoud and instead begin to see the world through his eyes, when we literally enter into the novel and find ourselves subsequently never able entirely to escape from its scenery and its citizens, then a kind of literary achievement has taken place that is complex and most personal—a real communication between reader and, in each of these novels, a dead man, an author who had incorporated so much life into his work that we have no choice but to be involved in that dead man's still-living power.

Though this achievement seems—if we think of it long enough—miraculous, it is achieved through miracles of technique. And it is technique, the process by which one man's words are transformed into another man's feelings, which most of the following essays most diligently explore. For it is one thing to be moved by fiction, quite another to know why one has been moved. In a world which seems to fall apart, some measure of joy may come to us in contemplating the structure of the structures that Joyce, Lawrence, Kafka, Conrad, Gide, and Faulkner, in defiance of time and the elements, built well.

A Portrait of the Artist as Achilles

EVERT SPRINCHORN

THE CONSTERNATION that first greeted Joyce's *Ulysses* was due less to its obscenity than to the fact that it was being read as a naturalistic novel rather than as a symbolistic one. What holds all that naturalistic detail together is not plot or characterization but symbols and parallels. Unless one is aware of them *Ulysses* collapses and crumbles into meaninglessness. To guard against that misfortune Joyce collaborated with Stuart Gilbert in drawing up a guide to the novel. There also exist one or more charts to aid the readers of *Finnegans Wake* who might otherwise still be all at sea. But strangely enough there is no adequate guide to Joyce's first novel, *A Portrait of the Artist as a Young Man.*

Perhaps everyone who reads the *Portrait* for the first time puts the book down with a sense of disappointment arising from the last chapter. There one finds that the autobiographical hero Stephen Dedalus has been transformed from a sensitive boy into an apparently insensitive, insufferable, and "indigestibly Byronic" [1] young man. How can one explain this change except by assuming, as some critics do, that Joyce intended to show his hero as an egotistic youth who will shortly get his comeuppance? And yet I wonder if this view does not offend the deepest instincts of every reader. During four of the five chapters in the book, the reader

---

[1] Hugh Kenner, "The *Portrait* in Perspective," in *James Joyce: Two Decades of Criticism,* edited by Seon Givens, New York, 1948, p. 173.

follows with great sympathy the attempts of Stephen to discover himself as an artist and to assert himself as a human being in a world where he has lived only a shadowy existence because he is half-blind, oversensitive, physically weak, and unhappy in love. At the end of the fourth chapter, in the memorable scene by the seashore, the miracle happens: Stephen is transformed. Is it at all likely that Joyce would have constructed his novel so that the regeneration of the sympathetic hero would be followed by his decline into a priggishness and egotism that alienates the reader from him? Aware that Joyce would scarcely have undercut his novel to this extent, the critics who think Stephen is insufferable have sought to detach the fifth chapter and to regard it as a separate work, different in tone and treatment from the others and serving as a bridge to *Ulysses*.[2] However, Chapter V is Chapter V, and what we wish to know first of all is how it follows from the previous four chapters, not how it anticipates another work. And what we wish to understand finally is how Stephen becomes an artist, not an insufferable young man with a chip on his shoulder.

In order to reveal to a select few the secret of the making of a dedicated artist, while at the same time concealing that secret from the insensitive and uncomprehending multitude, Joyce made use of all the characteristic techniques of the nineteenth-century symbolist, investing naturalistic detail with significance, implicitly comparing his characters to mythological, historical, and literary figures, transforming his symbols one into another in accordance with changes in mood or in point of view, minimizing external action in order to observe the movements of the soul, and constructing his work so that the relation of part to part conveys more meaning than what the hero does or thinks. The *Portrait*, not *Ulysses*, is the first novel in which Joyce perfected these techniques. One need only compare *Stephen Hero*, the early draft of the novel, with the finished *Portrait* to appreciate the extent to whch Joyce reshaped the factual, autobiographical material in accordance with symbolist principles. The *Portrait* cannot be read like an ordinary novel any more than *Ulysses* can.

[2] *Ibid.*

To get at the heart of this novel, and to appreciate fully the brilliant technical achievement represented by the fifth chapter, Joyce expects his ideal reader to pay minute attention to detail and to have an intimate knowledge of Christian lore, Greek myth, obscure initiation mysteries, and nineteenth-century literature.

In no other work was Joyce so secretive as in this, his most personal and most intimate work. It is significant that he never offered to help his readers with a key to the novel; he did not even provide an allusive title to hint that they should look for a key or that here was something more than the conventional *Bildungsroman*. Yet the secret of the artist lies there, buried in its quiet, dark depths, depths where the soul of an artist "has a slow and dark birth, more mysterious than the birth of the body" (203).[3]

Bird and Water

To penetrate those depths one might as well begin at the beginning and consider the symbols that face the reader on the opening two pages. Five symbols can be isolated: cow, rose, water (in the form of urine), colors (Dante's paint brushes), and the bird.[4] Each of these symbols, with one exception, is associated in Stephen's mind with something fairly pleasant. The exception is the bird, which here takes the form of an eagle that will pull out Stephen's eyes if he will not apologize for wanting to marry Eileen. In effect this last bit of the symbolic prelude conjoins girl, bird, and eyes in a complex image that might serve as an emblem to the *Portrait*.

Such a coalescence of symbols represents one of the basic techniques by which a subjective artist makes his most significant statements. In the first, fourth, and fifth chapters there occur moments crucial to our understanding of the *Portrait* in which the fragmentary symbols of the prelude are put together to form one

[3] All page references are to the Viking edition of 1964. For a list of corresponding pages in other editions, see the table on page 23.

[4] One's selection of symbols is bound to be somewhat arbitrary. For a slightly different approach see William York Tindall, A Reader's Guide to James Joyce, New York, 1959.

majestic mandala of harmony and wholeness in the mind of Stephen.

The first chapter describes Stephen's experiences at Clongowes Wood School. This is his first time away from home and, being the youngest boy at the school, he has a hard time of it. His weak eyes prevent him from taking part in games with the other boys. He is made fun of, pushed into a ditch, gets sick, and is sent to the infirmary. After the Christmas holidays he learns more of the unjust ways of the world when he is unfairly chastised for not having prepared his lessons, although he has been officially excused from his studies while his glasses are being repaired. Summoning up all his courage, he goes to the rector and obtains justice.

The narrative level of this chapter is supported throughout by symbolic underpinning. The two dominant symbols are bird and water. The bird is associated with Stephen's eyes on the playing field, where the football in flight looks like a heavy bird to his weak eyes. Already associated in the prelude with apologizing and eye pulling, the bird accumulates further unpleasant associations as Stephen's humiliation and pain increase. The chastising pandybat used at Clongowes is called a "turkey" (30), and later the sound of the cricket bats is linked with the pandybat (45).

In a similar way water in its various manifestations provides clues to Stephen's psyche. It appears first at Clongowes as the cold, slimy water or urine of the ditch into which Stephen is pushed. The image of this prompts a thought of mother and of a more pleasant kind of water, the tea that she used to serve (10). Subsequently the ditch water is associated with the wetness of a maternal kiss and with the question of whether it is right or wrong to kiss one's mother (14–15). The essence of Stephen's experiences at Clongowes Wood School is symbolized by the turf-colored bath water, the very thought of which fills him with a "vague fear" (22) and leaves an indelible impression on him; years later the image is still haunting him (160–61, 174). In the form of the stolen altar wine, water becomes a symbol of punishment. The episode of the stolen wine leads into the episode of Stephen's unjust punishment. These two episodes, which are really one, contain references to the stale urine smell in the square where the fellows were caught "smugging," and to the turf-colored bath water (43, 45, 54). The world as a cruel and unjust place is summed up in these images of water at its worst.

When Stephen achieves justice and when the world seems less unkind to him, the bird and water symbols also undergo transformations and are brought harmoniously together. The link between the two is the pandybat or "turkey." The bird symbol lurks behind both the pandybat and the football, the former standing for unjust punishment and the latter for a world of normal boyhood happiness in which Stephen cannot participate, and the cause of both the punishment and his separation from other boys is Stephen's weak eyes, with which the bird was first associated. Besides giving rise to thoughts of flogging, the pandybat also evokes the cricket bat of the playing field. And it is the pick-pock sound of the cricket bats that merges with the "pick, pack, pock, puck" of "drops of water in a fountain slowly falling in the brimming bowl." The bringing together of bat and water frames the episode dealing with justice (41, 59). When Stephen leaves the rector's office after having gained redress for his unjust punishment, the old painful and fearful thoughts are drowned for a while in the brimming bowl.

Another and more momentous transformation and coalescence of symbols occurs at the end of the fourth chapter, the climax of the novel, when Stephen cuts himself off from the church and family and commits himelf to art. Leaving home, he crosses a bridge, passes a squad of Christian Brothers headed in the opposite direction, and finds himself down by the sea. Here at the edge of the sea he had always dreaded (167), he experiences a transfiguration. In an ecstatic spell he arises "from the grave of boyhood" (170) and responds to the call of life. In the sublimest passage of the novel, the boy becomes a young man, the young man becomes an artist.

Here the symbols do more than reinforce the climax; they constitute it. All five notes of the prelude are here sounded together in one majestic chord. Water appears as the sea itself, the sea of life. The rose becomes the celestial rose to signify Stephen's transfiguration. The image I have labeled "colors" appears in the phrase "a day of dappled seaborne clouds" (166–67), which represents Stephen's commitment to the art of language, as he tries to put into words the feelings the colors of the day stir up in him. The cow is transformed into a bull when Stephen's friends, crying, "Bous Stephaneforos!" (168), greet him as the bull. (The whole scene, by the way, takes place on the breakwater known as the Bull.) And the bird is transformed into the vision of a beautiful, cranelike girl, standing in the water (171).

After this climactic scene the bird, which is the most important of the five symbols, is no longer fearful to Stephen; and in the last chapter it is actually identified at times with Stephen himself when he becomes Thoth, the ibis-headed god of writers, and Dedalus, "the hawklike man" (225) who will fly by the nets of "nationality, language, religion" (203). We might trace the development of this artist's soul by studying the transformations the bird undergoes from the terrorizing eagle of the prelude to the birdlike Dedalus of the last page. In Chapter II, where the bird appears in the guise of Vincent Heron, a boy with "a bird's face as well as a bird's name" (76), the symbol is still a very hostile one. Tormented and humiliated by Heron, Stephen is reminded of other humiliations and isolates himself from his comrades and from his father. The whole chapter is devoted to the exile motive, as the early references to the outhouse (60), to Napoleon (63) and the Count of Monte-Cristo (62–63) indicate. Most of the time Stephen pictures himself as the Count and dreams of the day when he will meet Mercédès, the heroine of Dumas's novel, in the real world. Anticipating the climax of the *Portrait*, Stephen has a premonition that if they should meet "he would be transfigured. Weakness and timidity and inexperience would fall from him in that magic moment" (66). Fitting Chapter II into the scheme of the novel, we sense that Stephen withdraws from family and friends and turns to the life of the imagination because his weak eyes separate him from the outside world and because the injustice he encounters in that world lead him to reject it. The withdrawal and the rejection are both due to the hostile bird; and when Stephen returns from his spiritual exile as a completely changed being, the bird reflects the transformation by becoming first a winged girl and finally the winged artificer.

But why should Joyce take the ninety pages of Chapter V to effect this final transformation? And what light does it shed on Stephen's conversion to the aesthetic life? Not very much—at least, not by itself.

The Wrath of Achilles

Relying only on symbols to guide us through the novel's "strange dark cavern of speculation" (178), we might never find our way in and out. Some other means must be employed. Now, if Joyce insists on comparing his hero to Daedalus, might he not elsewhere be drawing less obvious but still meaningful parallels to other mythical heroes? Not truncated parallels that are cut off after a few pages, as in the case of the Count of Monte-Cristo, but extended parallels that would link together the beginning and end of the novel.

At first glance Daedalus would seem to be the obvious choice, were it not for the fact that Stephen becomes an artist only in the last third of the novel. We need a hero who is early separated from his loved ones; who feels hurt and humiliated by an unjust world; who withdraws from it in disgust; but who finally gets hold of himself and re-enters the arena of life to do battle with his enemies. Drawing Stephen's story in such bold outline suggests immediately the hero Joyce had in mind: Achilles.

Like Achilles, Stephen is proud and swift of foot, running being the only physical activity he indulges in (61).[5] Achilles' mother rendered him invulnerable, except for his heel, by dipping him in the River Styx. The slimy, rat-infested ditch into which Stephen is pushed serves as his Styx, and the whole unfortunate episode is associated in Stephen's mind with his mother (14–15); and Stephen, like Achilles, also has a vulnerable spot, his eyes. Furthermore, like Achilles who was disguised as a girl to es-

[5] In *Stephen Hero,* he plays cricket and other games.

cape serving as a warrior, Stephen lives among women for a while and is even mistaken for a girl at one point (67–68).

But our main concern should be the events related in the *Iliad* and especially that part of it known as "The Wrath of Achilles." Agamemnon arouses Achilles' ire when he takes Achilles' concubine Briseis from him. Stung by the injustice of this, the warrior not only refuses to fight with his fellow Greeks against the Trojans but he prays for the intervention of Zeus against Agamemnon. To place the Greek leader in a difficult position Zeus sends him a misleading dream to the effect that the city of Troy is ready to fall. After the deliberations of an oneirocritic council of generals the war is resumed, the highlight of the first day of fighting being the indecisive duel between Paris and Menelaus. But the tide of battle gradually turns against the misguided Greeks, and Agamemnon, realizing now that he cannot capture Troy without the aid of Achilles, sends an embassy to the sulking warrior, offering to return Briseis. Achilles, with his close friend Patroclus, entertains the embassage but rejects the offer (Book IX). Also on the night of the embassy Odysseus and Diomedes go on a successful scouting expedition to capture Dolon, a Trojan spy sent out by Hector (Book X).

The first two chapters of the *Portrait* provide the parallels to these events. The Christmas dinner at the Dedalus home corresponds to Agamemnon's council of war, while the duel between Paris and Menelaus is fought out between the anticlerical, pro-Parnell Casey and the devout Catholic Dante in their memorable quarrel over the religious and political state of Ireland. If the situation by itself does not seem to justify my referring to it as a parallel, small details do. Dante, representing the average Irish citizen, is Menelaus, whose name means "might of the people"; and Casey, who has a "purse of silver in his throat" (28), is Paris, whose name means "wallet." The arrow that Paris shoots at Menelaus is transmogrified into the mouthful of tobacco juice that Casey spits into the eye of an old Parnell-hating harridan (36–37). Here Joyce is merely amusing himself, and the parallel has no great relevance to the principal theme of the novel.

Of greater relevance is the parallel to the scouting expedition. In Joyce the parallel is drawn in the section on injustice at Clongowes, which opens with some mysterious schoolboy pranks for which all the boys are to be punished (40–46). Later, and for a different reason, Stephen is wrongly punished, but he protests to the rector and scores a victory over Father Dolan. The change of one letter converts Dolan to Dolon, the Trojan spy. But, whereas Odysseus and Diomedes are the capturing heroes in the *Illiad*, Joyce makes Stephen-Achilles the hero in his version; and by doing so he relates the defeat of Dolan to the initial cause of the hero's wrath, while in the *Iliad* the capture of the spy has no direct bearing on Achilles.

Recalling the origin of the hero's feeling that the world is unjust to him, we come to the parallel that tells us most about the novel. Achilles is mad at the world because Agamemnon took his favorite girl from him. Stephen's sickness and disgust begin when he is sent off to school and separated from his mother. "Do you kiss your mother before you go to bed?" asks one of the boys at Clongowes, and Joyce makes the question relate directly to Stephen's being pushed into the ditch of slimy water and to his subsequent physical illness (9, 10, 14–15, 20). Here in the expository stage of the novel the incestuous attachment that will provide its overriding motive is stated for the first time. Once separated from his mother Stephen is "sick in his heart" (13) and "wastes his heart out sitting" (*Iliad*, I, 491–92) on the sidelines of life (cf. 67–70). Nor does his psyche recover its health until he is once again united with his mother. By keeping our eyes open to see how and when this happens, we can find our way through the "dark cavern of speculation."

In this Oedipal drama Simon Dedalus as father must play Agamemnon to Stephen's Achilles. In the *Iliad* Zeus answers Achilles' plea for justice by jeopardizing Agamemnon's position through a misleading dream. In the *Portrait* Stephen becomes the dreamer, but Simon remains the victim. Sick in the infirmary, Stephen dreams of the death of Parnell—a dream that will mislead us if we forget Stephen's ruminations about the death of a marshal on the battlefield (19) and the identification of Simon with the marshal (20: "His mother kissed him. Was that right?

His father was a marshal now."), and, finally, the association of Simon with the dead Parnell (39). Stephen's dream of Parnell's death is the expression of an unconscious wish that his father might die.

On the deepest level the second section [6] of Chapter I deals with a boy who is sick with life because he has been taken away from his mother and who blames his father for this cruelty. In the third section justice is temporarily restored to the world when Stephen goes to the head of the school to seek redress. In the corresponding scene in Homer, Achilles' mother, Thetis, goes to Zeus for justice. In the *Portrait* Zeus appears in the form of Phidias' awe-inspiring statue of him, fashioned out of gold and ivory, with four lions supporting the footstool, a work so magnificent that Zeus sent a bolt of thunder to show his approval. These attributes of the statue—gold, ivory, lions, and thunder—are glanced at in the opening pages of the section on injustice (40–42). That Stephen's victory in the rector's office represents a defeat for father is made clear on the Homeric level, where the unjust Agamemnon is disconcerted and punished upon the petition of Achilles' mother. The defeat for father must be understood as bringing Stephen unconsciously closer to a reunion with mother. This view is reinforced on the symbolic level, where the reunion is imaged at the end of the chapter by the brimming bowl of water—a maternal symbol.

Stephen's hostility toward his father is made obvious in the second chapter, where the father dies a second and lasting spiritual death, after which he fades from the novel. The chief incidents in the chapter are the Whitsuntide play, the humiliation of Stephen by three schoolmates in a flashback scene, and Stephen's visit to Cork with his father. The corresponding incidents in the Achilles story are, first, Patroclus' killing of Sarpedon (XVI); secondly, the embassy of Odysseus, Phoenix, and Ajax (IX), asking Achilles to end his exile and rejoin the Greek troops; and thirdly, the death of Patroclus (XVI).

The episode of Stephen's humiliation (78–82) is set within

---

[6] On the division into sections, see the table on page 23.

the episode of the Whitsuntide play (73–86) and is meant to relate to the main concern of the chapter: Stephen's loss of all respect for his father. The humiliation is prepared for by a little incident in which Stephen's father and Father Dolan have a hearty laugh together recalling Stephen's visit to the rector's office at Clongowes Wood School (72). What for Stephen had been an excruciating ordeal has become only a joke to Simon and Dolan. This brief incident corresponds to the moment in the *Iliad* when Agamemnon admits to having been wrong in his quarrel with Achilles and sends an embassy to lure the hero back to the battlefield. In the Joycean inversion of this scene, Simon-Agamemnon, far from making a gesture of reconciliation and admitting he is wrong, remains aloofly with the Jesuits-Greeks. Similarly, the three schoolboys, Heron, Boland, and Nash, who beat up Stephen and jeer at him for his heretical opinions are representatives of an Irish conformity that Stephen hates, just as Phoenix, Ajax, and Odysseus represent the Greeks whom Achilles hates. The bird that inflicts the torture on Stephen is a heron instead of a phoenix. Ajax ("of the earth") is Boland. Odysseus ("angry") is Nash (gnash). Phoenix is the envoy who offered Briseis back to Achilles; his Irish counterpart is Heron, who teases Stephen by saying that he saw Stephen's girl going in to the play and heard her talking about him to his father (76–77).

Performing in the Whitsuntide play, Stephen enjoys for a moment the happiness of boyhood (85), but immediately the play is over his joy turns to bitterness when he confronts his father, who by this time has become in Stephen's mind the chief advocate of Catholicism and Irish nationalism, of gentlemanliness and of everything that rings hollow in Stephen's ears (83–84). To find in the *Iliad* a parallel to this experience required considerable ingenuity, but Joyce worked it out. The theatre is described at some length as a festive ark (74, 85). Stephen's rejoicing in the ark is destroyed by his father's self-glorification or pride. In Joycean Greek this is rendered as "Patroclus kills Sarpedon," for Patroclus means "father's glory" and Sarpedon means "rejoicing in the ark."

Why does the episode occur at Whitsuntide when the church

commemorates the descent of the Holy Spirit? Joyce is either making a joke of the decline of Simon in his son's estimation, or suggesting that Heron who humiliates Stephen is the holy dove in another shape—and thereby further intimating that this kind of bitter experience, symbolized throughout by birds, is the making of Stephen as an artist and signifies the true descent of the Holy Spirit.

In the next section of Chapter II (86–96), Patroclus, that is "the glory of father," is utterly annihilated. Visiting Cork with his father, young Stephen grows more and more ashamed of him as one embarrassment follows another (93). The final blow is struck when Stephen realizes that Simon is old. In Homer, Patroclus was slain by Hector with the assistance of Chronos (XVI, 814–16). In Joyce, "the glory of father" is destroyed by Time—Chronos being the "brisk old man . . . called Johnny Cashman" [6a] (94–95)—with the assistance of that Irish traditionalism that is always hectoring Stephen.

After the death of his closest friend, Patroclus, Achilles in his hysterical, boundless grief defiles himself (XVIII). Joyce's Achilles in his loneliness, aware of "his own futile isolation," tries "to appease the fierce longings of his heart" (98) by abandoning his mind to orgiastic riots and his body to the whores he begins to visit at the very end of the chapter. The defilement continues through part of Chapter III.

In Chapter IV a reformed Stephen fights the "flood of temptation" (152). This may be an allusion to Achilles' fight with the River Scamandros (XXI), though I doubt it. In the climactic scene, however, at the end of the chapter, as Stephen contemplates the clouds and ponders the phrase "a day of dappled seaborne clouds" (432), the allusion is more obvious. In the corresponding scene of the *Iliad* (XVIII, 202–206), Achilles, beside himself with grief and rage, appears unarmed on the battlefield but is saved by Athena, who transfigures him by means of a cloud. The birdlike angel, wading in midstream, may be Athena herself, born of water, and the instructor of Daedalus in the arts that made him famous.

[6a] Time is money—hence the name Cashman.

Now, if the Homeric parallel would only continue through Chapter V, the problem of that chapter might be solved. An important event in the *Iliad* is the forging of Achilles' shield by Hephaestus (XVIII). In the *Portrait* the ugly dean of studies is Hephaestus beyond a shadow of doubt. His soul suggests a thundercloud; he builds fires; and he limps (184–88). (In real life the dean did not limp—nor does he in *Stephen Hero;* and his name was Father Butts, which accounts for the four candle butts he produces from the side pockets of his soutane.) However, Joyce makes a crucial change in his Hephaestus. From the verbal fencing that takes place between the dean and Stephen on the subject of language and aesthetics it becomes clear that Stephen has resolved to forge his own shield and that the priest is more enemy than friend (cf. 251). In a sense the whole chapter represents the shield of artistic creation that Stephen forges, which is not quite the same as the "conscience of his race" (253) to be forged after the novel closes. The *Portrait* ends with the hero about to do battle with his Hector, the old man with "redrimmed horny eyes," ignorant and Irish, with whom Stephen "must struggle all through this night till day come, till he or I lie dead" (252).

What has been said so far about the Achilles-Stephen parallel confirms the common view of this novel as being about a rebellious young spirit. But, more significantly, it brings to light a hidden aspect of the novel. The chief motivating force in this young man's life is an Oedipus complex, and the sickness of heart that incapacitates him throughout the first part is due to his having been separated from his favorite girl, his mother. A satisfactory conclusion should consist of a resolution to Stephen's psychological problem. Yet in Chapter V Stephen argues against Cranly's maternal allegiance and unregretfully repudiates his mother. What has brought about the change in Stephen from a shy, sick-of-life boy to a brash young man who will serve neither God nor mother? Instead of answering the questions I first raised, I seem only to have rephrased them. The illumination shed by Homer is not enough to lead us out of the dark cavern.

The Descent to Hell

If the Homeric parallel touches on only a few points in the fifth chapter, it seems to skip over virtually all of the third. Before we try to anwer the problem of the last chapter we might well ask ourselves what the relation of the middle chapter is to the rest of the work.

One quick glance tells us that it brings Stephen to the black pit of despair and then motivates his consideration of the church as his life's work. But if the extraordinary hell scene, which is the substance of the third chapter, represents the bottom of a pit, then the scenes preceding it may well represent steps leading down to it and the scenes coming after it may be steps leading up from it. To appreciate this aspect of the novel's structure it is necessary to ignore for the moment the division into chapters and consider instead the seventeen sections into which the novel is also divided. I can best do this by means of a table:

The table makes it clear that Joyce has constructed his novel so that the last eight sections reverse the action of the first eight. The ninth or middle section represents hell itself, and we should feel as we read the novel that we are descending into hell and rising from it.[7] At almost the dead center of the novel Stephen

[7] The 1964 Viking edition of the *Portrait*, edited by Chester G. Anderson and Richard Ellman and based on Joyce's holograph manuscript, divides the novel into nineteen sections by splitting sections 2 and 5 into two parts each. The first edition of 1916 had the seventeen sections I have listed, but with empty spaces on what are pages 27 and 78 of the 1964 edition. In 1917 Joyce submitted a list of errata directing the typesetter to insert asterisks in the empty space on page 27, add a space and insert asterisks on page 72, and eliminate the space on page 78. The English edition published in 1924 by Jonathan Cape adds yet another division, on page 70, making a total of twenty divisions. Even though it is known that Joyce read proofs of the Cape edition, Anderson in preparing the 1964 edition follows Joyce's 1917 list of changes. He argues that the 1924 edition is not authoritative because Joyce did not have his original manuscript on hand to refer to, and because Joyce, recuperating from an eye operation, did not read proof carefully. However, proceeding in that fashion, one might also question the authority of the 1917 errata on the grounds that Joyce did not have access to his original manuscript at that time either, and, furthermore, his mind was then occupied with *Ulysses*. (*Cont. p. 24.*)

* Viking edition, revised 1964. Also applies, with minor discrepancies, to Penguin Books edition.

† Viking Portable edition.

reaches the pit of his inferno and dies; but having touched bottom he immediately begins to rise.

> He had died. Yes. He was judged. A wave of fire swept through his body: the first. Again a wave. His brain began to glow. Another. His brain was simmering and bubbling within the cracking tenement of the skull. Flames burst forth from his skull like a corolla, shrieking like voices:
> —Hell! Hell! Hell! Hell! Hell!
> Voices spoke near him:
> —On hell.
> —I suppose he rubbed it into you well.

I would like to suggest, very tentatively, the following sequence of events giving rise to the discrepancy in the number of sections. Joyce wrote *Stephen Hero*, the original version of the novel, from 1904 to 1906. Between 1908 and 1914 he thoroughly reworked this material, boiling down the first 518 pages of the manuscript to the first two or three chapters of the *Portrait*. By the end of 1913 or early 1914, every aspect of the novel was clear in his mind, I think, except for the seventeen-section structure and the form the fifth chapter would take. The five-chapter division must have been clear in his mind from the time he started condensing *Stephen Hero*, for written in red crayon in the manuscript are the words, "End of First Episode of V" and "End of Second Episode of Chapter V" (see *Stephen Hero*, edited by Theodore Spencer, New York, 1955, pp. 31, 75). At the end of 1913 a publisher expressed an interest in the work, and Joyce gave his manuscript of the first three chapters to a typist while he set about writing the last two.

The idea of making the hell sermon the central episode in the novel may have come to Joyce when he started to write Chapter III. Probably the idea of the seventeen-section structure representing a descent to hell and an ascent from it did not occur to him until he started on Chapter IV. He realized he could incorporate this scheme into the basic design of the novel simply by making minor changes in the first two chapters to reduce the number of episodes to seven. However, in the meantime the typescript of the first three chapters had gone off to the publisher, so that Joyce had no opportunity to make those changes or even to determine precisely what they would be.

The *Portrait* was serialized in *The Egoist* in 1914 and 1915, with the printer getting so far ahead of Joyce that the installments had to be held up for five issues. Tear sheets of *The Egoist* provided the copy for the 1916 edition. The blank spaces there may indicate that Joyce had previously left instructions for making certain divisions in the first two chapters. But when Joyce drew up the 1917 list of errata, he may have forgotten, for the

—You bet he did. He put us all into a blue funk.

—That's what you fellows want: and plenty of it to make you work.

He leaned back weakly in his desk. He had not died. (125)

The reiterated "Hell!" forms the pivot on which the whole novel turns.

The references to blinds (window blinds) in the middle section (116, 127) serve also to remind us that Stephen is in the realm of the sightless presided over by Hades, the blind unseeing one. Later references to the blinds (153, 157) serve to identify the cadaverous and spectral priest who tries to prevail on Stephen

reasons mentioned above, how he wanted the first two chapters divided to bring them in line with the last two.

Frankly, I find it hard to believe that Joyce would ever forget such a matter. Two other possibilities are more likely. Either he abandoned the seventeen-section structural scheme as a bad job that could not be patched up properly, or he sent another letter or list of errata to supplement and correct the previous list. The first possibility is borne out by Joyce's acceptance of the 1924 edition with its twenty episodes. The second possibility finds some support in the strange fact that the American proofreaders, who corrected 147 of the 380 errors on Joyce's list, 99 percent of which are quite trivial, did not make the important one of inserting asterisks in the white space that was already available and would not require the resetting of any type. (See Peter Spielberg, "James Joyce's Errata for American Editions of *A Portrait of the Artist*," in *Joyce's Portrait: Criticisms & Critiques*, edited by Thomas E. Connolly, New York, 1962, p. 320 footnote.) It is to be noted that any of the dividing places indicated in the 1916 edition and the 1917 errata would work equally well in the scheme I have outlined, as long as there are just seven episodes in the first two chapters.

Joyce almost certainly got the idea for the seventeen-section structure from Strindberg's play *To Damascus,* Part I (1898). That play has seventeen scenes, the first eight showing the descent of the protagonist to the psychological inferno of the ninth scene, and the last eight reversing the order of the first eight as the hero works his way toward a new outlook on life. It is also, like the *Portrait,* a highly symbolic work filled with naturalistic detail, and it makes use of parallels to adumbrate the life of the hero, who is compared to Saul, Jacob, Jesus, and others. Beginning about 1907 Strindberg was one of the most talked about writers in Germany. Joyce could have read this play in the German translation that appeared in 1910, that is, before he started to write the last half of the *Portrait.* I suspect the Swedish dramatist was a major influence on the Irish novelist after 1907.

JOYCE

to enter the church as Hades himself. Joyce has in effect consigned the church to the ninth circle of the inferno. It is Stephen's turning away from the church and from religion that represents his rebirth. The central sermon on hell may describe the consequences of the sin of pride, of not serving God; but it is by not serving God, it is precisely by asserting his selfhood that Stephen climbs out of the inferno. The humility that the church teaches helps Stephen only as far out of the pit as the fear that the church instills had forced him down into it. He finds joy in life to the extent that he spurns the church and proudly recognizes his own individuality. Those who turn in revulsion from the sermon on hell should realize that in Joyce's eyes Stephen's pride is his greatest virtue and not a sin at all. The point needs to be emphasized since attempts are continually being made to palliate the blasphemy of Joyce's novel and to extenuate Stephen's pride as mere youthful error. But the blasphemy is there for all but the blind to see. Stephen's decision *not* to serve is the saving of his soul (cf. pp. 117, 161, and 239). To watch Stephen's boyish soul gradually withering away through the first eight sections, to see it virtually die in the ninth section as he succumbs to the humbling spirit of the church, and then to see Stephen come to life in the last eight sections and emerge with all the brashness of cocky youth in the last chapter is to experience the novel in the spirit with which it was written.

That the last eight sections do form counterparts to the first eight sections is clear enough from the table, but some of the entries require further explanation. In section 6 Stephen loses all respect for his irresponsible and disorderly father. In section 12 Stephen considers the "grave and ordered and passionless life that awaited him" (160) as a novice. A moment later he realizes that "his destiny was to be elusive of social or religious orders" (162). The connection between the two sections becomes apparent when Stephen smiles "to think that it was the disorder, the misrule and confusion of his father's house . . . which was to win the day in his soul" (162).

I have discussed the Whitsuntide play of section 5 as showing Stephen's disgust with his father. At the culmination of the

26 /

episode Stephen comes out from the theatre and expects to be greeted by his girl friend. Not finding her, he turns his back on his father and rushes off "amid the tumult of suddenrisen vapours of wounded pride and fallen hope and baffled desire" (86). The implication of this highly emotional response is that Stephen blames his father, who has no status of any kind, for his girl's desertion. The complement to this scene occurs in section 13 where Stephen wins his girl in the form of a seaside angel.

The various girls that appear throughout the *Portrait* merge one into another. Joyce's intention is to make us think of these various women as forming one figure. Whatever her name may be, The Girl is the second lead in this drama of the growth of a young man. Sections 4 and 14, like sections 5 and 13, show Stephen winning and losing his Girl; and Stephen's loss of The Girl in section 14 (183–84, 202, 215–16) is of great symbolic moment and should help to explain what happens in Chapter V.

The relationship of section 15, in which Stephen composes a poem, to section 3, in which Stephen goes to the rector for justice, may seem obscure at first. But a moment's thought makes us realize that both sections show Stephen accomplishing something worthwhile, with the brimming bowl and chalice, both symbolizing the water of his life in its most attractive aspect, serving as a manifest bond between the two sections. What should arouse our interest all the more here is that section 15 deals with artistic creation. If this novel is indeed about the making of an artist, this section should be the most important of all.

The Initiation Rites

Seeing the *Portrait* in terms of its seventeen sections incorporates the fifth chapter as part of the overall design. But anyone who rereads it now will certainly feel that there is still too much in that overlong chapter that neither Stephen's ascent from hell nor the adventures of Achilles can explain. Where can we look for further clues? Let us gain some perspective by considering a few of the most obvious aspects of the novel: the artist as a young man, a young man's first love affairs, a boy who is deeply attached to his mother and is separated from her, who harbors monstrous thoughts, who masturbates, who frequents whores. In a word, the novel is largely about puberty and adolescence. If it were exclusively so, the crucial scene might occur at the end of section 7, where Stephen visits the brothels of Dublin. Wandering into the maze of dirty streets, Stephen sees "before the doors and in the lighted halls groups . . . gathered arrayed as for some rite" (100). Which rite? Here the sense of strain or irrelevance in the description gives Joyce's secret away, as does the placement of the episode at the end of a chapter. If this rite marks the end of one chapter, might not other rites end other chapters? Or might not all the chapters comprise parts of one long ritual? Now what ritual that has to do with adolescence could Joyce have had in mind? The first guess is likely to be the right one: the initiation rites of ancient Eleusis, the so-called Great Mysteries.

For our purposes the best description of the Eleusinian mysteries is that given by Theon of Smyrna (fl. A.D. 130), an obscure explicator of these rites, but, as far as I know, the only one who establishes five grades. He must therefore be the one Joyce consulted. Theon says:

> The parts of the initiation are five. The first is purification. . . . Next after purification is the administration of the rite. The third is the so-called *epopteia* [the beholding of the secret rites]. The fourth, which is also the end of the *epopteia*, is the crowning and laying-on of the garland, which empowers him, after becoming a *hierophantes* [shower of holy things] or *daidoûchos* [torchbearer] or other official, to administer the rite to others. And the fifth and last is the blessedness which comes of enjoying the love of the gods and feasting with the gods.[8]

These mysteries represented the confluence of two primitive traditions, the one having to do with the seasonal renewal of the crops, and the other with the transition from boyhood to manhood. The first was embodied in the story of Demeter and Persephone. Lured to the underworld by Hades, Persephone was the object of a long search by Demeter, the Great Mother of Asiatic religions.

[8] Quoted by George Thomson, *Aeschylus and Athens*, 2nd ed., London, 1946, p. 125.

Hades was reluctant to let Persephone go after she had been found, and an arrangement had to be worked out in which Persephone, like the crops she personified, would spend one third of the year in the underworld. The ritual enactment of the joyful reunion of the Great Mother and her daughter, signifying the annual rebirth of the crops, constituted the heart of the Eleusinian Mysteries. To this vegetation rite the rite of adolescence was joined, since the change in the young man was looked upon as equivalent to a death and a rebirth.

Here was grist for Joyce's mill. A descent to the underworld, death and rebirth, the suggestion of a reunion with mother, and all the mythological elements associated with these events fitted perfectly with the shape Joyce had already given to the story of his archetypal hero. Using these Mysteries, Joyce could impose a pattern of meaning on the chaotic material of *Stephen Hero* and convert it into the *Portrait*.

Chapter I shows the candidate for initiation being purified. In the Eleusinian Mysteries the candidate went down to the sea. Stephen has to settle for a dunking in the square ditch, but he is surrounded by water in much of the chapter, from the bed wetting on the first page to the brimming bowl on the last.

Once he had been purified the candidate was taken from the house for women to the house for men. In Chapter II the description of Stephen sitting out life among old and young women (67–70) works on both the Homeric and Eleusinian levels. In the last two sections of the chapter Stephen goes first to Queen's College, where he realizes "his childhood was dead" (96), and then to the brothel, where he is initiated into sexual intercourse. Both the college and the brothel may be construed as houses for men.

In the third grade of the Mysteries the qualified candidate beheld the innermost secrets that he must under no condition reveal, although Aeschylus inadvertently did reveal part of them in one of his plays and was quickly brought to court. From the scanty evidence available some scholars have conjectured that the candidate witnessed a terrifying drama of the journey of the soul to the underworld, then a symbolic sexual union as Demeter married off her daughter Persephone, and finally a burst of light to mark the happy event. In Chapter III the sixteen-year-old Stephen is forced "to reflect on the mysteries of holy religion" (109) and to listen to the horrendous sermon on hell and judgment day. In the middle of it a symbolic marriage takes place. Stephen, imagining a pure and soulful love for Emma in place of the lustful one of his "monstrous dreams," has his hands placed on Emma's by the Virgin Mary (115–16), who may be taken as the counterpart in the Christian religion of the Great Mother of pagan religions. In this marriage ceremony Stephen becomes Iacchos, bridegroom of Persephone and one of the numerous incarnations of Dionysus, who as god of fertility is torn to pieces and reborn. Finally, as for the burst of light, Stephen's joy after having confessed his sexual sins is caused by the "light of God's mercifulness" (145) shining on him.

The descent to hell suggested by the seventeen episodes dovetails perfectly with the stages of initiation suggested by the five chapters. Central to both is a journey to the underworld. Foucart, whose exhaustive studies on the Mysteries appeared between 1895 and 1914, argued that in the *dromena* or sacred pageant of the Mysteries the neophyte was taken through certain underground rooms and passageways at Eleusis to simulate the journey of the soul to the underworld. Foucart was led to this belief by a passage in Themistius' essay "On the Soul":

> The soul (at the point of death) has the same experiences as those who are being initiated into great mysteries. . . . At first one wanders and wearily hurries to and fro, and journeys with suspicion through the dark as one uninitiated: then come all the terrors before the final initiation, shuddering, trembling, sweating, amazement: then one is struck with a marvelous light, one is received into pure regions and meadows with voices and dances and the majesty of holy sounds and shapes: among these he who has fulfilled initiation wanders free, and released and bearing his crown joins in the divine communion, and consorts with pure and holy men, beholding those who live here uninitiated, an uncleansed horde, trodden under foot of him and

huddled together in mud and fog, abiding in their miseries through fear of death and mistrust of the blessings there.[9]

This reads almost like a synopsis of the third and fifth chapters of the *Portrait*.

Furthermore, the scene with the girl at the seashore in Chapter IV almost certainly derives from Joyce's reading on the Eleusinian Mysteries. The bridge Stephen crosses at the beginning of the episode (165) may owe something to the bridge of the Rheitoi that the neophytes were compelled to walk across in the procession from Athens to Eleusis.[10] After crossing the bridge the candidates would rest along the shore of the bay until sunset.

> It was perhaps during this period of respite by the seaside that Phryne's famous exhibition took place. "At the great assembly of the Eleusinia and at the festival of Poseidon," states Athenaios, "in full sight of the whole Greek world, she removed her cloak and let down her hair before stepping into the water." [11]

Stephen's girl at the seashore, an "angel of mortal youth and beauty" (172), bares her thighs "almost to the hips. . . . Her slateblue skirts were kilted boldly about her waist . . ." (171). The fact that this Phryne was the celebrated hetaera who inspired Praxiteles and Apelles to create their statues of Aphrodite reinforces our initial impression that it is the vision of this girl at the seashore which makes Stephen take up his calling as an artist.[12]

[9] Translated in Lewis Richard Farnell, *The Cults of the Greek States*, Vol. III, Oxford, 1907, p. 179. See Paul Foucart, *Les Mystères d'Eleusis*, Paris, 1914, p. 393.

[10] George E. Mylonas, *Eleusis and the Eleusinian Mysteries*, Princeton, 1961, p. 246. Cf. Foucart, pp. 304–305.

[11] Mylonas, p. 256.

[12] The business with the watery tea and the box of tickets at the beginning of Chapter V may also relate to the Eleusinian Mysteries. The initiate was required to participate in some kind of sacrament for which the ritualistic words were: "I have fasted, I have drunk barley water, I have taken things from the sacred chest; having tasted thereof, I have placed them in the *kalathos* [basket] and again from the *kalathos* into the chest." (Farnell, pp. 185–86.)

JOYCE

The Mysteries also provide an explanation for the Greek words with which Stephen's friends, splashing in the water, greet him as he walks along the breakwater. "Stephanos Dedalos!" they shout. "Bous Stephanoumenos! Bous Stephaneforos!" (428). Only in a symbolist novel would untutored Irish urchins hail the hero in Greek as a garlanded and victory-crowned bull! They do so because Stephen, having witnessed the secret rites, now enters the fourth grade of his initiation and is given a garland in token thereof. It must have warmed the cockles of Joyce's heart to discover that the name he had given his hero in allusion to the martyred saint meant garland and could be used with perfect appropriateness in the climactic scene of the novel. Moreover, the diving boys also recognize in Stephen the bull that participated in the rituals of Dionysus, the bull that incarnated the god. Stephen's transformation as a bull signifies his initiation into manhood. But this transformation calls our attention to another level of meaning incrusted on this scene. By becoming a bull Stephen breaks with his childhood, his mother, and his mother church, all of which are suggested by the cow that appears recurrently throughout the book (7, 63, 111, 118). Nor is this all. Joyce has overlaid the scene with yet another meaning, for the boys, diving through the air, hail Stephen as Daedalus, the fabulous artificer.

> His throat ached with a desire to cry aloud, the cry of a hawk or eagle on high, to cry piercingly of his deliverance to the winds. This was the call of life to his soul, not the dull gross voice of the world of duties and despair, not the inhuman voice that had called him to the pale service of the altar. An instant of wild light had delivered him and the cry of triumph which his lips withheld cleft his brain.
> —Stephaneforos!
> What were they now but cerements shaken from the body of death—the fear he had walked in night and day, the incertitude that had ringed him round, the shame that had abased him within and without—cerements, the linens of the grave?
> His soul had arisen from the grave of boyhood, spurning her graveclothes. Yes! Yes! Yes! He would create proudly out of the freedom and power of his soul, as the great artificer whose

32 /

name he bore, a living thing, new and soaring and beautiful, impalpable, imperishable. (169–70)

At the climax of the novel not only do the symbols coalesce but the Homeric, Ovidian, and Eleusinian lines converge to celebrate the death of an unhappy boy, sick at heart and afraid of life, and the birth of a life-embracing artist, glorying in his intellectual courage and finding strength in his loneliness.

Since the third and fourth parts of the initiation as Theon gives them are really one, both the third and fourth chapters of the *Portrait* depict Stephen's rebirth. Nearly all writers on the Mysteries distinguish only four, and often only three, grades, since the fifth and last grade, admission to the company of the gods, can only come at the end of one's life on earth.[13] Joyce of course apotheosizes his alter ego here on earth. When the young Stephen places his faith in art, art becomes his religion. And in the hierarchy of that religion, Joyce gives Stephen pride of place.

The Artist as Christ

Even a casual reading of the last chapter discloses Stephen as Jesus Christ. Leaving home on his walk to the university, Stephen hears a mad nun screeching, "Jesus! O Jesus!" (175) as he passes by. A few moments later he meets on a bridge a man wearing a brimless hat and holding a furled umbrella a span or two from him (177). This is Pontius Pilate (Pons = bridge; pileatus = wearing a skull cap; or pilatus = armed with a javelin). Seeing him, Stephen realizes it must be eleven o'clock (177), time for his ascension, the culmination of his rise from the pit of the inferno.

The cock crew
The sky was blue:

[13] Theon divided the initiation into five stages to accommodate the Eleusinian Mysteries to his philosophy. The best evidence indicates there were actually only three stages: "the preliminary initiation into the Lesser Mysteries, the initiation proper into the Greater Mysteries, known as the *telete,* and the *epopteia,* or highest degree of initiation." Mylonas, pp. 238–39.

The bells in heaven
Were striking eleven.
Tis time for this poor soul
To go to heaven.
—*Ulyssees,* Chapter II

The actual ascension takes place immediately after the last diary entries, which present Dedalus poised for his flight from Ireland.

If Stephen is Jesus, we may expect to find the rest of the blessed company hovering around him. Cranly is emphatically and repeatedly identified as fig-chewing John the Baptist (178, 233–35, 239, 248). This explains another one of Joyce's little jokes. During the roll call in the physics class (191), someone responds to the name Byrne, which was Cranly's name in real life, but no one responds to the name Cranly. A student calls out, "Try Leopardstown!" a not very helpful suggestion since Cranly seems to have no interest in horse racing, the only thing for which Leopardstown is known, but more relevant if one recalls that John was baptized at Bethnemra, "the place of the leopard."

The four evangelists, Matthew, Mark, Luke, and John, are only a little less difficult to identify. The dean of studies who functions as Hephaestus on the Homeric level of the narrative is Matthew the tax collector on the Christian level. Stephen sees him as "a levite of the Lord" (185) and "that disciple who had sat at the receipt of custom" (189). Also, Matthew's iconograph is a face, and Stephen is fascinated by the dean's face (187). Luke the physician, generally represented with an ox lying near him, turns out to be Dixon, the medical student who is seated in the library near a book, *Diseases of the Ox,* opened at the frontispiece (227). (Remembering Stephen's transfiguration as an ox or bull, we can expect some further significance to attach to this book.) St. Mark appears as Glynn, a tutor who carries a portfolio of papers to mark (238). He contributes nothing to our understanding of the *Portrait.* But Davin the athlete contributes a great deal. He is the disciple John, who is patron of net makers and whose emblem is the eagle. As Davin, he dwindles in Stephen's mind to a "tame goose" (181, 201), a conventional person who helps make those nets of nationality, language, and religion that Stephen must fly past in order that his soul may be born (203). More importantly, John was the Beloved Disciple. But rather than have Davin loved by Stephen (although there may be a strain of homosexuality in their relationship), Joyce makes him loved by all the girls, as Stephen is not. Just as John was present at Jesus' agony, so Davin is present in Stephen's mind when Stephen realizes that girls prefer other boys to him (228, 234).

Among the remaining disciples, the most important in this last chapter is of course Judas Iscariot, who turns out to be Lynch, the student Stephen harangues with the long lecture on aesthetics. "It was a great day for European culture when you made up your mind to swear in yellow," says Stephen to Lynch (204). Swearing in yellow, the color of Judas, betrays Lynch as the disciple who betrayed Jesus. But how does Lynch betray Stephen? On the library steps Lynch whispers that Stephen's girl friend is present.[14] Thus suddenly reminded of her lack of interest in him, Stephen loses all interest in aesthetic theory; his mind is emptied of intellectual courage and his heart is filled with bitterness (215–16). Underwritten as all of Joyce's momentous scenes are, this on the library steps prepares the episode that will resolve all the issues raised in the novel. More of that in a moment.

Andrew, the first of the disciples, usually pictured with gospel in hand, is reincarnated in Joyce's Dublin as the president of the college, "reading his office" (200); James the Less, or shorter, as the "squat" professor of economics (192); Bartholomew, the mystic disciple, as the professor of mental science (192); Jude, author of one of the epistles, as the little priest "who wrote devout verses" (192); and Barnabas, who was guilty of dissimulation and who founded the church in Bergamo, as the professor of Italian with rogue's eyes (192), who gives Stephen a

[14] Lynch's role in the *Portrait* scarcely seems to justify setting him up as Judas. The ulterior reason is found in Joyce's life, not Stephen's. Lynch was modeled on Vincent Cosgrave, who boasted to Joyce in 1909 that he had seduced Joyce's mistress, Nora Barnacle.

recipe for *risotto alla bergamasca* (249). Doubting Thomas, patron saint of masons, emerges as the professor of physics who is rumored to be "an atheist freemason" (191). I must not overlook Peter and Paul. Peter, a bald old man who was converted by Jesus and who became patron saint of Flanders, is recognizable as the prefect of the sodality, a descendant of Baldhead, king of Flanders (229–30) and a married man before he was converted (199). Paul, whose emblems are an open book and a sword, the former signifying the new law he propagated, the latter his martyrdom, and whose heart spouted milk instead of blood, not unexpectedly shows up in twentieth-century Ireland as MacCann, who urges Stephen to sign the petition for disarmament (194–95), who preaches the "new gospel of life" that will secure "the greatest possible happiness of the greatest possible number" (196), who is accused by Stephen of flourishing a wooden sword (197), and who keeps next to his heart a bar of milk chocolate (196).

A few non-Christians also put in an appearance in Chapter V. In addition to Pontius Pilate we can pick out from the crowd of Biblical figures Herod Antipas and the high priests Caiaphas and Annas. Herod, who ordered the execution of John the Baptist, is Temple, whose anti-Catholicism infuriates Cranly. When Cranly pursues him, Temple flies like "a wild creature, nimble and fleetfooted" (237). If this does not remind us of Jesus' calling Herod a fox, then the very name "Temple" should call to mind the great palace associated with Herod's reign. Caiaphas, who presided at the council that condemned Jesus to death, can be no other than Father Moran with whom Stephen's girl has been keeping company (216, 220). When Lynch-Judas betrays the presence of Stephen's girl in front of the library, Stephen thinks "with conscious bitterness" of this priest (216). The high priest Annas is of no consequence to the thought of the chapter, but those who are curious to know where he may be hiding can find him, by punning on his name, disguised as the "stinkpot" Goggins who farts briefly (230).

Now that the cast is before us what are we to make of this fifth and last act in the drama of an emerging artist? Joyce has placed his autobiographical hero in the realm of the blessed, but surely the longest chapter of the book must tell us something more than that Stephen is the most blessed. The impression left by the chapter is that Stephen-Jesus is set apart from the Christians as well as from the Romans and the Sadducees. Yet he must have something in common with the Christians or there is no point to the analogy. Most of the Christians as they appear in the *Portrait* are emasculated creatures, wearing skirts instead of pants, and gamboling with each other in an obscenely old-maidenish way (155, 192, 199, and elsewhere). Even Cranly–John the Baptist is described as having "womanish" eyes (178). In contrast to them stands Stephen, the bull-like creator. At first glance, Davin–John the Beloved, who appears to lack any effeminate traits, also seems to be contrasted with the other Christians. But that is not the point. It is his normality, his conventionalism, his philistinism that opposes him to Stephen in the design of the chapter. All the Christians, Davin included, have one thing in common: they are all mother's boys. Stephen is not. They are Madonna worshipers and Mariolaters, whereas Stephen represents the true and pristine faith and not the church that Peter built. It is Stephen's rebellion against mother and all that she stands for that is the making of him as an artist. That may be only part of the truth but it is the heart of the matter.

The last chapter is devoted entirely to mother. From the first page to the last she is ubiquitous, whether she appears as Stephen's mother or as the Blessed Virgin or as a ghost haunting the thoughts and language of the Christians. "I hope the matric men will all come" (199), says the prefect of the sodality, quite innocently. When Davin first meets Stephen, he asks the way to the matriculation class, "putting a very strong stress on the first syllable." Stephen asks himself, "Is he as innocent as his speech?" (202). And what is that ball Cranly plays with throughout the chapter if not a homespun version of the ball and cross carried in church processions to represent the glorified Madonna? More than anyone else Cranly stands for devotion to mother. "He had spoken of a mother's love. He felt then the sufferings of women, the weaknesses of their bodies and souls: and would shield them

with a strong and resolute arm and bow his mind to them" (245).
Understanding that, Stephen knows he must break with Cranly.
It is that rupture that quickly brings the novel to a close.

Cranly as John the Baptist can figure as a precursor of
Stephen-Jesus (248) because both have a strong incestuous attachment to their respective mothers. Stephen, however, is aware
of his incestuous desires as Cranly and the others are not. Compared to Cranly and Davin, the perceptive Stephen is a sexual
monster (203, and see also 90–92, 115–16). But Stephen is able
to resolve his incestuous desires by becoming the rebellious artist,
while the others meekly bow their heads before mother in whatever domineering form she takes—mother church, mother country, mother of the family.

The Monster in the Labyrinth

Becoming an artist, Stephen invests himself simultaneously
with the robes of Jesus as priest of eternal imagination, and with
the wings of Daedalus, the fabulous artificer. The epigraph to
the *Portrait* reminds us that Daedalus "turned his mind to
unknown arts that seemed to outwit nature" when he fashioned
the wings with which to escape from Crete and King Minos. It is
time now to consider the events that led up to this escape.

Minos' wife, Pasiphaë, harbored a lust for a sacred white
bull, and, seeking to consummate her lust, instructed the royal
artisan Daedalus to fabricate a wooden cow in which she might
conceal herself. Daedalus did as he was told; the sacred bull
responded as Pasiphaë hoped; and the result was the monstrous
Minotaur. Now the embarrassed king had to find a place to con-
fine the monster. Again Daedalus was called upon, and this time
he constructed the labyrinth at Cnossus.

The long last chapter of the *Portrait* is the labyrinth the
dedalian Irishman built. Precisely in the center of it he placed a
wooden cow (214), used by Stephen to illustrate a point in his
lecture on aesthetics. Precisely two-thirds of the way through he
placed an ox, in the frontispiece to a book on the diseases of the
ox (227). (May I remind the reader that the pivotal hell scene
occupies the exact center of the novel, and that the climactic

vision of the girl at the seashore occurs precisely two-thirds of the way through the novel.[15]) We can now diagnose the principal disease of the ox as unrealized incest or as an Oedipus complex, a diagnosis corroborated by the fact that the book belongs to Cranly. The real monster is of course Stephen, whose sexual thoughts and acts appall and frighten Davin (202–203) almost as much as they frightened little Stephen himself when, visiting Queen's College, he saw the word *Foetus* on a classroom desk as if carved there by his father. The extraordinary impact this word had on Stephen, causing swarms of "monstrous reveries" to spring up before him from some "den of monstrous images," can only be attributed, considering the context of the incident, to the existence in Stephen of an Oedipus complex (89–93).

When Ariadne wanted to help Theseus enter the labyrinth and slay the Minotaur, she too asked Daedalus for help. He came up with the ball of thread that Theseus would unwind going into the labyrinth and wind back up to find his way out. For his act of treason, Daedalus was himself imprisoned in the labyrinth. Joyce also provided an Ariadne's thread to his labyrinth, but he took much greater pains to keep anyone from getting their hands on it than on the keys he provided for *Ulysses* and *Finnegans Wake*. The reason is clear. The latter are rather impersonal works, whereas the monster to be hunted down in the *Portrait* is Joyce himself.

Once we understand, as the clues in the first two chapters give us to understand, that the *Portrait* is fundamentally about a young man's incestuous attachment to his mother, then the labyrinth can be mapped out.

Mass of the Catechumens

To orient ourselves in this maze we must face the central fact in the life of a Christ figure: the crucifixion. The ultimate ar-

---

[15] I suspect that the thinness of the fifth chapter is due to the fact that Joyce had to fill a certain number of pages. When he turned his holograph manuscript of the first three chapters over to his typist, he took note of the page number of the "Hell! Hell! Hell! Hell! Hell!" line and set himself the task of doubling that number of pages.

tistic expression of Jesus' agony, death, and resurrection is the Mass, and it is the Mass that gives shape and significance to the sprawling fifth chapter.

This particular Mass takes place on Maundy Thursday (177, 210), and the ministers are Cranly as chief celebrant, attended by Temple as deacon and Stephen as subdeacon (158–59, 199). I scarcely need to add that the only priest at Mass is Jesus.

The first part of the rite is the Mass of the Catechumens, but this chapter begins with the preparations before Mass. The washing before vesting and the Blessing of Water (rain) occupy the opening pages (174–78), with Pontius Pilate, the man on the bridge, now doubling as the wielder of an aspergillus in the form of a furled umbrella or divining rod.

Introibo ad altare dei (178–80). The opening part of the ceremony, the prayers at the foot of the altar, reveals Stephen meditating on the words "ivy" and "ivory," the former symbolizing the resurrection, the latter the Virgin Mother. Stephen's relationship to his mother will be one of the two chief factors in his being resurrected from the death of the spirit he experienced as a boy. The other factor is language. Jesus as the second person of the Trinity is the Word.

Confiteor (180–83). Davin–John the Beloved confesses when he tells Stephen of the Irish peasant woman who tried to seduce him. This is Joyce's version of the woman taken in adultery.

The Kissing of the Altar (183–84) is parodied in the brief incident of the flower girl. Stephen refuses to reverence Irish girls or Ireland.

The Censing (184–90). When the dean of studies, already familiar to us in the guises of Hephaestus and Matthew, lights the fire in the physics theatre, we are to understand that the ritual incensation ("setting fire") of the altar is taking place. The bucket and lamp alluded to several times function together as the thurible. The deity to whom the incense is offered is the spirit of language, and in the worship of that deity Stephen is the true devotee, the dean merely a lax and lukewarm soul. Compare 251.

Introit (190–91). The students pour into the physics theatre. The roll is called.

The *Kyrie eleison* (191–92). Known also as the formula, the kyrie is parodied here as a mathematical formula discussed by the atheistic professor of physics.

The *Gloria in excelsis* (192–94) is intoned in a droning voice by the professor as he explains electric coils, a fitting symbol of the modern god, as Henry Adams discovered while he was being educated. Stephen jokes about offering himself as a subject for electrocution, read: crucifixion.

The Collect (194–95). The congregation petitions God in this part of the ritual. Here MacCann urges the gathered students to sign his peace petition.

The Epistle (195–99). The epistle is generally from St. Paul. Here MacCann (Paul) delivers his gospel of utilitarianism and quarrels with Stephen. "If you must have a Jesus, let us have a legitimate Jesus," says Stephen.

The Gradual (199–204). These versicles were originally sung on the step or *gradus* of the lectern, where we find the dean of studies, "a foot on the lowest step," when this gradual begins. The subject matter of the gradual refers back to the epistle, and such is the case here too, where Stephen announces his intention to fly past the nets of nationality, language, and religion.

The Tract (204–10), which is intended for a great solo voice, replaces the Alleluia on Maundy Thursday. Here Stephen delivers the first part of his tract on aesthetics to Lynch.

The Sequence (210). Fervid hymns fill out this part of the ritual. On the verge of revealing the secret which informs the entire novel, Stephen naturally thinks of Aquinas' hymn *"Pange lingua"* ("Now my tongue, the mystery telling").

Ordination (210–11). Mass on Holy Thursday commemorates the ordination of the apostles. Here the seven deacons (students) who aided the apostles are admitted to holy orders by partaking of a stew that in this parody replaces a more formal Last Supper.

The Gospel (211–15). The reading of the gospel brings the Ante-Mass to its climax. In it Christ teaches us what to believe and what to do. Here Stephen, the voice of incarnate God, finishes his lecture on aesthetics, his concluding words comparing

/ 41

the artist to the indifferent god of creation. It is unfortunate that Stephen's aesthetics, which are neither original nor profound, should have provided the occasion for so much empty discussion. Joyce obviously had much more interesting things to say about art than Stephen has. Stephen's callow theories are simply meant to be the gospel of a very young man who has just discovered himself as an artist.

The *Credo* (215–16). The medical students in front of the library who chant in Latin of the bloody cruel life of a doctor correspond to the holy doctors who first expounded the credos of the church. During the *Credo* the corporal representing Christ's body is spread on the altar to signify that the sacrifice is imminent. While the medical students are talking, Lynch betrays the presence of Stephen's girl. His whispered "Your beloved is here" is equivalent to the Judas kiss that betrayed Jesus on a Thursday evening. Stephen's sacrifice and crucifixion are imminent. Thus ends the Mass of the Catechumens and section 14 of the *Portrait*.

The Crucifixion

The Mass of the Faithful or the Mass of the Mysteries begins with section 15, which along with the scene in hell midway through the novel and the climax at the seashore two-thirds of the way through, is one of the three main pillars on which the edifice rests.

The Offertory and the Preparation of the Bread and Wine (217). With his soul lying "amid cool waters," conscious of "faint sweet music" (the Oremus) and of seraphim "breathing upon him," Stephen feels poetically inspired and begins to compose a villanelle that sings of the end of his love for the girl. The words that haunt his imagination represent the bread and wine of this sacrament. "In the virgin womb of the imagination the word was made flesh."

The Preface and *Sanctus* (217–18). The introduction to the Sacrifice itself takes the form of Stephen murmuring the first verses of his villanelle as smoke and incense ascend from the altar. As the morning light gathers, the faraway sound of a bell and the twittering of three birds marks the light-bringing *Sanctus* or *Trisagion*.

The Canon or *Epiclesis* (218–20). This part of the ritual symbolizes Christ mounting the cross. The descent of the Holy Ghost is invoked by the ministrant in verses that commemorate the living, primarily the Virgin Mary. Stephen remembers the hours he spent with his girl; and he remembers Father Moran too, the priest with whom his girl has been flirting.

The Elevation of the Host and the Chalice (220–22). Recalling this flirtation, Stephen feels a "rude brutal anger" bursting from his soul. The passion of Stephen-Jesus begins. Railing at the "priested peasant" whom his girl prefers, Stephen sets himself up as a "priest of the eternal imagination, transmuting the daily bread of experience into the radiant body of everliving life." Out of his bitterness and despair he sings his poem, a eucharistic hymn in which "sacrificing hands upraise / The chalice flowing to the brim." (The host is also raised: there is a sly reference to Jacob's biscuit factory.)

The *Anamnesis* or Commemoration of the Dead (222). Stephen's recollection of his past friendship with the girl corresponds to that part of the Mass in which the celebrants remind themselves that the consecration is done in remembrance of Jesus. In effect, the *anamnesis* provides a résumé of the Mass.

The Little Elevation or the Thanksgiving (222–23). As Stephen continues to reflect upon his girl, his anger changes to compassion, for she too has known humiliation. Reconciled to her in thought, he feels a sensual desire for her. "Her nakedness yielded to him" and as he thinks of this the eucharist hymn, the villanelle he has been composing, flows forth "over his brain." In the Mass this elevation of the host and chalice, both raised together, was formerly the more important, for now the bread and wine are become one with the Body and Blood of Jesus. In Joyce's parable the body and blood of Stephen have become Jesus, the Word. But the significance of the scene extends far beyond this.

It is this section of the novel that provides the final answers to the questions I raised at the beginning. Here we learn once and for all how essential the fifth chapter is to the meaning of the whole work. Here we come to understand what it is that makes an artist of Stephen.

The making of this particular artist involves an Achilles' heel, an Oedipus complex, and an ineffectual father. Stephen's vulnerable spot is his weak eyes that made him turn to the world of imagination in the first place. But there must also be some emotion, some source of energy that will impel him to create, or some goal or desire toward which the energy may be directed. This factor is supplied by Stephen's parents. Longing for his mother's love and attributing all his sense of loss, his pain, and his humiliation to his father, Stephen unconsciously attempts to take revenge on his father and win his mother's love through artistic creativity. His first attempt at poetry is a poem about Parnell. Remembering that Stephen's dream of Parnell's death was a death wish directed at Simon Dedalus, we can understand the unconscious reason for Stephen's choice of subject—and also understand why Stephen chooses to jot the poem down on the back of one of his father's unpaid bills, of all places. However, this hostility against his father is a negative influence on Stephen's creative urges. Emotions are merely released without being gathered together again. The creative effort is aborted and the poem remains unfinished. Better luck comes with Stephen's second poem, a poem about an undefined sorrow in the hearts of a boy and girl at the moment they kiss. After writing this poem, Stephen goes into his *mother's* bedroom and gazes "at his face for a long time in the mirror of her dressing table" (70–71). In this episode Joyce distills the essence of the whole novel. Separation from his mother has made Stephen sick at heart, and only a reunion with mother in the deepest sense can bring him back to the source of his being and restore to his soul that balance and harmony out of which he can create.

The Homeric analogue conveys the same idea. The wrath of Stephen-Achilles cannot be appeased nor can he be made to enter the battlefields of life again until "the glory of the father" (Patroclus) is slain. And furthermore, Stephen-Achilles cannot be armored for battle until "with my own eyes I see [my mother] come back to me" (*Iliad*, XVIII, 189–90).

The same point is made on the symbolic level. I have discussed how the bird and water, the two chief symbols, are fused together in Chapters I and IV to reflect a harmonious state of soul. In the villanelle scene of section 15 the final fusion occurs and provides the structure of the novel with its capstone.

To begin at the beginning: Stephen's separation from his mother pollutes the water of life, transforming it into the turf-colored water at Clongowes, then into the horse stale that Stephen smells after he discovers his girl has not waited for him at the Whitsuntide play, and finally into the liquid corruption of the hell scene (120). The water becomes sweeter according as the bird becomes less unpleasant and frightening. When Stephen goes to the rector for justice, the bird merges with the water in an image of harmony; and in the climax of the novel the bird becomes the beautiful girl wading in the water. But this scene does not represent the ultimate condensation of symbols. Stephen is still not in the water of life, as the boys are, and the girl is still not his mother with whom he must eventually be united. Hence section 15 is necessary to complete the symbolic development. Here Stephen is finally immersed in the water, now become the "liquid letters of speech" (491). Here Stephen himself becomes the bird-man Daedalus. And very shortly his mother will also become a bird.

Not only do the symbols coalesce in the villanelle scene, but all the threads of the novel are brought together to reveal the pattern of the whole work. "The brimming chalice" in the poem recalls the brimming bowl of water in section 3 and suggests that now Stephen has risen triumphantly from his inferno. As an initiate into the Eleusinian Mysteries, Stephen attains *eudemonia*. On the Homeric level the hero forges out of language the shield with which to do battle against home, nation, and religion. On the Ovidian level Stephen becomes the birdlike artificer Daedalus. On the Christian level Stephen crucifies himself on the altar of language. All of this is balanced on the simple psychological point that Stephen has learned to live without love.

The liturgy of the Mass reminds us that the Elevation signifies Christ's Passion. In writing the villanelle Stephen-Jesus suffers his passion. His realization that conventional love will be denied him in life is his calvary. Out of the pain of this realization he creates his poem. And in the act of creation he escapes from his pain and is reunited with his mother. This occurs at the exact moment (223) when the girl of his imagination yields her nakedness to him and enfolds him "like water with a liquid life"; when the "liquid letters" of the villanelle flow forth over his brain; when "the chalice flowing to the brim" is elevated. For this Little Elevation of the Host and Chalice signals the moment when Christ was nailed to the cross. And, according to St. Augustine and other theologians, when Christ was nailed to the cross He was united with the Holy Mother.

Ite Missa est

After the Little Elevation the liturgy continues with the *Pater Noster* (224–25). This is Jesus' own prayer. Corresponding to it is Stephen's invocation at the beginning of the sixteenth section to the spirit of "the hawklike man whose name he bore" and to the spirit of Thoth, god of libraries and of writers. The swallows that wheel about Stephen's head as he stands on the steps of the library refer not only to the winged Daedalus and the ibis-headed Thoth, but also to Stephen's mother, whose image he sees in the temple of air that these birds build (224). The library and the birds and the water imagery serve to link this scene with the library scene at the end of section 14 (Lynch's betrayal) to create the impression that the villanelle scene of section 15 takes place at the library. The library is the Acropolis, the temple of Athena, who was goddess of learning and Daedalus' teacher. The references to dew and rain (216–17) suggest the earliest priestesses of Athena, who were personifications of wetness.

The Fraction or Breaking of the Host (225–26). The gathering swallows also remind us of the moment of Christ's death, when swallows hovered over the cross crying "*Svala, svala*": console, console. As augur (blind Tiresias, probably), Stephen interprets these auspices to mean departure or loneliness.

Agnus Dei (226–32). This passage in the liturgy represents John the Baptist hailing Jesus. And Stephen-Jesus discovers

Cranly-John with a copy of *Diseases of the Ox*. The incest motive sounded by this title is repeated a moment later in the otherwise inexplicable episode of the dwarfish man who is rumored to be the offspring of an incestuous love. The dwarf is Wagner's Mime; the smiling Dixon is Siegfried; and the signet ring Dixon diplays is the ring of the Nibelungs. Siegmund and Sieglinda appear as the brother and sister who embrace passionately in the park, with the brother turning out to be Davin. Dixon will later (237) whistle the bird call from Siegfried behind Stephen and Cranly. These allusions to incest serve as a prelude to the final dialogue in which Stephen comes to understand the source of Cranly's suffering and enters the "strange dark cavern of speculation."

The Priest's Communion (232-34). In the liturgy the minister consumes the Host and Blood. In the novel the Body and the Blood turn to lice and urine as the poetic thoughts Stephen entertains about his girl turn to ugly thoughts, and the joy he momentarily experiences when she passes by turns to the despair of knowing she prefers another.

Communion of the People (234-38). This passage needs scarcely any comment after all that has been said before about Temple and Cranly, Davin and Stephen.

The Post-Communion (238-47) is given over to the private devotions of the assemblage. Now Stephen and Cranly have their last long talk and confide in each other. Stephen informs him that he has broken with his mother and with the church. "I will not serve," he says. Cranly, on the other hand, defends a mother's love as the one sure thing in this world. Stephen understands that, like himself, Cranly has an Oedipus complex. On the mythical level of the narrative the suffering Cranly is Talos ("suffering") who was the rival of Daedalus as an inventor. Suspecting Talos of having incestuous relations with his mother, Daedalus flung him down from the Acropolis. So on the primary level Stephen breaks with Cranly because they stand at opposite poles on the mother question. Stephen repudiates his mother only to be reunited with her in a more profound sense. By doing so, he finds his way back to the source of creation. Cranly and the others cannot forswear their love for mother, and hence they can-

/ 47

not create. They remain conventional in their thought, frustrated in their emotional life, and moribund in spirit. Having been resurrected from ordered daily life by abjuring church, family, and nation, Stephen is the only one who is truly alive at the end of the book.

Ite Missa est (247–53). The diary entries that conclude *A Portrait of the Artist as a Young Man* correspond to the dismissal of the Mass. Arming himself for the fight against his Hector, an old Irishman with "redrimmed horny eyes" (252), and putting on his wings for his flight into self-imposed exile, Stephen gives final utterance to an exultant pride of youth and scorn of love, two virtues which this novel seeks to inculcate upon those who may be suffering under the burden of the conventional virtues.

One entry in Stephen's diary deserves brief comment. On the morning of March 25, Stephen records a troubled night of dreams. He has dreamed of small men advancing as from a cave. A little Freudian insight reveals why Stephen was troubled. The cave is a womb, and the small men are kin to that dwarf who was rumored to be the offspring of an incestuous union. For Stephen-Jesus, March 25 would inevitably be the occasion for such a dream of incest since, according to Tertullian, it was the date of Christ's Passion, and, according to any calendar of the liturgical year, it was the date of the Annunciation to the Virgin Mary.

Thus ends this Daedalian novel whose intimate secrets Joyce revealed to no one. There was no reason for keeping his trade secrets and technical novelties to himself after he had provided Gilbert with the key to *Ulysses*. Yet he kept silent. His position on the *Portrait* was more consistent than the position he took on *Ulysses*. One writes a symbolist novel in order to conceal while revealing, revealing to the world at large only so much as one wants them to know while concealing the ultimate truths from all but a few initiates who can understand "the unspoken speech behind the words" (242) and who will respond in the proper spirit.

Ulysses is painted on a larger canvas than the *Portrait,* but it is no more clever and no more profound. And certainly it is less original. Both technically and thematically, it is only a complement to the *Portrait*. The *Portrait* ends with a Mass and *Ulysses* begins with one. Having written his *Iliad*, Homeric, half-blind Joyce was ready to write his *Odyssey*. And having brought about the mystic union of a mother and the son who forsook her, he could next contrive the mystic union of a father and a son who were not even related.

Postscript on Influences

Shortly before and during the time Joyce was writing his autobiographical novel there appeared a great number of psychological and anthropological studies that Joyce probably read. The Oedipus complex comes of course from Freud, who was getting to be fairly well known about 1910. In the footsteps of Freud came Jung, whose *Wandlungen und Symbole der Libido,* 1912, stresses two ideas that are crucial to the *Portrait:* first, the transformation of symbols in a myth reflects changes in the hero's being; and second, the individual human being cannot, on the one hand, find his own identity unless he breaks with his mother, nor can he, on the other hand, be creative unless he returns to the source of his being, his mother, and is united with her. The solution to what looks like an impossible situation is achieved in the realm of the spirit as revealed in all the great myths. The mythic hero learns to overcome his fear of incest, symbolized by a monster, the Terrible Mother—consider Stephen's "monstrous" thoughts—and channels his libido into the symbolic equivalent of mother. Without Jung the *Portrait* would not have taken its present shape. Another student of Freud was Otto Rank, whose *Der Mythus von der Geburt des Helden* (1909) reduced all heroic myths to one basic story and advanced the idea that the artistic, creative type is bisexual, an idea that flickers behind much of Joyce's novel. Rank also wrote a very exhaustive study of incest in literature, *Das Inzestmotiv in Dichtung und Sage,* 1912, which Joyce might have dipped into.

Among the anthropological studies that apparently influenced Joyce are Paul Foucart's *Les Grands Mystères d'Eleusis,* 1900, and van Gennep's *Les rites de passage,* 1909. But the period from 1890 to 1915 was especially rich in works on ancient rituals. Besides the earlier researches of Foucart, published in 1894 and

1895, there were Goblet d'Alviella's *Eleusinia*, 1903; Farnell's monumental *Cults of the Greek States*, of which the third volume, 1906, dealt with the Eleusinian Mysteries; and Jane Harrison's *Prolegomena to the Study of Greek Religion*, 1903, and *Themis*, 1912.

Among artistic or creative works that may have left a direct impress on the structure of the *Portrait* are Strindberg's *To Damascus*, mentioned above; his autobiographical novel *The Son of a Servant;* and Wagner's *Parsifal.* Though the idea of modeling the last chapter on the Mass was probably original with Joyce, he may possibly have got it either from Strindberg's novel, in which the author impiously compares himself to Christ, or from Wagner's opera. The end of Act I, the love feast of the Grail, was inspired by the Eucharist, and Wagner presents a condensed Mass in which the procession of the knights of the Grail forms the Introit; the long plaint of the sinner Amfortas corresponds to the *Confiteor;* the chorus of boys in the darkening room to the Offertory; the raising of the Grail accompanied by a burst of light to the Consecration of the Host; the repast of wine and bread to Communion; and the *"Dort hinaus"* of Gurnemanz to the Dismissal. Joyce need not have seen the opera or read the libretto; he could have learned of Wagner's "heretical" use of the Mass in Max Nordau's widely read denunciation of the artistic vanguard, *Entartung*, printed in 1892 (English translation 1895). But it is interesting to consider that, though *Parsifal* was at Wagner's insistence staged exclusively at Bayreuth for a number of years (except for the unauthorized New York production of 1903), it was staged by nearly every major opera house in 1914, immediately after the copyright expired; and 1914 was the year in which Joyce wrote the last chapter of the *Portrait*.

As a matter of fact, each and every one of the cardinal ideas in Joyce's novel could have had its immediate source in a work published or made easily accessible between 1895 and 1914, or, to put a fine point on it, between 1906 and 1914, the very years Joyce is known to have been reshaping the unwieldy and naturalistic *Stephen Hero* into the polished perfection of the symbolic *Portrait*.

The Contravened Knot

L. D. CLARK

WITH THE WRITING OF *Women in Love*, D. H. Lawrence entered the full maturity of his art. His dominant theme had always been love, but now an attitude which had been latent in his previous work assumed control and imposed a religious tone on all of his later writing. The task of understanding love became a quest for its ultrahuman sources and the nurture of right relationship to its power. And since for Lawrence life and art moved together like John Donne's stiff twin compasses, he brought forth some of his greatest work just when he was most passionately involved in life. Introducing *Women in Love* to Americans in 1920 (where, because of the hesitation of his English publishers, it appeared first), he called it "a record of the profoundest experiences in the self" (*WL*, x).[1] These were the experiences of his initial years with Frieda, and of the First World War, which filled several of those same years with horror and disaster. A summary of what lay behind the writing of *Women in Love* is essential to comprehension of the book itself.

In April of 1912, Lawrence, son of a coal miner, met Frieda von Richthofen Weekley, daughter of a German aristocrat, wife of a professor, mother of three children. Their attraction to one another was immediate and decisive: in May they eloped to the Continent. But the adjustment was a stormy one, and so absorbing that the mutual accommodation of the male and female

---

[1] The edition of *Women in Love* used is that of the Modern Library, Random House, New York.

/ 51

spirits in the intimacy of love became for Lawrence an earthly *discordia concors* echoing that of the macrocosm: like all great artists, Lawrence thought of both his problems and his solutions to them as universal. It is impossible to imagine the Lawrence of *Women in Love* without Frieda, or without the First World War; for while the public world suffered the disintegration of hate, their private world enjoyed the hard-won growth of love. The war Lawrence saw as the first act of civilization's end, but, believing in cycles and in himself as the forerunner of a new age, he incorporated this faith with his faith in marriage into a creed of physical mysticism and natural aristocracy.

The writing of *Women in Love* cost Lawrence more effort than that of any of his other books. On Christmas Eve, 1912, after *Sons and Lovers,* the summation of his old life, had gone to press, he was "writing a bit of a new novel" (*Letters,* 171),[2] which gave him "a curious pleasure—venomous, almost" (*Letters,* 176). Through several rewritings, with large changes prompted by his own doubts and the advice of others, this work was to mature as *The Rainbow* and *Women in Love.* It will be profitable to dwell at length on the struggles of composition out of which the two novels grew in those crucial years when Lawrence rose from uncertain learner to assured artist. Between Christmas and mid-January he produced eighty pages (*Letters,* 178); by March 5 he could announce that his novel, which he called *The Sisters,* was "half-written" (*Letters,* 193). Then he put it aside as "too improper" (*Letters,* 197), but he soon returned to it. Swelling to two hundred pages by April 5, it had shrunk to one hundred and eighty by April 18, and to one hundred and forty-five by April 26, as reshaping proceeded (*Letters,* 203). Still, by May 19 he had completed and sent the first half to Edward Garnett, his editor at Duckworth's, and by early June the second half, willing, he said, to revise any faults Garnett might find. Perhaps fearing that the tone was too personal, Lawrence had volunteered earlier that "the novel is *not* about Frieda and me" (*Letters,* 194), but now

---

[2] All page numbers of *Letters* refer to Volume I of *The Collected Letters of D. H. Lawrence,* 2 volumes, edited with an introduction by Harry T. Moore, The Viking Press, New York, 1962.

he admitted that it depicted "Frieda's God Almightiness" (*Letters*, 208). Garnett suggested that he rewrite it in the third person.

He began to do so in Germany, in August, 1913, and continued in Italy. He was happier, now, with what he was doing; the book became *The Wedding Ring*. Frieda and he were achieving a more tranquil understanding, and his style softened: "The Laocoon writhing and shrieking have gone from my work, and I think there is a bit of stillness, like the wide, still, unseeing eyes of a Venus of Melos" (*Letters*, 241). This gentleness almost survived the portion of the work that became *The Rainbow*.

Edward Garnett continued to counsel, and Lawrence to listen. In February, 1914, Garnett was still not satisfied and Lawrence was beginning "for about the seventh time" (*Letters*, 264). In April he had altogether over a thousand discarded pages. But he was not discouraged: "Thank God, Frieda and I are together, and the work is of me and her, and it is beautiful, I think" (*Letters*, 269). He finished in May, he and Frieda returned to England, in July they were married, and in August the war began. Accompanying this succession of climaxes came a change of publishers. Garnett now objected to the fundamental psychology of the characters, which he found "incoherent." In a famous letter written from Italy on June 5, 1914, Lawrence explained the doctrine of character which had been taking shape in his imagination as he wrote, and which reading the pronouncements of the Futurists had helped him to formulate. Conflicting views between him and Garnett led to impatience, a Duckworth executive was brusque, Methuen stood waiting with £300—and Lawrence was in acute need of money.

Although he had balked at further changes for Duckworth, Lawrence rewrote for Methuen. But the inconsistency was probably due to reconsideration rather than perversity. He did not relinquish his new-found theory of character, but he did come to recognize that the people of his envisioning spanned the reach between the old creation and the new, and accordingly split his work into two novels. The first he brought to rapid completion and saw published in September, 1915, as *The Rainbow*. His old way of writing is still paramount here: the emphasis on conscious personal experience; but exploration into the unconscious and the impersonal brings about at intervals a shift in perspective. In the last two chapters especially, the tone approaches that of *Women in Love*. And because *The Rainbow* is transitional it lacks integrity of form. The movement of Ursula Brangwen from dead past to living future, coming near the end of the novel, powerfully depicts the rhythm and scope of her emotions, particularly in the horses scene, but the rainbow as an all-embracing symbol of her new state enters as a sudden intrusion, without the inevitability that the symbolism was to have in *Women in Love*.

Two months after its appearance, *The Rainbow* was suppressed for indecency, and perhaps unadmittedly because it belittled the military spirit in the midst of war. In any event, the suppression and the war became inseparable in Lawrence's mind, and he turned bitterly upon the world: "I feel as if the whole thing were coming to an end—the whole of England, of the Christian era. . . . I cannot bear it—this England, this past" (*Letters*, 379).

Men were not only so mad as to slaughter one another, but also to close their ears to the voice of the prophet.

Lawrence and Frieda passed the war years in a state of poverty. He was rejected three times as physically unfit for active military service, and, although in the last of these examinations he was classified for "sedentary" work, the war ended before he was called up. Each of these momentary exposures to officialdom enraged him further, and, still worse, he and Frieda were forcibly moved out of Cornwall because of some vague suspicion among ignorant neighbors that they were communicating with German submarines.

After writing sporadically on his "philosophy," reading early American literature and what he could borrow on Egypt, Druids, and Orphic rites, Lawrence began work in May, 1916, on what was left over from *The Rainbow*, at first calling it "the second half" of that novel, but soon "a new novel" (*Letters*, 449, 451). Again it was a matter of experiment, of casting and recasting for six months. He was on the fourth draft by July 21, writing longhand and then, to save money, typing from the manuscript himself. But he had to give up this mechanical task, for which he was ill-suited, sending the last half of the book to his agent to be typed, in November, after yet more revisions.

Now that the novel was done, he brightened. "The world of my novel," he said, "is big and fearless" (*Letters,* 477). At another time he called it "the book of my free soul" (*Letters,* 454). But the freedom was dangerous, too: "The book frightens me: it is so end-of-the-world. But it is, it must be, the beginning of a new world too" (*Letters,* 482). It was finality, and a new dawn. He thought of calling it *The Latter Days,* or, at Frieda's suggestion, *Dies Irae;* or, later, *Noah's Ark.* The eventual title was one he had offered tentatively near the end of the writing.

Women in Love was not published until four years after completion, after the war had ended, and after the fears of the publishers from the battle of *The Rainbow* had subsided. But Lawrence was in no hurry; the time of recognition would come. As he stepped back to survey his achievement, modesty had never hampered him less: "It is a very good piece of work: in fact, a masterpiece" (*Letters,* 495). And so it is.

As already suggested, *The Rainbow* and *Women in Love* stand in sharp contrast to each other. *The Rainbow* is a brilliant re-creation of individual and family experience—the discovery of the world and love by adolescent and adult, and a chronicle of generations. But the characters partake of the human condition as sublunar beings, distinguished only by the uniqueness that each person attributes to his own life. When forces beyond the personal move them, these are commonly social; the mystical eye into the dimness of metabiological experience opens but rarely. But in *Women in Love* the transcendent vision supersedes all other; with singular devotion Lawrence pursues new meanings for love, and through them new communion with the supernatural.

Our century has seen great concentration upon form in fiction, but far from indulging in technical pastimes for their own sake the modern novelist has been preoccupied with shaping vessels to contain our multitudinous life, whose new wine has burst the old bottles. Aldous Huxley brought musical form to the rescue of fiction; James Joyce called upon the aid of Homeric epic to lengthen the stature of the common man. But Lawrence's way was not so deliberately intellectual as Huxley's nor so painstakingly comparative as Joyce's. His erratic genius plunged through several strata of the past, recapturing wherever he found it the matter to give body to his fiction and the forms in which to mold it. Though the world he created is modern and overripe with civilization, it is one where a Hebrew prophet glowers and prowls; where the more ancient world of primitive sculpture and dance ruffles the smooth deceptions of society; where out of the blackness peers that inscrutable presence which Lawrence convincingly describes as the first intimation of immortality that the earth knew. The later novels of Lawrence vibrate with the tone and rhythm of ancient myth, of gospel and apocalypse, improbably combined with the tone and rhythm of the novels of Jane Austen or George Eliot. The wonder is that such disparate elements cohere at all; the triumph is that they combine so well as to produce a form of novel that is uniquely Lawrence's own and one of the century's most significant contributions to literature.

Women in Love owes its chief debt of form to the Bible. The world in which Birkin preaches salvation is a gospel world, active in the letter of the law but moribund in spirit, in mortal need of new access to divine love. With a contest between the powers of good and evil enveloping the action and destruction hanging imminent, *Women in Love* is apocalyptic. Remaking the savior image and setting the orthodox world straight in its thinking on the first and last parts of the New Testament became the later Lawrence's special province. Besides Birkin, Lilly of *Aaron's Rod,* Kangaroo of *Kangaroo,* Don Ramón of *The Plumed Serpent,* and the man of *The Man Who Died* are chief among Lawrence's company of messiahs. And, following other such efforts, he devoted what was to be his last book, *Apocalypse,* to explaining that the Book of Revelation is a natural consequence of gospels that preach the wrong kind of love and power: the frustrated power impulse turns vengeful. The author of Revelation endeavored in vain to justify his bottom-dog thirst for retribution and glory by patterning his work after the initiation rites of some early mystery cult. If we translate from exposition to fiction, penetration to the animistic substratum under newer forms of religion is also Lawrence's intent in *The Man Who Died*. The Christ of this excellent fable, refusing godhood in a religion of spiritual love as sensational and unnatural, accepts instead the role of Osiris offered him by a priestess of Isis through connubial rites in the temple. His visitation complete, he leaves his seed to increase in the priestess's womb and descends a current of the sea, prepared to return, like a vegetation god, in his season.

While *The Man Who Died* was Lawrence's most direct experiment in rewriting the Christ story on pagan principles, *Women in Love* was his first, and as a novel it remains one of his best, in part because Birkin is a mixed creature, now assured in proselyting, now diffident: a reluctant savior who grapples with his own soul and thereby gains in humanity what he loses in divinity.

Women in Love is only in part about women in love; its men in love carry equal burdens of theme. Its meaning evolves through the progress of two love affairs: one between Ursula Brangwen and Rupert Birkin, the other between her sister Gudrun and Gerald Crich. The love of Gudrun and Gerald betrays and devours, opening the way for Gerald to the void of despair and death, for Gudrun to depths where vitality is totally perverted. The love of Ursula and Birkin sustains bodies and souls in balance and leads to participation in the hidden powers of life. Relationships between the two men and between the two women are important but subordinate.

The story proceeds episodically until well into the last half of its course. The figures move from one country house to another, to the school where the Brangwen sisters teach, into the soiled environs of coal mines, briefly to the decadent circles of Bohemian London—to a variety of other settings, as well, in park and village and country. The action covers several months from spring to Christmas, which in this book is more a season of death than of birth. The movement of the early part is diffuse, even repetitious on the surface; the development becomes tightly knit only when the affair of Gudrun and Gerald gathers momentum in approaching its disastrous end. There are lengthy stretches of prose where the emotional involvement of the characters loses all but a thread of development. But in spite of periodic looseness of structure, the whole form of *Women in Love* is a maze where strands of theme wind about and turn back on themselves with intricacy and subtlety. Like Birkin's life at the outset, it is a "contravened knot" (*WL*, 142). We shall attempt to follow these strands as clues to the central meaning of the novel.

To bring this complex work as near as we can to simple understanding, it seems best to discuss character and symbolism, before going on to show how these elements of the novel fit into the total structure.

The question of character in *Women in Love*, perplexing to Edward Garnett, has remained so to many later readers. For elucidation we may turn to what Lawrence says, to what his characters say, and to what his characters do. The first of these sources, and more especially the third, will give us sufficient answers—if we do not lose them among the inconsistencies of the second. For no characters were ever more contradictory and obscure in talk. But far from negating Lawrence's intent, the irrationality of their speech only brings it to realization. Dark utterance is no more than we would expect from those whose thought and speech well from the dark underground of the soul. Announcing the exploration in his manifesto and making the discoveries in the characters of *Women in Love*, Lawrence reached consistency of essence underlying accidental form. He declared his independence from the old method: "To conceive a character in a certain moral scheme and make him consistent." He abandoned "the old stable *ego*" of character and embraced "another *ego*, according to whose action the individual is unrecognizable, and passes through, as it were, allotropic states which it needs a deeper sense than any we've been used to exercise to discover are states of a single radically unchanged element" (*Letters*, 282). The new *ego* of Lawrence's definition distinctly resembles the *id* of psychiatric parlance, or again, a collective unconscious whose workings are hidden from the rational individual.

Though Lawrence found his way to practice not far from his theory, one deceptive term arises to forbid simple identity of the two. In spite of his public repudiation of a "moral scheme," he held fast to morality, if by morality we understand the necessity of choosing between good and evil. The cosmos of *Women in Love* is permeated by divine instinct or intuition—Lawrence and his prophet would not give it a more exact name. Salvation for the inhabitants depends in part upon achieving complete integrity as individuals and equally complete polarity with other individuals in marriage or friendship, but it depends even more upon submission to this universal instinct or potency, which to breathe is their life and to refuse is their death. The world of *Women in Love* is a world of free will, where choice abides with the single soul, and within the course of the action all declare themselves among the children of salvation or the children of damnation. The dialogue we hear may be misleading, and the action we observe may at times appear ambiguous—for in *Women in Love* as in life the perverted seeks to approximate the normal—but the resolution of the universal conflict at length divides itself clearly into victory and defeat, when the deeds of the characters issue in results. By their fruits we know them.

The four-square foundation of human character in *Women in Love* is composed of Gerald Crich, Rupert Birkin, Ursula Brangwen, and Gudrun Brangwen, reinforced by the elder Crich, Hermione Roddice, and the sculptor Loerke. With all of them, to speak of the particular is to speak of the universal.

Gerald, like the other three principals, contains within him the seeds of salvation as well as those of destruction.[3] He is endowed with all the surface gifts of fortune: intelligence, beauty, and wealth. Hating school but suffering through to graduation, a noble primitive in his way, he turned his back on the industrial world of the family mines, seeing life as "a condition of

[3] Lawrence's practice of referring to Gerald Crich as "Gerald," and Rupert Birkin as "Birkin" is followed throughout this essay.

LAWRENCE

savage freedom," "a wilderness where one hunted and swam and rode" (*WL*, 252). By turns a soldier, explorer, and social reformer, he comes to the knowledge, never more than half-articulated, that the modern world suffers from some dreadful impairment. Seeing his duty plain, as an aristocrat, to set his bit of the earth right, he takes control of the mines, which have languished under his father's dominion, with all his innate energy and decisiveness: in the mines he has "a vision of power" (*WL*, 253). The universe becomes to him a vast machine, in which men like himself are the visible gods, ruling, as it were, by the divine right of natural aristocracy. "Translating the mystic word harmony into the practical word organization" (*WL*, 259), this early organization man creates, through hyper-efficiency, great profits and high wages. More important, he generates in himself and in the miners a passion for what they are doing: "The men were satisfied to belong to the great and wonderful machine, even whilst it destroyed them" (*WL*, 263).

While following Gerald's rise to greatness as "industrial magnate" in a chapter so named, we follow also the decline of his father, industrial magnate of another breed: the humanitarian. The failure of the elder Crich is the failure of economic paternalism, of the mistaken hope that Christian charity can be applied to industrial civilization. But the tenets of this creed—profession of abstract love for humanity and denial of the glory of great place—violate the natural laws of love and power and lead to rapid deterioration in society, facilitating the overthrow of the system by the new and apparently vital pragmatic system promulgated by Gerald. The withering and death of the elder Crich symbolize the passage of the old order.

Secure for a time in the uncontested triumph of his industrial religion, Gerald slips by degrees into the knowledge that "substitution of the mechanical principle for the organic" is but "the first and finest state of chaos" (*WL*, 263). The sin of the father may have been based upon a mistaken conception of life, but the worse sin of Gerald denies life altogether, viewing men as cogs in a social mechanism. With one order gone and a second going, *Women in Love* remains uncertain about the establishment of the

third, the order of Birkin, to be ruled over by the spontaneous
love of human for human, not indiscriminate love for humanity,
and by the quest to harmonize man and nature, not to organize
him around the machine. The men of all three orders, besides
going their individual ways, are figures symbolizing what Lawrence thought of as three stages in the wayfaring of European
man—a duality of role for his characters that he was to attempt
again and again, but never with more notable success.

In the last months of his father's illness, Gerald comes "under-
the influence of death, and of Birkin's talk, and of Gudrun's pene-
trating being" (*WL,* 252). He has been clutching at salvation in
debauches with desperate women; he half perceives but cannot
choose the course of Birkin, whose "odd mobility and change-
ableness" seem to him "to contain the quintessence of faith"
(*WL,* 265). Having betrayed the organic to the mechanical, he
has left no outlet for the life of the senses but the obscene, and in
this his perdition is accomplished, through the agency of Gudrun,
whose desperation, underneath a controlled exterior, is more profound than that of the avowed prostitutes.

Gudrun, the woman of *Women in Love* who surrenders her
being to negation and perversion, is the most beautiful of her
company, as Gerald is the most handsome of his. As an artist returned from a Bohemian life in London to teach at the grammar
school of her native town, she is following a pernicious urge to do
what she cannot bear to do, all with an air of "confidence and
diffidence" (*WL,* 8). "Fatal desire" and "fatal callousness" attend
her life among the village miners; she finds them "potent and half-
repulsive" (*WL,* 130), and in truth would like to see them
annihilated. She clings silently in spirit to her sister Ursula,
though she is the ostensible leader—a "cleaving" which is "ultimate but treacherous" (*WL,* 103). Most of her gratifications are
submerged and grounded in cruelty. Violence involving animals
holds a ritual attraction for her. On seeing Gerald spur the blood
from his Arabian mare to make her stand at a crossing gate while
a train passes, Gudrun enters a trance, as into "a vision isolated in
eternity" (*WL,* 127), then cries out encouragement to her future
lover "like a witch screaming out from the side of the road" (*WL,*

127). Even her gratuitous dance before some Highland cattle in a later chapter, begun in a spirit of instinctive response to another life form, becomes an invitation to violence which, when it is not done upon her, she turns upon Gerald by striking his face and leaving at the same time the impress of fatality upon his heart. This instance, however, is one of those in which she rouses briefly to the flow of sympathy that is one of the twin forces of salvation in Lawrence's world; the opportunity of response is not denied to the worst of that world's inhabitants.

This portrait of the artist as a demon is matched by another: that of Loerke, purely talented, purely loathsome, in league with whom Gudrun assists Gerald to his destruction and with whom she leaves the book, unredeemed, unpunished, but certainly unenvied.

As Birkin is the first Lawrence character whose predominant role is that of savior, so Ursula is his first embodiment in a woman of the human soul in quest of salvation, although "quest" is perhaps too energetic a word for the pilgrimage of Ursula, who is not so much engaged in seeking as in waiting upon the salvation of the lord. While Gudrun has been away tasting the world and finding it rotten, Ursula has stayed at home teaching in the grammar school, knowing that her life is "obsolete," hoping that marriage will "tempt" her. So far it has not. Still she looks ahead with "a strange prescience, an intimation of something yet to come" (*WL*, 10). In a passive but sensitive state that grows more active but no less delicate after the first ten chapters, she receives influences from all around her: from Gudrun, from Birkin, from Hermione, that "modern free woman." The first stirrings of recognition of Birkin as her destined lover do not come, although she has known him for some time, until one of his routine visits to her classroom as school inspector places him in unexpected strata of light and dark where the flowers of botany class flicker forth in mystic appeal to the profound vibrations of the soul, and Hermione, Birkin's current mistress, appears to do battle with him over the meaning of knowledge, goading him into a sermon that blesses the sensual and curses the sensuous. If the verbal meaning is ambiguous, the effect of the words is not. Ursula is left alone afterwards "bitterly weeping." Whether "for misery or joy" (*WL*, 49), she does not know, but all her heart is shaken. While it needs Birkin to open the subliminal ways of love to her understanding, definitions as such do not go deep with Ursula. She has little regard for Birkin's contortions in making articulate his doctrine of love that is not love but something else, of sensuality that is not sensuous. But although she has no compulsion to expound, herself, and dislikes the "Salvator Mundi" tone of Birkin's discourses, she would be lost without the complement of the male, who must strive in word as well as deed.

Ursula feels as little necessity to create as she does to state. Much of the opposition between the souls of the two sisters, so carefully approached and so significant finally, emerges through art. For example, while Ursula follows butterflies along a stream, as unconscious as they are, Gudrun can communicate with plants only by sketching them, in a "stupor of apprehension" (*WL*, 134). The fulfillment that Ursula experiences directly from the beyond and in her relationship to Birkin, Gudrun must absorb at one remove through her art, not near enough to save her from completely distorting it. The imperative to create is impure by most of the standards of *Women in Love*.

Although Ursula is pre-eminently the disciple and Birkin the master, she has the advantage over him in insouciance, that habit of taking no thought for the morrow which, on Birkin's strong recommendation, she acquires in more effective quantity than he, and which in the interflow of saving grace between them is Ursula's contribution to healing the physician.

Birkin is the keystone in the character structure of *Women in Love*. Without him, Gerald would be a common instance of the magnate overtaken at last by the failure of his successes, Gudrun would not have full occasion to spread the poison of her influence, and Ursula would not be exposed to salvation. Had Lawrence made him a thorough-going holy man, Birkin might still have prompted the other three characters to actions they perform, but then the story would have been more a fable, like *The Man Who Died*, than a novel. Birkin is messianic, to be sure, but, laboring under doubts and in need himself of being saved, he is also of this world—the most human of Lawrence's prophets—and also the world of a novel. He has "travestied himself" (WL, 22) to fit the ordinary and allowed himself to be possessed by Hermione "as if it were his fate" (WL, 24). He comes near submitting to death at her hands, and even after this, is slow to break free from her domination. Conflict is a condition of humanity, and in a novel human doubts stimulate a deeper interest than the certainties of divine anointment. Preaching a new gospel of love, Birkin becomes most fascinating in his struggle to practice what he preaches. He resists Ursula and the feminine principle made incarnate in her, though clearly recognizing their mutual accord, as he never resisted the always parasitic Hermione. Even as a savior, he wavers. While Gerald both opposes and implores the aid of his teaching, Birkin dissipates his message in contradictory pronouncements, shrugging off the latent power he has over the other man.

So far we have come upon little to distinguish character formation in *Women in Love* from that of the traditional novel. The people of fiction have always represented a class and symbolized a condition of humanity; if they did not, they would not appeal to the human beings who read their stories. And the four characters discussed above are certainly recognizable as individuals—in seeming refutation of the central theory of Lawrence's manifesto. What, then, is meant by the desire of the coalminer's son to reveal the darkness of carbon and ignore the sparkle of diamond?

The English novel as Lawrence knew it had followed paths which though they proceeded in various directions had all led to narrowing limits of exploration. Creating the people of fiction meant shaping them in relation to the codes—social, political, or moral—of the existing system. Some, like Jane Austen, might never think to question these; others, like Dickens, might wish to reform them; but few ever got beyond preoccupation with them. Traditional human institutions had come to look like forms having ultimate rule over human life. The straitened laws of society had led to Henry James and John Galsworthy, and those of science to George Moore and Arnold Bennett. The mysterious workings of vitality seldom intruded upon the world of a Galsworthy club or a James drawing room, and the specimens of characters in naturalistic fiction had indeed become mechanical products of mechanical forces, reduced from men to things.

Lawrence attempted to crack the shell of circumstance and probe nearer the essential source, but he was not so much making discoveries as rediscoveries. He saw that Melville and other "classic" American novelists had reached for expression of the hidden energies behind the outlines of society. He began to use means of insinuation into the depths of experience that had long been at the service of poetry but had remained nearly untouched by the art of fiction. And, allowances made for the changed aspect of psychology in his time, he returned to the universal pilgrimage theme of Dante and Bunyan and Blake: the life of men seen in relation to those enormous realities in the presence of which they live and move and have their being: the world of myth, of epic, and of the Bible.

The attitude of Lawrence toward human experience is expressed in *Women in Love* by methods that today are commonly grouped under "symbolism." He thus belongs to a body of novelists whose innovations are similar and whose efforts transformed the English novel in the early twentieth century, even though his fiery insistence on prophetic message and the direct clash of forces of creation and destruction set him apart from the rest. It is the object of symbolism to make a work—the components and the whole—the outward witness to inner forms of thought and feeling.[4] And since what any novel conveys to the reader is the direct experience of its characters, it becomes a symbolic novel when the direct gives simultaneous voice to the indirect, the describable to the indescribable: unlike the classical Dr. Johnson, whose opinion it was that if a man has experienced the inexpressible he has no business trying to express it, the more romantic Lawrence made just such an endeavor his chief concern.

One of the chapters of heightened symbolism in *Women in Love* is "Water-Party." In this, before surveying the general structure of the novel with symbolism fitted into a proper perspective,

---

[4] William York Tindall, *The Literary Symbol,* Indiana University Press, Bloomington, 1955, pp. 3–6.

we can see at closer range how Lawrence manipulates the palpable and the impalpable. In this chapter Ursula comes to realize that she is "deeply and passionately in love with Birkin" (*WL*, 216); Gudrun feels certain, for the time being, that for her Gerald is "the final approximation of life" (*WL*, 206). It is here also that Gerald, released from his self-consciousness, "lapsed out for the first time in his life, into the things about him" (*WL*, 202), and that Birkin foresees rebirth in the "ultimate and triumphant experience of physical passion" with Ursula (*WL*, 213). "Water-Party" is an episode in which love and death are intertwined. Each is of two kinds: destructive love and creative love; final death and death preparing for resurrection. Old emotions die to give birth to new. The death by drowning of Gerald's sister Diana lends physical dimension to its moral counterpart, and, being ultimate, this event is a prelude to the annihilating love that begins to evolve here between Gudrun and Gerald. Both love and death, in "Water-Party," are inseparable from dancing. Diana does a wild dance on the roof of a launch cabin, falls into the water and drowns both herself and the young man who dives in to rescue her. In contrast to this dance of death, Birkin performs a "slack-waggling" step for Ursula on a remote shore of the lake, making her start with fright and fascination. Gudrun's dance for the half-wild cattle, more difficult to classify at first, is soon identified as destructive by the impure motive that occasions it— defiant emulation in motion of Ursula's still participation in the life flow through singing—and by the witchlike ardor that seizes Gudrun as she dances.

In this Heraclitean chapter, where all things are a flowing, the pervading symbol of water is intensified by the shifting of light and darkness. The banks of the lake, with their confluence of people from all classes invited by the elder Crich, witness the last surge of this mock-charity togetherness before the death of the girl hastens the final extinction of the elder Crich and the disappearance of his kind of faith in such community endeavors. The realistic Gudrun offers in contrast to this strained festival a description of a savage fight for thrown pennies among slum boys on the banks of the Thames.

To escape the crowd, the sisters request a canoe in which to paddle away, as over the Nile, to a cove of their own. Gerald arranges for the canoe, warning them to be careful and asserting his desire for control in a phrase that turns out to be ironic: "I'm responsible for the water" (*WL*, 185). Just how little responsibility an industrial magnate can exercise over such forces as water is revealed by the course of events.

Bathing like nymphs in their remote inlet, picnicking, Gudrun doing eurythmics to Ursula's singing, the girls achieve a precarious happiness that even isolation by water is not enough to maintain for long. For Gerald and Birkin join them, and as Gerald chases Gudrun chasing cattle Birkin preaches to Ursula a sermon on waters, dividing them into the "silver river of life" and the seething "river of darkness" (*WL*, 196). The Aphrodite of modern love flowers, in his belief, from the "universal dissolution" of the black stream, a dark lily holding sway over such as Gudrun and Gerald. He inveighs against creatures born of too much water, quoting Heraclitus's "a dry soul is best." Ursula's temporary agreement with Gerald that Birkin would limit them to a knowledge of death indicates that as yet she does not understand the difference between one kind of death and another.

With night comes time to return to the main party. Gudrun rows herself and Gerald: a hand he has injured in the machinery of his industrial world will not allow him to exercise even this much of the control he has claimed over the water. But a current of sympathy, with only slight undercurrents of corruption, begins to run between him and Gudrun. Earlier, lighting paper lanterns to hang on the boats, they came even closer together, in "luminous union" (*WL*, 199). In "Water-Party" all glimpse the sources of salvation and hesitate in the face of choice. But even in the glow of lanterns Gudrun cannot entirely suppress her evil nature. Since her subconscious is attuned to hard, scuttling forms rather than to the flowing of "soft streams," she demands the lantern with "black crabs" and abandons to Ursula the one with "a great white cuttle-fish" (*WL*, 199).

When Diana's plunge breaks in upon their peaceful course, and Gerald dives again and again in search of her, both he and

Gudrun suffer new and fearful relationships to water. He recognizes an underworld over which he cannot extend his kind of responsibility, and she becomes terrified, also, by the infinite subspaces. But the overpowering presence of water unites Birkin and Ursula. To facilitate dragging for the bodies, they go to open the sluice gates of the dam, and the outrush, the "great steady booming of water" (WL, 210), torments Ursula and sends her to the arms of Birkin; clinging in mute contemplation, they consider renewed life, the anticipated "little death" that will bring them to resurrection.

The "flow" that has brought all things to pass in this chapter is doubly symbolic, then: to some a current of destruction, to some of life, the direction determined by moral choice. While "streaming" has proved obviously inimical to the love of Gerald and Gudrun, and they turn in the future from its symbolic import, Birkin and Ursula come back to it with natural affinity at important junctures of their relationship. Birkin's is a fluid soul, Gerald's is hardened beyond all change, constantly painted in symbolic association with ice and eternal snows. It is Birkin's portion to flow and live, Gerald's to shatter and die.

The method and scope of "Water-Party" are those of the whole of *Women in Love*. While exploring the multiple images of experience, Lawrence never loses sight of his single theme: the mystery of interdependence between unity and duality. The rhythm of the book's structure, a rhythm magnified by the lens of symbolism, is one of ebb and flow, of climax and subsidence, best described by Lawrence himself in his foreword to the first American edition as a "pulsing, frictional to-and-fro which works up to culmination" (WL, x). In *Women in Love*, where all things are double, experience oscillates between the consummation of attraction and the consummation of repulsion.

Marriage, understood not as an institution but as a state of perfection, is the most ubiquitous face of the theme. In the first talk between the sisters, Ursula looks forward to marriage with anticipation, Gudrun with hopelessness. They immediately go to witness a marriage, where the bride, seeing the groom arrive late, races him from the road to the altar. Gerald condemns this breach of etiquette, believing in the maintenance, if not the value, of convention; Birkin approves the action as stemming from the spontaneity of true freedom—and thus an early step is taken in the progression of theme from simple to complex.

On the way to the church, Gudrun is repelled by the ugly village. Seeing Gerald for the first time, she experiences "a strange and overwhelming sensation" (*WL*, 16). Hermione is "rapt, triumphant" (*WL*, 24), in possession of Birkin's arm. All these are subordinate consummations repeated from chapter to chapter, as when Ursula reacts in a "spasm of anger and chagrin" (*WL*, 49) after the botanical episode in "Class-Room," and Gudrun feels "damned" (*WL*, 52) by her envy of Gerald's physical freedom in the chapter called "Diver." But comprehending the structure of *Women in Love* is a matter of moving from one significant culmination to the next.

The first of these, in "Crème de Menthe" and "Totem," is a travesty, a favorite device of Lawrence's, one that has not been sufficiently appreciated. This is Gerald's affair with the degenerate Pussum, whose psyche is that of the "violated slave" (*WL*, 89), pregnant by one lover, seeing in Gerald another through whom to stir the jealousy and force the submission of the first. That the unnatural bears a surface resemblance to the natural seems consistent in a book where "sensuousness" is said to be the reverse of "sensuality." In a parody of Laurentian blood mystery, the Pussum "(unfolds) like some red lotus in dreadful flowering nakedness" (*WL*, 77), and Gerald is stimulated by "magnetic darkness . . . concentrated at the base of his spine like a fearful source of power" (*WL*, 81). The symbol of this episode, the "totem," is a primitive African carving of a woman in childbirth, the "extreme of physical sensation, beyond the limits of mental consciousness" (*WL*, 83). The young magnate, about to go to bed with a woman carrying another man's child, wants to know if that statue is not "rather obscene" (*WL*, 83). Next morning his spirit affirms before his ego can deny that the statue objectifies his knowledge of Pussum. Then, as the industrialist turning to the prophet for a definition of art, he demands enlightenment of Birkin, whose bluntness is far from reassuring.

The place of art as symbol in *Women in Love* is not to be judged alone by the obvious fact that the artists portrayed therein are on the side of the devils. Birkin explains to Gerald that the statue "contains the whole truth of that state," a state "so sensual as to be final, supreme" (*WL*, 88). Another African fetish from the same collection, remembered in the turmoil of the chapter "Moony," becomes for Birkin a crucial step in seeing beyond the dead end of such sensuousness into a new and creative union of opposites in himself and Ursula. The artist Loerke, handing round a photograph of a statuette he has done representing Lady Godiva as a bud of a girl on a terrible stallion, maintains that art is pure form, unrelated to the living world. The sensitive Ursula guesses rightly that the girl is one whom Loerke has betrayed, and joins battle with Loerke and Gudrun: "The world of art is only the truth about the real world, that's all—but you are too far gone to see it" (*WL*, 491)—as indeed they are. What Ursula here states explicitly applies implicitly to art, if not to artists, in the novel as a whole.

The abortive love of Birkin and Hermione—a culmination of repulsion—reaches a crisis at Breadalby, her country house. In a "consummation of voluptuous ecstasy at last" (*WL*, 118), she attacks him with a lapis lazuli paperweight. Shielding himself with a thick volume of Thucydides but not escaping without a bruised head, Birkin retreats to an ultrahuman source of power. In a damp grove, naked, he paddles among the primroses and rolls in the hyacinths, in the healing solace of the "lovely, subtle, responsive vegetation" (*WL*, 121). This, he finds for the time being, is his marriage place, and he leaves it feeling that he will be satisfied forever with this vegetable love. Later, in the chapter "An Island," he has a change of heart in and about the plant world, with vegetation, water, and an island forming for him and Ursula one of their preliminary Edens. But this one proves unsatisfactory because Birkin persists in being a teacher rather than a lover.

The chapters "Rabbit," "Moony," "Excurse," and "Death and Love," forming the heart of the action in *Women in Love*, celebrate the rites of matrimony according to the opposing mystiques of good and evil. "Rabbit" and "Moony" are ceremonial; "Excurse" and "Death and Love" are co-responsive to ceremony in direct action. Alternation between the differing complexities of love as embodied in the two pairs of lovers traces the main structure of the book, and these chapters stand in culmination of that structure. With all the comprehensiveness of Lawrence's art, they intertwine consummations of attraction and consummations of repulsion, with attractions which to the reader are often repulsive and repulsions which are sometimes attractive.

Gudrun is now at Shortlands, the Crich estate, as tutor to the youngest Crich daughter, Winifred. Beneath the physiognomy of innocence, the child is a demon artist in the making; through inborn misanthropy and the maternal adoption of her dog and rabbit, she contributes to the "Rabbit" theme of humanity depraved to bestiality. In Lawrence's system, man has his own sensuality, which is able by means of his body, the utterance of his soul, to commune with the god-mystery. It is not an evolutional system; the vital impulse does not progress from stage to stage in either its natural or its supernatural manifestations. Rather, it leaps across gaps between universal cycles, from incarnation to incarnation in creatures, from apotheosis to apotheosis in gods. The hierarchy of Laurentian being is not a great chain, descending link by link through heaven and earth, but a great order in which polarities vibrate from plexus to plexus. For a creature to deny its place in the natural order, its own specific kind of polarity—which is possible for man, at least—is the unforgivable sin. This sort of negation, in Gerald and Gudrun and Winifred, has led to reversion. The rabbit, true to his own creation, is not obscene, not "rabbit-mad" (WL, 276); but the transfer of human emotions to his sphere, by Gerald and Gudrun as lovers and by Winifred as "mother," immerses them all in obscenity and brings Gerald another step closer to the madness that finally entraps him.

These "abhorrent mysteries" (WL, 275), brutish and raging, involving both the subjection of masochism and the mastery of sadism, begin when Gudrun lifts Winifred's "pet" rabbit by the ears and he claws gashes in her wrist. Gerald arrives, seizes hold of the rabbit's ears, strikes him on the neck to subdue him. In the dreadful temple of Gudrun's psyche the screams of the animal rip the "veil of her consciousness" (*WL,* 274), and Gerald has "knowledge of her in the long red rent of her forearm" (*WL,* 275). Then Gerald carries the rabbit to an enclosed grass court, throws him in, and man, woman, and child watch him alternate from violent running to quiescent crouching; Gerald and Gudrun enjoy invisible initiation together in the "obscene beyond" (*WL,* 276). Winifred creeps into the court, "softly conjuring the rabbit" to let "mother stroke its fur" (*WL,* 277).

The first portion of "Moony," following at once upon "Rabbit," is a contrasting ritual, linked, however, to its predecessor by Ursula's preference for animal company in her temporary "repudiation" of mankind. But her proper sphere is the lunar, that of the full moon whose "great presence" (*WL,* 279) causes her to shrink but whose brightness she radiates. She takes a path to the bank of a millpond, welcoming the shelter of trees against exposure to her luminary, and there spies Birkin prowling near the water, who suddenly begins to damn Cybele and, as if really attacked by lunacy, to hurl stones at the moon's image in the pond. The splashes sounding and echoing, the shatter and restoration of the reflected orb invade the soul of Ursula-Cybele and reduce it to primal moon and water. When she at last approaches him and begs him to stop, he does so, but he demands the gift of "golden light" (*WL,* 284) from her. They must find release from opposition in a brief argument before surrendering to "gentle communion" (*WL,* 288), which on this occasion seems perfect without the extremities of physical passion, but in spite of which the mooning Ursula remains for some time to come in "a complete bright world of her self alone" (*WL,* 296). This incident is one of the prose triumphs of *Women in Love,* and Lawrence is due praise not only for making it so, but for making it more enthralling than the ceremonials of "Rabbit." It is not the ordinary way of novelists to create good more engrossing than evil.

The consummations of "Rabbit" and "Moony" are more psychic than physical, but in "Excurse" and "Death and Love" the balance reverses, and each pair of souls gives utterance to its composite nature in the body. "Excurse" discovers Ursula and Birkin fleeing to an inn, to Sherwood Forest—yet another Eden —to ultimate communion as lovers in and out of this world. Birkin has prevailed, for the concept of love that he has preached in obscurity now dawns upon Ursula, and the "golden light" in her goes free (*WL*, 358). Love emerges as "mystically-physically satisfying" from profundities "deeper than the phallic source" (*WL*, 359)—paralleling Birkin's previous vision beyond the impasse of sensuousness depicted by the African statues. In these climactic moments Lawrence always introduces the occult and the biblical. To Ursula this love means resting "steadfast in perfectly suspended equilibrium, pure mystic nodality of physical being" (*WL*, 365); it also signifies "the old magic of the Book of Genesis, where the sons of God saw the daughters of men, that they were fair" (*WL*, 357).

The chapter "Death and Love" might also have been designated "Death in Love." Despite some touches of hope in its earlier stages, the affair of Gerald and Gudrun arises from desperation and flowers in voracity disguised as passion. After the death and burial of his father, Gerald is driven one night to revisit the muddy graveyard, where terror awaits him and where as a last measure he resolves to enter the Brangwen house by stealth and seek out Gudrun in her bedroom. He succeeds in reaching her, and releases upon her "all his pent-up darkness and corrosive death," while she receives him "in throes of acute violent sensation" (*WL*, 393). But an "awful, inhuman distance" remains between them (*WL*, 395); he is a "burden upon her" that she is offended at having to bear (*WL*, 398); there is to her "something monstrous about him, about his juxtaposition against her" (*WL*, 396).

The union of Ursula and Birkin is a figure of supernal marriage, while that of Gudrun and Gerald is a similitude of infernal nuptials. Lawrence has now arrived at the fullest statement of the contrasted consummations, psychic and physical, whose fires illumine the dual forces of good and evil in his emotional universe.

After "Excurse" Ursula and Birkin submit to legal marriage,

and now even the surviving conflicts between them only attest to their essential unity: the creative unity that is attained through the continuous reconciliation of opposites. The progress of Gerald and Gudrun now assumes dominance over that of Birkin and Ursula, devastation running its final course for the magnate who was already in the "first and finest state of chaos" (*WL*, 263). The symbolism of fixity and frost, always attached to Gerald, now becomes more pronounced. Recalling Lawrence's manifesto on character, we may consider snow and water as "allotropic" states of the same substance and recognize that the difference of state makes all the difference: Birkin as "water" is a creature whose mobility enables him to encompass the subtleties of existence, but Gerald as "snow" is crystallized in a state whose limits of tolerance are narrow and inelastic. This "flame of ice" (*WL*, 458) conveys himself and Gudrun to frigid consummation and death in the Bavarian Alps. Birkin and Ursula are there too, and all formulate their last testimony on the meaning and purpose of life in Gerald's element among the peaks, a "perfect cradle of snow" (*WL*, 453)—more nearly a coffin. Birkin seldom enters the action now, but he is clearly content. To Ursula the alpine air is "murderous," yet she feels reborn "here in the high snow, against the stars" (*WL*, 466). But for her ambiguity soon turns to certainty, and, fighting off the winter that is "slowly strangling her soul" (*WL*, 494), she has Birkin take her away to the lower world. The battle between Gerald and Gudrun, already intense enough, flares higher after the departure of the Birkins. With their last restraint gone, Gerald and Gudrun can now contend in the open. Under the preponderant urge of each to inflict cruelty is the inseparable urge to submit to it: to destroy or to be destroyed, with no middle ground. Gudrun's love of these diabolical opposites draws her into closer affinity with eternal frost as she slowly annihilates Gerald, creature of that frost, turning his own weapon against him. She breaks her unholy pact with Gerald to go far beyond him in the mysteries of iniquity with Loerke. At the boundary of his tortured life, knowing that his last ecstasy must transpire in the arctic barrens, Gerald stumbles upon a choice that stirs for him the sympathy of the reader. "One convulsion of his will" would translate him into a soul "impervious, self-completed, a thing isolated" (*WL*, 508)—would make of him, that is, a being like Gudrun or Loerke. But to bring about this kind of isolation he feels that he must murder Gudrun, and at the last instant he recoils from the act, wandering off to his own death in the snowy night. He is overpowered, finally, by the stigma of Cain: having accidentally killed his brother when they were boys, he has carried that guilt all his life. In the snow, with the eyes of delirium, he sees himself murdered by his own ghost.

Now that we have considered the chief framework of *Women in Love,* other components will fall naturally into place. Although the perplexities of amatory love fill most of the novel, the question of sympathy within the sexes, especially between man and man, occupies a high if lesser position. Birkin and Gerald, though enjoying a "powerful and suppressed friendliness," do not at first profess belief in "deep relationship between men and men" (*WL*, 37), and sometimes even hate each other (*WL*, 62). Or again, Birkin expands with the pity of a wiser for a weaker man. Often on the point of asking what he must do to be saved, Gerald would be a disciple if he could only follow a strong propensity in himself, but he is prevented by the reluctance of Birkin's saviorhood and by his own inclination to scoff. In one of the two chapters devoted primarily to their relationship, "Man to Man," Birkin proposes a *Blutbrüderschaft* and is met with evasion: the suggestion may hold a frightful irony for a man who unintentionally committed *Brudermord* early in life: a deed that both Birkin and Ursula speak of as a compulsive accident—and considering Gerald's end they may be right. The intimacy of the other chapter, "Gladiatorial," a brotherhood of sorts, is something for which Lawrence has been more often condemned than lauded. Physical closeness between males is easily suspect. To the reader it may seem that to insist on a difference between outright perversion and nude wrestling in private into a state of unconsciousness is to draw a nice distinction—though Lawrence would have thought semi-nude wrestling on television before an audience of thousands obscene by comparison. But, judging within the context and by the standards of the novel, hopeful to avoid overdrawing conclusions, we may say that the incident attempts to solve a problem which plagued the artistic honesty of the author. If love is to be physical and not spiritual, then physical communication without abnormality must be possible within as well as between the sexes. And so the wrestling contest is interpreted as "inspiration" (*WL*, 308) and as a way of keeping sane (*WL*, 310). But, still following the book's criteria, the companionship of Birkin and Gerald turns out to be a failure. Birkin does not save Gerald; at one point he even recommends Gudrun to him. The two men at last "revoke" each other (*WL*, 497), and, after the death of Gerald, Birkin is left with only his faith, barren of works, that "love" without dishonor is possible between men.

Even more subdued, but far from negligible, is the response of woman to woman. Except between the two sisters, and sometimes then, such understandings are usually confederations against men. On one occasion, when Birkin is being his usual difficult self in the presence of both his former and his prospective mistresses, Ursula joins with Hermione in opposition to him, but this influence Ursula throws off even before she and Birkin come together as lovers. The gradual separation of the sisters is far more significant. The impressionable Ursula admires her younger sister "with all her soul" (*WL*, 10)—but not quite all, for Gudrun causes in her "a certain weariness" (*WL*, 14). As Gudrun's time at home from London lengthens, exchange of confidences and a common front against hostile conditions increase sisterly affection, but then the girls tend apart until finally it is Gudrun who admires—and despises. At leavetaking in the Alps, the last time they see each other before Gerald's downfall, Gudrun sneers at Ursula's discourse on love, echoed from the master. The "quest of Rupert's Blessed Isles" is not for her (*WL*, 500). Upon Ursula's tearful condolence after the death of Gerald, Gudrun can only hide her face on Ursula's shoulder, not "escape the cold devil of irony that froze her soul" (*WL*, 542)—the further irony is that now Gerald is dead his icy demon has joined the legion in her soul.

As previously stated, discourse in Lawrence is confused by the annoying habit his saints have of sometimes talking like sinners, and, to a lesser degree, his sinners of talking like saints. But yea is as yea does, not as it says, and so is nay. Gerald the denier is dead, having put himself beyond the reach of salvation, and Birkin can only grieve that this is so. Love in *Women in Love* has had its defeat in the actions of Gerald and Gudrun, in the actions also of Gerald and Birkin, but its triumph in those of Ursula and Birkin. The failure of brotherhood precludes Utopia, yet the success of matrimony confirms the possibility of establishing a more perfect society, to be built by the few upon the ruins of a society of abstract love or of mechanism, the first represented by Gerald's father, the second by Gerald himself. The victory of two, of Birkin and Ursula, stands above the loss of all the rest to declare *Women in Love* a document of love and affirmation in spite of the large shares of misanthropy and negation that darken its pages.

Disgust and damnation for the majority of mankind are consistent with the New Testament prophet in Lawrence: which brings us again to the evangelistic and the apocalyptic and to the discussion of form. To see Lawrence the artist in these terms is to understand best what he was and what he was about. Not that he was an official adherent to Christianity, but that the tone and form of his creation are those of Christianity in its most primitive state.

Whatever its claims to being a religion of love, Christianity has always envisioned a heaven for the beloved few, a hell for the despised multitude. Its attitude is thus compounded of the charity preached in parts of the Gospels and the hatred proclaimed by much of the Book of Revelation. What Lawrence says about these two sides of Christianity in his book *Apocalypse* applies as well to his art as to that religion. We discover in *Women in Love* the same paradox of the prophet: the apocalyptist in him fulfills his wish to be rid of a troubled and troublesome society, while the evangelist in him proposes a new heaven and earth founded upon love. The good news of this novel is that of the messianic savior; the rest is that of the prophetic avenger.

Lawrence's art is generated, then, like the religion that controlled his imagination if not his allegiance, out of contradiction, with victory and affirmation emerging in the same proportion in the one as in the other. It is the nature of paradox to refuse logical explanation, and perhaps because of its very nature to exert strong influence upon the human spirit, in both art and religion. Whether or not Lawrence's art makes any sense as religion is beside the point. *Women in Love* employs form, tone, and symbol from early Christianity to illuminate the experience of modern characters in such a way as to make strong appeal to the imagination. Having succeeded in so much, the novel has succeeded in all that can be demanded of a work of art.

The Inwardness of the Understanding

DOROTHY TUCK

> The matter of prime importance was, of course, that he should be understood; the inwardness of the understanding would consist precisely in each individual coming to understand it by himself.
>
> SØREN KIERKEGAARD, *Concluding Unscientific Postscript*

FAULKNER FREQUENTLY WROTE what might be called psychological mystery stories; he was a master of suspense, of the beguiling and ambiguous hint of dark secrets soon to be unveiled, of the presentation without comment of mystifying actions, only afterward offering possible motivations. Because of this, there is really no such thing as reading Faulkner once and being done with him, for only at the end of the initial reading do we have all the pieces in the puzzle (or at least as many as Faulkner ever intends to give us), and only then do we attain the perspective from which the entire action can be viewed meaningfully. With most authors, a certain amount of mystification is simply a device for keeping the reader's attention, for making him want to find out what happened. In Faulkner's work, however, the gradual revelation of motive and clue, fact and speculation, serves a far more important function than the creation of suspense per se; it makes the reader himself a participant in the unfolding of meaning. As a result, he is almost literally subjected to the fictional experience, rarely only an objective observer of it.

As life is a process of discovery, so fictional experience in Faulkner is a constant re-enacting of the drama of awakening consciousness, both for reader and character. But Faulkner's characters, by and large, fail to make the final thrust toward realization that would give them perspective on their past errors and the moral vision with which to confront the future. Thomas Sutpen dies an ironic rather than a tragic figure for his failure to recognize his "mistake" in equating moral action with debts owed and discharged. Even gentle Ike McCaslin can see no way to act morally within the framework of the world created by his grandfather, and so withdraws from it entirely. But if Faulkner's characters persistently fail to achieve self-knowledge or, gaining some insight, fail to act upon it in any positive sense, it is in order that the reader might learn from their negative example. "We have had the experience but missed the meaning," says T. S. Eliot. Faulkner's people, who come to the end of their fictional lives without quite grasping the meaning, provide for the reader the opportunity that lies beyond the final page: an understanding and assessment of the fictional experience that restores it in a fuller and more complete form, beyond any statement that can be easily articulated.

The narrative techniques that Faulkner generally uses to intensify reader involvement are variations of the stream of consciousness: more or less complete immersion within the immediate mental processes of a character, so that the reader himself experiences (rather than is told or shown) both the character's inner reality and the total complexity of the action. Thus the essence of the Compson family and its world is reborn in the reader as he experiences Benjy, Quentin, and Jason in *The Sound and the Fury;* thus in *As I Lay Dying* the tensions and relationships among the members of the Bundren family emerge into multidimensioned reality as we see the action from within the minds of some fifteen different characters; thus in *Absalom, Absalom!* we recreate the reality of the Sutpen family and the Old South out of the contradictory and subjective medley of the narrators' stories.

If for the reason of technique alone, *Light in August* is something of an anomaly among Faulkner's most impressive early works. Written in the middle of his phenomenally productive

1929–1936 period, it is the only one of the major novels [1] not
markedly experimental in structure and technique. In contrast to
the intense subjectivity of the experimental novels, *Light in
August* is relatively objective, focusing on the actions of the characters far more than on their internal states, and even describing
the characters' inner experience in a more or less objective fashion. Mystification that is a natural result of the subjective approach, when the reader is limited to the contents of one character's mind and perceptions at a time, becomes in *Light in August*
almost entirely dependent upon structure—the order in which the
action is unfolded. Faulkner's various structural and technical
devices for the withholding of meaning, most brilliantly displayed
in *Absalom, Absalom!*, are reduced in *Light in August* to the form
of simple and objective flashbacks.

Yet, though it uses a very minimum of these technical devices, *Light in August* achieves the same effect as the experimental novels: the immersion of the reader in the artistic creation so
that he experiences the "inwardness of the understanding." How
the novel does so, it seems to me, is by a peculiar kind of direct
indirection, an objective presentation of a situation through
which glimmer suggestive outlines of some profound and subjective apprehension of human experience. Interestingly enough, in
doing so the book partakes not only of the elements of the psychological mystery, but of the more straightforward popular detective story as well.

All of Faulkner's major novels are studies in meaning, of
past experience reconsidered in order to illuminate the reality of
the present. Like the typical detective-story writer, he is concerned with discovering the truth, though it is a different kind of
truth and so there is accordingly less emphasis on *who done it*

---

[1] In addition to *Light in August* (1932), the major novels are probably
The Sound and the Fury (1929), *As I Lay Dying* (1930), and *Absalom,
Absalom!* (1936). *The Hamlet* (1940) and *Go Down, Moses* (1942) are
sometimes considered major works, though it seems to me that neither is
of the stature of the least important of the earlier group. *A Fable* (1954), a
relatively late work, is a complex and awesome philosophical novel that
fairly shouts its importance, but it suffers under a heavy load of abstractness
and ultimately fails (it seems to me) as a work of art.

and more on *what is it:* what really happened, what are the real sources of the action. However, unlike the mystery writer, Faulkner rarely provides us either with one guilty individual or with a single "true" account of the facts. This suggests not only a parallel but a new twist, a striking and ironic contrast to what might be called the detective-story syndrome.

Part of the appeal of the detective story may very well be, as W. H. Auden [2] has suggested, that it reduces to an allegory of guilt and innocence in which the reader experiences a psychological revalidation of his innocence when the murderer is unmasked and the other members of the group, until now equally shadowed by the suspicion of guilt, are cleared; it is a simplified and somewhat altered version of the archetypal Fall in which the protagonist is finally proved innocent and restored to Edenic bliss, the murderer-scapegoat assuming all guilt and removing it from the group with his conviction and/or death. This is a relatively simple, wish-fullfillment type of story, frequently referred to (not without some sense of superiority) as escape literature. Quite often (particularly in the hands of lady writers) it tends to have an element of romance involved in it. However, the dectective story's most striking characteristic is its lack of moral ambiguity. Though ideally the reprehensible elements of the murderer's character should not be at all apparent until his unmasking, his evil traits should then be so clearly revealed that there is little or no sympathy for him. In cases where the murderer tends to enlist our sympathy, he is usually given the opportunity to commit a decent suicide. In a word, the detective story rarely raises moral questions; the guilty are always caught, the innocent vindicated, and the society or group, temporarily disordered, is set right again. It provides a deeply ironic contrast between the world as we are pleased to see it and the world as it actually is.

A summary of *Light in August* can be made to read like a parody of our typical detective story: It begins with a romance interest in the person of pregnant Lena Grove seeking Lucas Burch, her defected sweetheart. Lena arrives in Jefferson at the

[2] Cf. W. H. Auden, "The Guilty Vicarage," *Harper's Magazine*, May, 1948, 406–12.

time of the discovery of the murder of Joanna Burden. A prime suspect appears at first to be Lena's lover, who has assumed the name Joe Brown and lives in a cabin on the murdered woman's property; the supposititious Brown tries to clear himself and get the reward by accusing his partner and roommate, Joe Christmas, who Brown claims has Negro blood. Brown is believed, and a manhunt for the "nigger murderer" of a white woman is begun. After hiding in the nearby woods for a week, Christmas walks into a neighboring town and lets himself be arrested. Two days later, being transferred from the jail to the courthouse, he breaks away and flees. He is pursued by a militant young deputy, Percy Grimm, into the house of a former minister named Hightower, who tries to protect him. Cornered behind a kitchen table, Christmas is shot and castrated by Grimm. The romance interest is picked up at the end as Lena, with her new baby, travels on, accompanied not by her worthless lover but by the faithful and honorable Byron Bunch.

This summary, of course, is grossly unfair to the depth and complexity of the novel; while the superficial facts may fit, the essence of the story is destroyed, the emphasis on the characters of Joe Christmas, the Reverend Hightower, and Joanna Burden are not taken into account, and the polarities and contrasts that Faulkner underlines at every opportunity are not even mentioned. And yet, is not the above summary essentially what the townsfolk in the novel believe has happened? They are experiencing a murder, a manhunt, and an execution which is precisely parallel in psychological effect to the discovery and expulsion or death of the scapegoat that takes with it the guilt of the people. It is only to the reader that the multiple ironies of this literal and psychological expunging of guilt become apparent. From the point of view of the townsfolk, there is no moral ambiguity whatever; and Gavin Stevens, as the voice of the people, further underlines their (literal) black-and-white approach to morality in his explanation of Joe's good and bad actions as dictated, respectively, by what Stevens assumes to be Joe's white and black blood.

In one of its aspects *Light in August* is an ironic recasting, into another and more meaningful dimension, of the detective story's allegory of guilt and innocence. Much of the meaning and power of the novel stems from a series of ironic inversions of similar mythic or archetypal situations. The crucial figure in these half-mythic designs is the hostile, opaque anti-hero, Joe Christmas.

In terms of space devoted to him, Joe clearly occupies the center of the book. One is tempted to call him the hero, except for the fact that he is so patently unheroic; one can pity him to a certain degree and empathize with him under certain conditions, particularly in the scenes where he strikes his foster father and then rides to get Bobbie, and in the description of his actions during the twenty-four hours before he murders Joanna; but one rarely feels sympathetic toward him or understands the internal sources of his deeds. Ruthless, lonely, violently aggressive, and inflexibly passive by turns, he elicits neither our perverse admiration for wickedness nor grudging recognition of good. He seems his own worst enemy, persistently daring Fate to stand aside and let him destroy himself. He is a negative character in an almost photographic sense, as well as in the figurative sense of lacking positive or "likable" qualities. Yet he is unquestionably not a villain nor, like Faulkner's inhuman and vicious characters, Flem Snopes and Popeye, is he two-dimensional. This is an important distinction; Joe is never a caricature. The very opaqueness of his character, the fact that we almost never are taken into his mind or his confidence, contributes to the sense of density and three-dimensional reality that he conveys. We may never really understand why he acts as he does, and shruggingly agree with the behaviorists that he was conditioned to doom by his heredity and environment. We may never really sympathize with him, and may even actively dislike him, but we can also not quite escape the feeling that these reactions are irrelevant, for his essential and puzzling humanity remains. To the end, he is a mystery; but he is always Joe, a man.

On the most realistic level, Joe is simply the isolated man seeking his identity. His close similarity to the archetypal Wanderer, the isolated Cain, is readily apparent, and suggests his ironic affinities with other mythic figures. The circumstances surrounding his birth, the mystery of his identity, his being found in a basket on the doorstep of an orphanage, his upbringing by foster parents, his flight from home—all these factors fit in the general pattern of the early life of the mythic hero.

Joe's childhood is a kind of parody of the innocent youth of the mythic hero, and there is a tremendous dialectical tension between the actual Joe and the archetypal echoes his actions suggest. The inflexible child who refuses to learn his catechism is described as resembling a picture of religious ecstasy. The stoical young Joe occasionally reveals an Adam-like innocence, and strikes out in vicious despair at the bitter taste of the apple of knowledge. Each of his most climactic early experiences is a "fall" —almost a sudden, headlong plunge—into a further (and, to Joe, repellent) realization of mankind's bondage to nature. Thus he sacrifices a sheep in a paradoxical attempt to buy immunity from the hated knowledge of menstruation, to cancel, as it were, blood with blood. Significantly, he was "not hurt or astonished so much as outraged" (164). The outrage is the instinctive reaction of a man who discovers himself not a child of the gods, a creature of spirit and light, but an animal trapped in the natural cycles of birth and death from which his mortal flesh cannot escape. Joe can live with the abstract knowledge, but when he is forced to face it in his own life (on his first assignation with Bobbie Allen, he realizes that her "sickness" is menstruation) he reacts violently, striking her and fleeing into the woods, where in rage and revulsion he vomits. The contrast between the timeless, deathless perfection for which he longs and the earthbound actuality he has been made to face is emphasized in his impressions during his flight through the trees: "He seemed to see a diminishing row of suavely shaped urns in moonlight, blanched. And not one was perfect. Each one was cracked and from each crack there issued something liquid, deathcolored, and foul" (165).

Joe's relationship with Bobbie is a parodic inversion of idyllic romance and first love. In his incredible, blind innocence he makes love to Bobbie as if no one had ever made love before, as if it were not only his first love but the first love in the world. He hears the conversation of Bobbie's "managers," Max and Mame, "as if they talked at and because of him, in a language which he did not understand" (169). He visits Bobbie's room two nights a week, not knowing at first that anyone else had ever done such a thing. When he discovers—as one would expect him to have discovered at the very beginning—that she is a prostitute, his response is pure understated pathos: " 'I thought you knew,' she said. 'No,' he said. 'I reckon I didn't' " (173). And, in despair at his knowledge, he begins to smoke and drink, to ape Max's mannerisms, and to call Bobbie, even in the presence of others, his whore.

On three later occasions Joe is brought up short with a recognition of reality that he reacts from violently but fails to assimilate. First, he is betrayed by Bobbie, whom he has come to take away with him after he has struck and perhaps killed his foster father; she curses and reviles him, lets her friends beat him up, and abandons him. Later, a Northern white prostitute indifferently reveals to him that she will accept a Negro as readily as a white customer, and in outrage at her moral betrayal of the white race he tries to reject his whiteness completely and goes to live entirely among Negroes. And finally Joanna Burden, who has claimed him as a Negro in a last, violent expression of her sexuality, perversely betrays his perverse acceptance of her as the embodiment of female corruption and moral perfidy; her apparent pregnancy is actually the onset of her menopause, signalling to her and Joe the end of her sexual life. Each of these "falls" is occasioned by a woman and takes place in a sexual context; this underscores Joe's identification with Adam, who was prevailed upon to eat the apple by Eve and who, having eaten, saw that he was naked and was ashamed.

But Adam's loss of innocence is also a climbing toward consciousness, a moving away from the slumbering matrix of nature toward a sense of separateness and self-awareness; and the paradox of the fortunate fall exists not only in the religious sense of making possible Christ's willing sacrifice for man's redemption, but as a metaphor for man's emergence into the sphere of moral responsibility. In Joe's case, however, each further loss of innocence leads him not to self-knowledge but away from it, not toward a reconciliation of the opposites symbolized by his sense of himself as having black and white blood but toward a sharper separation of them, until finally, with Joanna, he is a white man by day, a Negro by night. And, as he fails to reconcile and integrate the disparate elements of himself, he fails to grow. The street he enters at eighteen flows past his fleeting feet like mechanical scenery operated by the treadmill on which he paces unawares; the street continues moving on for fifteen years, while Joe tirelessly pumps the mechanism and remains in the same place. Not until after his murder of Joanna and his week-long sojourn in the woods does he come to a realization of all he has been. Then he sees his life as a circle made by a street which ran for thirty years, a circle that he is still inside, though he has traveled further in the last seven days than in the thirty years before. Ironically it is a circle, double-edged symbol of both wholeness and nothingness, with which Joe expresses the futility of his frantic attempt to make himself what he chooses to be.

During his days in the wilderness Joe comes closest to an acceptance of his human condition and its inevitable bondage to the cycles of nature and death. In acquiescing to the nature from which he has held himself, all his life, rigidly apart, he paradoxically becomes freed of the demands of nature. Living in the woods, in the very heart of nature, he loses the need to eat, to sleep; he loses an awareness of time and in a sense steps outside of time. "All I ever wanted was peace," he thinks despairingly before he kills Joanna. Finding "peace and unhaste and quiet" in the woods, he accepts his fate as man: he is described as sitting on the seat of the wagon that is taking him to Mottstown, while on his feet are the Negro shoes, "that mark on his ankles the gauge definite and ineradicable of the black tide creeping up his legs, moving from his feet upward as death moves" (297). Literally, he is going toward the death he has invited with his murder of Joanna; but he is also accepting Adam's fate, the death that mocks all mankind's efforts. For the first time in his life he moves out to confront the world and human experience without defensive hostility, with the quiet acceptance of a man who has seen his guilt and knows that his only freedom lies in bearing it willingly.

An aspect of *Light in August* that has been persistently puzzling to readers is the presence of a fair amount of what seems to be Christ symbolism connected with Joe. This has been explained away variously by reasoning that Faulkner may have originally conceived of Joe as a Christ figure, got carried away and created a very un-Christlike character, but forgot to go back and take out the now-misleading clues; or (somewhat more realistically) that Joe is a negative Christ figure, implicitly compared with Christ to show how thoroughly un-Christlike Joe is. It seems to me, however, that Joe functions as an ironic archetype of Christ. This is neither to say that he in any way resembles the Jesus of the Gospels or that he is identified with Christ as a purely religious figure. Joe serves the community as the archetypal Christ or scapegoat, the victim (willing or otherwise, divine or otherwise) on whom is placed the guilt of the people, and whose death destroys that guilt. He also figures as an ironic inversion of the archetypal dying god, in whose death there are elements both of sacrifice to a higher and more fearful power and of the communion with the god and with one another granted to the partakers of his body. Thus the archetype of Adam, the guilty man sentenced to death, evolves into the archetype of Christ,[3] the innocent taking on the guilt of others.

Joe has killed Joanna Burden, so we can hardly call him an innocent victim. Yet, that he is victimized is shown by the enormous discrepancy between the actuality of his deed and the interpretation placed on it by the townspeople. His personal guilt is great enough, but hardly so overwhelming as to deserve the end that awaits him. Though the murder is premeditated, almost

[3] The idea of Christ as the "new Adam" is a common religious concept and has been seconded in Jung's psychology of archetypes; cf. Jung, *Symbols of Transformation,* p. 262: "Not unjustly is Christ called Adam secundus." Both figures, of course, are archetypes of the Self. For an interesting discussion of the figure of Adam as a primary expression of the concept of the hero in American literature, see R. W. B. Lewis, *The American Adam.*

precommitted ("I had to do it," he says, speaking of it as though it were already accomplished), it is also, strictly speaking, in self-defense: when Joe refuses to pray with her, Joanna pulls a gun with the intention of killing them both. From a rather extreme point of view, it can even be argued that Joe acted as an agent in another's suicide and that, therefore, the murder scarcely exists as a murder.

Murder is not only man's most violent act against man but also one of his most violent acts against the state. It challenges the entire structure of society, the laws and covenants by which men live together. Until the murder is avenged or otherwise compensated for, it throws the community into a state of moral, if not literal, anarchy. As Faulkner comments, "It was as if the very initial outrage of the murder carried in its wake and made of all subsequent actions something monstrous and paradoxical and wrong, in themselves against both reason and nature" (259). Until the murderer is captured and punished, everyone in the community shares his guilt; as long as he remains unpunished, the community is giving its tacit consent to his act. Everyone is a moral murderer and, until the temporary anarchy is put down by the communal reaffirmation that murder is forbidden, everyone is a potential murderer.

However, in Joe's case both the murderer and the victim are isolated from the community to such a degree that they are members of it only technically, by virtue of their physical presence within the physical boundaries of the town. They seem to exist something like trichinosis cysts in the muscles: encapsulated, almost a part of the surrounding area yet completely cut off from it. Few of the townsfolk know Joe by sight; almost none of them have any kind of acquaintance with Joanna, and they know her only in terms of their exclusion of her. It would seem that, from a community point of view, Joe's murder of Joanna would be relatively unimportant. Yet, ironically, this most trivial of murders becomes, in its Southern context, the most horrendous of all crimes: the murder of a white woman by a Negro.[4] This is the

___

[4] Cf. the townsfolks' first reaction to the thought that Joanna was murdered by a Negro: "They were gathering now about the sheriff and the

crime that most profoundly shakes the oganization of the community.

In reality, the alien Christmas has killed the isolated nigger-lover Miss Burden; in the minds of the community, the treacherous Negro has brutally violated and murdered Southern Womanhood. As his crime is converted into an act of mostrous implication by the townsfolk, so his death is transformed from a lynching [5] to an event of ritual significance that parallels the communion sacrifice through which the partakers are united with their God and with one another. Thus, Joe, on the one level merely a fleeing criminal, is also a strangely godlike figure from whose manacled hands and nickel-plated pistol flashes the lightning of the reflected sun. His pursuer, who is, strictly speaking, a dedicated and overconscientious upholder of law and justice, is

deputy and the Negro . . . with faces identical one with another. It was as if all their individual five senses had become one organ of looking, like an apotheosis, the words that flew among them wind- or air-engendered *Is that him? Is that the one that did it? Sheriff's got him. . . . By God, if that's him, what are we doing, standing around here? Murdering a white woman the black son of a* None of them had ever entered the house. While she was alive they would not have allowed their wives to call on her" (254–55).

[5] As Cleanth Brooks has pointed out, a lynching constitutes an act of two or more individuals to dispense punishment without recourse to legal means, and thus that, since Grimm alone shot him, Joe cannot be said to be the victim of a lynch mob. Technically, Mr. Brooks is right, and his distinction between the act of Grimm and the will of the community is important. Faulkner, however, maintains a careful ambiguity: it is clear that Grimm alone kills and castrates Christmas; it is mentioned that one of "the others" vomits at the sight of Grimm mutilating the dying man, and this is taken to mean that he, at least, does not consent to this particular act of brutality. However, the townsfolk are a party to Joe's death, morally if not literally, as is shown by their new acceptance of Grimm "with respect and perhaps a little awe and a deal of actual faith and confidence" (400) after he mobilizes his "protective" unit. Furthermore, the same savagery that infects him and leads him, in spite of his outspoken desire to prevent violence, to fire at Joe before Joe has shot at him and without first asking him to surrender, infects the men who follow him: "It was upon them, of them: its shameless savageness. Out of it their faces seemed to glare with bodiless suspension as though from haloes as they stooped and raised Hightower, his face bleeding, from the floor. . . ." (405–406).

described as a young priest, a man whose face "had that serene, unearthly luminousness of angels in church windows" (404–405). And while Grimm the deputy does his grisly work on the dying criminal, Grimm the priest offers the sacrifice for the people. The intensity with which the scene is brought to a close grows out of this ironic juxtaposition of the gratuitous cruelty of Grimm's act and the cool serenity of its ritualistic parallels. With a final ironic turn Joe becomes not only the murderer, not only the victim, not only the furious god he had resembled moments before, but "the man," so that all of his attributes are subsumed under his achievement of humanity. His apotheosis is human, not divine, though his death serves the normally religious function of binding together the community in the intense sharing of a common vision:

> . . . the man seemed to rise soaring into their memories forever and ever. They are not to lose it, in whatever peaceful valleys, beside whatever placid and reassuring streams of old age, in the mirroring faces of whatever children they will contemplate old disasters and newer hopes. It will be there, musing, quiet, steadfast, not fading and not particularly threatful, but of itself alone serene, of itself alone triumphant. (407)

The Phoenix-like image of the man that rises from the collapsing body and the rushing forth of pent black blood hold archetypal suggestions of resurrection or rebirth, as does the sudden transition from the horror of the death to the triumphant serenity of the eyes "empty of everything save consciousness . . . peaceful and unfathomable and unbearable" (407). And, in an ironic and terrible way, Joe's death saves others; most directly he serves as the means by which the lost and lonely Percy Grimm is restored to a sense of community he felt had been denied him by his being born too late to be in the First World War. More tangentially, Joe's actions trigger the events that lead to the moral salvation of Hightower and plunge timid Byron Bunch into love and a new awareness of life.

It might seem, on first glance, that there is little real connection between Joe, literally and figuratively at the center of the book, and Lena Grove, Hightower, and Byron Bunch, more or less on the periphery. Joe's story is framed by the placid travels of Lena, with which the book begins and ends and through which Byron and Hightower are precipitated into the action. The obvious relationship of Joe and Lena (they never meet) is one of tonal and thematic contrast: the circle made by the placid, life-bearing Lena surrounds, as with a nimbus, the tormented and destructive Joe. If we view them for a moment as abstractions, we see that they are polar opposites, embodying the antinomies of human existence from the basic separation as male and female, the aggressiveness and passiveness, respectively, with which each is traditionally identified, to the more abstract oppositions of dark and light, fragmented complexity and simple wholeness, civilization and nature, and so forth. Significantly, it is the *intersection* of the paths of Joe and Lena that brings Hightower and Byron into crucial involvement with life and makes possible their moral salvation. It is merely an additional irony that these metaphorical godparents of Hightower's and Byron's spiritual rebirths should never meet each other in the flesh, for their metaphysical conjunction is unmistakable. This conjunction is further pointed up in Mrs. Hines's confused (but spiritually accurate) belief that Lena has given birth to a child that is in her mind alternately (and perhaps even simultaneously) Joe's child and the infant Joe himself.

It is easy to overstress the dichotomies predicated by Lena and Joe and so to see them as alternatives rather than as parts of a whole. Thus many critics, while admiring Lena's charming simplicity and placidity, cannot help but object to her naïve faith in the worthless Burch, her almost vegetable imperturbability, and her decided lack of critical intelligence. This, however, is to miss the point. Lena is not set up as a model of desirable attitudes or behavior, however preferable her calm fecundity might be to Joe's angry destructiveness. She forms, with Joe, a broad spectrum that contains all the aspects of life and that posits a concept of wholeness, a potential reconciliation of the opposites which neither of them can individually achieve, but which may be momentarily created by their interaction in the perspective of the reader. As the complex, involuted style and multiple narrators of *Absalom, Absalom!* reflect the shimmering, shifting, never fully apprehensible complexity of life, so in *Light in August* the constant emphasis on contrasting characters, situations, myths, and so forth serves to remind us that there is always more to the picture than what appears on the surface, that reality—whether considered in terms of a single character, the interaction of several characters, or the entire action of the book—is immensely complex, never, perhaps, completely explicable, never fully reconcilable in the world of time.

Lena, within her limitations as an individual, accepts life fully. While she is not unaware of the accepted standards of social morality, she is not particularly concerned with them. She knows instinctively what is important—that a family should be together when a child comes—and is utterly confident that the Lord will see to it. She has an innate courtesy and decorum that are the natural and unaffected source of "polite" social behavior, the little graces that make possible smooth contact between people; but she does not, like the women of Jefferson, confuse things of importance with the more superficial aspects of morality, such as a strict concern for the appearance of virtue.[6] In the fullness of her beautiful, cowlike nature she is destined to breed and bear children, which she sets about doing with complete aplomb; and her acceptance of herself leads others to accept her grudgingly at her own valuation and suspend their normal moral judgment of a "fallen woman." Thus the sharp-tongued, highly moral Mrs. Armstid is moved, almost in spite of herself, to give Lena her egg money; thus all the men with whom she comes in contact respond to her with pity and kindness, as she knows they will. Her "knowledge," her serene confidence in the rightness of her actions, is a result of her perfect equilibrium with nature; stemming from nature, it is an encompassing knowledge, a subrational sense, perhaps, but one that instructs her truly.

Completely opposite from Lena is the madman Hines, in

---

[6] The community's concern with appearances reaches heights that would be almost ludicrous were they not so serious. Lena is about to have a baby and therefore is both in need of care and protection and completely unavailable as a sexual object; in spite of this, even the compassionate and understanding Hightower feels he must warn Byron against risking the appearance of evil by camping near the cabin where Lena is staying alone.

whom Lena's natural certainty is transformed into narrow-minded bigotry and fanaticism. Whereas Lena calmly accepts life as a whole, Hines carefully divides it in two, seeing it as a battle-ground between God and Satan in which he himself and the male white race in general are on God's side and women (as sexual objects) and Negroes on the side of the Devil. Hines claims divine instruction for the atrocities he commits, and demonstrates it by his preternatural knowledge both of the Negro blood [7] in Joe's supposedly Mexican father and of the fleeing man's exact whereabouts. The fact that Hines's information on the latter count is accurate, from whatever recess of his mad brain it comes, leads us to suspect an ironic parallel to the old association of manic and mantic, mad and divinely inspired. As Lena suggests the more benevolent aspects of the earth goddesses of pre-Christian Greece, so Hines is a kind of ironic parody of a satyr, a goat god whose natural lechery has been transformed into its opposite, a Puritanical and lecherous hatred of "womanflesh" and "woman-sin."

Both Lena and Hines serve as contrasts to the character of Joanna Burden, who is barren as Lena is fertile and an abolitionist as Hines is a racist. But Joanna is a complex character, who to be understood fully must first be considered in terms of her ancestors. Her grandfather, Calvin, was a man of massive vitality with a thorough disregard for maintaining an appearance of consistency in his actions: the son of a New England minister, he was converted to Catholicism, lived for a year in a monastery, and ten years later denied Catholicism and reverted to the religion of his forebears—all with no pain of soul or self-searching doubt. Outspoken, vigorous, unself-conscious and untroubled by delicate moral problems, the ancestral Calvin has an integrity that is utterly unshakable. As a patriarch he is at once magnificent and ludicrous; his complete possession of himself

[7] Hines claims to "know" that the man is part Negro, and seems to be vindicated when the circus owner "come back and said how the man really was a part nigger" (330). However, Faulkner never conclusively settles the question for the reader, and Joe himself, though he believes he is part Negro, does not know for sure.

suggests the superb tranquillity of Lena, whose nature, like his, is utterly fulfilled. And, as Lena's pastoral idyl is essentially a comic one, so Calvin's history has overtones of the exaggerated comic stance of the frontier tall tale. The union of the sublime and the ridiculous in Calvin's position is nowhere better expressed than in the picture of his homecoming on Saturday nights when, full of whiskey, he would wake his son, saying, "I'll learn you to hate two things . . . or I'll frail the tar out of you. And those things are hell and slaveholders. Do you hear me?"

"Yes," the boy would say. "I cant help but hear you. Get on to bed and let me sleep" [8](212).

In Calvin's son Nathaniel, however, the patriarch's hatred of slavery and hell becomes more articulate and less spontaneous, more theoretical and at once less immediate and more influential. The moral simplicity of Calvin becomes tortuous reasoning in Nathaniel, who tells the child Joanna: "Your grandfather and brother are lying there, murdered not by one white man but by the curse which God put on a whole race before your grandfather or your brother or me or you were even thought of. A race doomed and cursed to be forever and ever a part of the white race's doom and curse for its sins" (221). And Joanna, raised on doom and gloom, isolated from normal, healthy existence, comes in her turn to do her father's concept of the "curse" one better: "The curse of the black race is God's curse. But the curse of the white race is the black man who will be forever God's chosen own because He once cursed Him" (222).

Rejected by the community for her New England descent and her forebears' abolitionist feelings, taught by her father to compound that rejection by reasserting, in her own person, the Burdens' fight for Negro rights, Joanna is largely a victim of her history. She has a marked ability, however, to externalize her

---

[8] Calvin is forever threatening to frail the tar out of his offspring, but his own wholeness makes his physical assaults on them spiritually harmless, if not necessarily beneficial. On the other hand, the pietistic beatings administered to young Joe Christmas by his foster father, McEachern, have very different results. McEachern's arrogant aesceticism, which operates in terms of spiritual as well as material self-denial, makes Joe resist him with every fiber of his being.

"burden," to discharge it in action—and this is the source of Joe's almost unwilling attraction to her. Joe's conflict is internal, and his fits of seemingly irrational violence the result of the boiling-over of that internal contradiction. In Joanna, however, he not only sees obsessions being acted out, but is invited to take part in the drama himself, to play the chthonic Negro to Joanna's bacchantic nymphomaniac. Here Joe can, for the first time, accept and express himself without conflict as a Negro precisely because of the elements of play-acting—of ritual—involved. Joanna's extreme behavior is a kind of pantomiming, a discharging in ritual action of the tremendous energy generated by the sudden confrontation of her disparate and previously rigidly separated selves. She can indulge both because she overacts, externalizes the conflict between them to such a degree that the drama quite literally takes place outside herself. With the onset of her menopause one of the conflicting terms is removed, for she feels that she is no longer a sexual being. Except for the fact that she feels she must expiate her sins, it is as if her affair with Joe had never happened, and she settles with almost no sense of transition back into her role as the benevolent spinster dedicated to the physical and spiritual uplift of the Negro. But Joe will not follow her, for here the inner dialectic of their drama ceases: he is to become wholly and simply a respectable Negro, she his white benefactress. Rather than submit—and not only to her but to the chilly Puritan God whom Joe had spent his childhood resisting—and rather than consent to the death that she offers as the only alternative to submission, Joe kills her.

Named after Juana, her father's Mexican ("black")[9] wife, Joanna is in many ways a mirror of Joe, similar yet opposite. Symbolically black and white, as her naming suggests, she is as positively obsessed with Negroes and religion as Joe is negatively obsessed by them. As Joe has no past, no corpus of family identity from which to take the materials to build his self, so Joanna, his

[9] Cf. grandfather Calvin Burden's comments on the marriage of his dark-complexioned son, French on his mother's side, to a Mexican woman: "Another damn black Burden. . . . Folks will think I bred to a damn slaver. And now he's got to breed to one, too" (216).

mirror image, is strangled by a family identity and its roots in history so strong that her own self has no chance to develop its individual potential.

Particularly in this last respect Joanna has thematic affinities with Hightower, the ironically-named broken minister who has been an outcast in Jefferson for twenty-five years. The grandchild, like Joanna, of a man of swagger and confidence supremely at home in himself and his world, he grew up in a house peopled with ghosts: his shadowy and elderly (though still living) parents, and the far more vital ghost of his lusty and sacrilegious grandfather, dead twenty years before his birth. But where Joanna is for all practical purposes *forced* to take up the cross of her grandfather's life, Hightower *chooses*, over and over again, to pursue his grandfather's spirit at the cost of his own life. He enters the seminary not simply because he believes in the church but in order that he may be called to Jefferson, where his grandfather was killed; he learns to finagle and dissemble in order to achieve this end; he preaches to his congregation not "the crucified shape of pity and love" but a "swaggering and unchastened bravo killed with a shotgun in a peaceful henhouse" (428); and he drives his wife to despair and suicide by revealing to her "not only the depth of [his] hunger but the fact that never and never would she have any part in the assuaging of it" (427).

Like the young Joe, the young Hightower is alarmingly innocent; he believes at first that the simple fact of his obsession with his grandfather will be reason enough for his church to send him to Jefferson. Disabused of this notion by the girl he is to marry, he soon comes to realize that love is not what he had believed it to be—and, after his wedding, that marriage is not, either. But these confrontations with reality drive him not, like Joe, into raging despair, but further into the security of the past, and marry him more firmly to the ghost of his grandfather. Both he and Joe desire perfection, a life of purity and harmony and peace, symbolized for both in the image of an urn[10] strongly

[10] Cf. the imagery of the "suavely shaped urns," cracked and leaking a foul liquid, associated with Joe's emotional reaction to the knowledge that Bobbie Allen is menstruating. In the seminary Hightower thinks of "his

suggestive of Keats's urn of timeless and changeless beauty. Both, finding reality imperfect, attempt to buy immunity from it, Joe by sacrificing a sheep to the aspects of nature he hates and fears, Hightower by accepting scorn and even physical violence as the price of being left to live in Jefferson in peace.

But Hightower is a considerably more intelligent and perceptive man than Joe, and works out his escape from the world quite ingeniously. He creates for himself an approximation of that longed-for serene and classic vase in his vision of the thundering cavalry that descends on him at twilight. The eternal "wild bugles and the clashing sabres and the dying thunder of hooves" (432) sound across his consciousness with the perfect and immutable splendor of the youth pursuing the maiden of whom Keats wrote, "Forever wilt thou love, and she be fair!" Deliberately turning away from the world and living human beings to dedicate himself to his vision, he courts the world's contempt. He does not do this consciously, perhaps, but nevertheless he is secretly glad for the pain of losing his church, for the martyrdom he supposes he bears when he is taken out one night and beaten by a group of outraged townsfolk. With the rational man's clever confusion of arithmetic and morality, he uses his ill-treatment by the world as justification for renouncing his moral responsibility as a member of the living human community. He keeps up a tenuous contact with the doings of the present only through Bryon Bunch, who, though living normally in the community, is as removed from any real perception of the immediacy of events as is Hightower.

Byron is a comic inversion of Hightower, a smaller, less intense, and less dramatic figure whose comic and pathetic discovery of reality parallels the minister's more tragic realization. Fittingly, Byron's confrontation with reality begins when he falls in love. As contrasted with Joe, whose love affair with Bobbie Allen brought him bitter knowledge of reality and despair, Byron's love is in the best tradition of happy bucolic romance, given a slight ironic twist in the fact that the lovely Lena is enormously preg-

future, his life, intact and on all sides complete and inviolable, like a classic . . . vase" (419). It is an image of which Faulkner is particularly fond (cf. "The Bear").

nant. This, however, simply arouses all of Byron's sleeping instincts of chivalry and protectiveness, and he sets about the somewhat ludicrous task of taking care of her.

As he hears Byron tell of Lena, Burch, and the murder of Joanna, Hightower realizes the younger man's as yet unrecognized involvement with Lena, and almost immediately senses, with fear, that he himself will be drawn into the living present through the events born of Lena's arrival and Joe's crime. Torn between an intense compassion for Joe and the fate he knows is in store for him, and an equally intense fear of his own involvement, Hightower becomes a battleground on which his human and ghostly selves fight for supremacy. At first he rationalizes that, even assuming his willingness to re-enter life, he may already have irrevocably cut himself off from the world: " 'I am not in life any more,' he thinks. 'That's why there is no use in even trying to meddle, interfere. He [Byron] could hear me no more than that man and that woman (ay, and that child) would hear or heed me if I tried to come back into life' " (263). But he knows—whether or not he will admit it—that this is merely an excuse, that the question is not whether he is able but whether he is willing. He is free to choose, and on two occasions (when he learns from the grocer that Christmas' trail has been found, and the following Sunday night when he refuses Byron's plea to give Christmas an alibi) he chooses not to be involved. On both occasions he is almost physically overcome by the intensity of the conflict, and reacts with almost identical violence: "I wont! I wont! I have bought my immunity. I have paid. I have paid" (270). And later: "It's not because I cant, dont dare to . . . it's because I wont! I wont! do you hear?" (342).

As Hightower struggles in the meshes of his ghosthood, Byron quietly accepts the chance to love and learn to live that has been offered him; and, as he takes up responsibility for Lena and then for Joe's grandparents, he comes to walk with pride and to speak in a new voice, "each word definite of meaning, not fumbling" (274). As Byron is drawn more deeply into the circle of action, he pulls Hightower with him; and a crucial occurrence for both of them is the birth of Lena's child. Byron, hearing the child

/ 99

cry, is struck with knowledge as if with lightning, and realizes for the first time that Lena exists independently of his imagination's rose-colored vision of her. His idealized picture of her as "placid, unchanged, timeless" (350) dissolves before the terrible awareness that she is not a virgin. "If I had known then," he thinks, referring to the time of his riding for the doctor that morning, "I would have turned my back and rode the other way. Beyond the knowing and the memory of man forever and ever I reckon I would have rode" (351). But he did not know then, and the scales are stripped from his eyes whether he wills it or not; he sees the thoroughly unvirgin Lena, he knows of her relationship with Burch, and he knows that he himself is nothing to her. His realization immediately recalls the parallel discovery of Joe's that Bobbie Allen was a prostitute; but, while their confrontations with reality are similar, their responses are almost diametrically opposed. Joe accepts the abstract fact of Bobbie's profession but does not let it become emotionally real to him, as is evidenced by his foolish but unquestioned belief that she would run away with him. Byron, on the other hand, swallows his knowledge and gains moral strength from it. Now that he *knows* that Lena belongs to another, he is too honest to come between them, even given the excuse that Burch is shiftless and probably unwilling to marry Lena should she ever catch up with him. With a nobility that is only slightly comic he arranges to have the slippery Burch delivered to Lena's cabin and then departs (as he thinks) forever. Even when he catches up with Burch, not realizing that his rival is abandoning Lena, he fights with him as a kind of benediction: "And now there is one more thing I can do for him. I cant marry them, because I aint a minister. And I may not can . . . whip him . . . because he is bigger than me. But I can try it. I can try to do it" (373).

As Joe's ironic rites of passage into adulthood end with the physical ordeal of being beaten half senseless by Bobbie's friends, so Byron is confirmed in manhood by being beaten by Burch. Both emerge from the timeless limbo of semiconsciousness into a new relationship with the world: Joe is committed to a lonely street that never ends, while Byron, the happiest of his mirror images, walks forward to the "hope unbelievable and certainty incontrovertible" (386–87) of his right to stay with Lena.

With his delivery of Lena's child, Hightower breaks through the barrier of his ghosthood and into a warm and glowing awareness of reality. Having helped life into the world he has been brought back to life himself. For the first time in twenty-five years he moves like a man with a purpose; he responds joyously to the earth and woods and fertile countryside with which Lena is associated, and he looks on Lena and the child with an expression "gentle, beaming, and triumphant" (357). He even hopes, rather pathetically, that Lena might name the child after him. But this happiness is only half of the total experience of life; and as Lena, the life- and light-bearing,[11] has brought him to an awareness of life as animal joy and responsiveness, so the darkly tormented Joe presents him with the reality of death and precipitates Hightower's ultimate confrontation with himself.

The final irony, of course, is that the former man of God is powerless to save the doomed Joe, while Joe, the God-hater and desecrator of churches, becomes the unwitting agent of Hightower's moral salvation. That night, after the violence and the agony of Joe's death, Hightower relives in memory his history and his life, and comes at last to the terrible realization of all that he has done and been: not simply a phantom that had chosen death to life, but the betrayer of his parishioners and his church, the debaucher and murderer of his wife, and a man who under the guise of serving God and man rejected both and turned to the inhuman worship of a dead and phantasmal past. The horror with which this knowledge approaches him is magnificently suggested in the image of the sandclutched wheel of thinking that turns "with the slow implacability of a mediaeval torture instrument, beneath the wrenched and broken sockets of his spirit, his life" (430). With his realization and acceptance of his responsibility for his wife's death comes the knowledge that he has been nothing, that "for fifty years I have not even been clay: I have been a single instant of darkness in which a horse galloped and a gun

[11] Lena is a diminutive of the Greek name Helena, which means a torch or a light one.

/ 101

crashed" (430). Yet this devastating knowledge is a triumphant achievement, for it signals his emergence into the sphere of moral awareness [12] and makes him, in the fullest sense of the word, a conscious being. And, underlining the positive, integrative nature of his moment of consciousness, there comes out of his confrontation with inner reality a sense of reconciliation. The wheel whirls away and becomes a halo full of faces "not shaped with suffering, not shaped with anything: not horror, pain, not even reproach. They are peaceful, as though they have escaped into an apotheosis; his own is among them" (430). Also among them is Joe's face, less clear than the others, blending and then freeing itself from the face of Grimm; even Joe, this image seems to suggest, is reconciled to his murderer, as Joe's death has reconciled Grimm to the community.

Of the dark trinity formed by Hightower, Joe, and Joanna, Hightower comes the closest to attaining tragic stature because of the deliberateness of his choice and his realization of his failure. If he is a tragic figure, however, it is still one cast in an ironic mold. We are not given a noble and unjustly broken man but a bloated, stale, musty ex-minister who, with our last glimpse of him, still clings to the phantoms for which he has sold his life. Though he attains insight of a very real kind, it is followed not by an affirmation in action but by a visitation of the ghostly cavalry. The total effect is rather like that of a symphony which, after a triumphant final movement, ends on a subtly unresolved chord. Yet, within the limits of this irony, Hightower rises to a nearly tragic realization of his responsibility for his wasted life.

In spite of their isolation from the community, Hightower, Joe, and Joanna reflect the dominant problems of the community: the relationship of the past (particularly the Civil War past) to the present; [13] the relationship of Negro and white; and the rela-

[12] Whether or not he will act on this new awareness and abjure his ghosthood by committing himself to reality and the present is another question, and one that Faulkner (perhaps wisely) does not answer.

[13] Though emphasized in the relation of Hightower and Joanna to their families' Civil War past, this theme does not dominate *Light in August*. It is given much greater stress in other novels, particularly *Sartoris* and *Absalom, Absalom!*

tionship of religion to life. Joe, utterly deracinated, is as crippled by his lack of familial and social tradition as Hightower and Joanna by their excessive familial and historical dependence. Either extreme is destructive. The one deprives Joe of a sense of his membership in something larger than himself—the family, the society, and, in its largest extension, humanity as a whole—and thereby dooms him to a psychological aloneness that, once created, acts upon itself and utterly prevents moral or spiritual contact with others. At the other extreme, Hightower and Joanna turn away from the reality of the present and address themselves to the spirit of the past; Hightower communes with a ghost and denies the living, and Joanna approaches the reality of the present in terms of her grandfather's abolitionism, regarding Negroes as objects for her benevolence rather than as human beings with whom she is in relation.

Joanna's attitude reflects the community's attitude toward the Negro, in spite of the fact that Joanna is dedicated to lifting the Negro to the white man's level and the community is interested in keeping him in his place. These two superficially opposing views reduce to a similar moral failure in that both regard individual Negroes as expressions of an abstraction, not as human beings.

Religion assumes an importance in *Light in August* that it has in no other Yoknapatawpha County novel. The majority of the characters [14] are in one way or another associated with religion, and the townsfolk in general are frequently seen in their capacity as churchgoers. Their religion provides a frame of reference in which to view the world and their experience, and as such is as important in their conception of themselves and their relation to the world as is their sense of being Southern and white. If

[14] Hightower is a former minister; his father was an unordained preacher; Byron Bunch conducts the choir in a country church; Doc Hines, a religious fanatic, preaches a white God to Negro congregations; McEachern is a stern Presbyterian; Joanna Burden's great-grandfather was a minister and his descendants, including herself, are deeply imbued with New England Puritanism; Joe's hatred of religion is as much a recognition of its importance as the other characters' positive involvement with it. The only characters of any significance that are not concerned with religion are Lena Grove (who is a kind of nature goddess herself) and Lucas Burch.

their religion is authoritarian, stern, repressive, and joyless, it is because the people have failed it as much as it has failed them. Hightower, finding the Church to be full of human faults and not the pristine and inviolable sanctuary of truth for which he longed, refused his human (as well as sacred) obligation to work within its institutional limitations and oppose "the professionals who control it and who have removed the bells from its steeples" (426). Acquiescing in its failure, Hightower has contributed to that failure. The townsfolk, too, are responsible, for they have reduced their religion to a system of moral imperatives that, by eliminating self-doubt and the necessity of choice, equally eliminates the possibility of existentially responsible action.

Light in August is many things. It is one of Faulkner's loveliest books in terms of its evocation of place, the tranquil and summer-still August countryside, and in its lyric simplicity of description and narrative. Occasionally the narrative structure is complex, but its complexity is so deftly handled that it passes almost unnoticed. It flows; and in its fluid present we hear the voices of many narrators, some speaking from a clear individual perspective, as does the furniture dealer who ends the book, most emerging out of the tender drone of the omniscient author and briefly defining the focus of the action with their own vivid idiom.

The novel is generally agreed to be among Faulkner's most powerful works, though there is less agreement as to why this is so—and there are several reasons why it should not be so. For instance, a number of important actions are left unexplained: Why, after his passive surrender, does Christmas try to escape? (Gavin Stevens' theory that Mrs. Hines persuaded him to do so is, at best, dubious.) Where does he get a pistol? If (as seems unlikely) he deliberately goes to Hightower for protection, how does he know where the house is, and why does he strike Hightower down? We can invent answers of a sort, but they have about them that vaguely specious quality of rationalizations. We are forced, at last, to accept the action as given, but this raises still another problem: because of the apparent arbitrariness of his final acts, Christmas ends much more as a ritual figure than as a personality in his own right, and the burden of centrality falls fully upon Hightower. How Faulkner manages this shift of emphasis with such success is a mystery.

The book is also marred by an undeniable carelessness about facts. Joe is said to be thirty-three at the time he first comes to Jefferson, three years before he is killed. From the various references at the end of the novel to the thirty years of his conscious life, or to the fifteen-year-long street he entered when he was eighteen, it would seem that Faulkner was still thinking of him as being approximately thirty-three at his death. The parallel to the age of Christ at his crucifixion, which must have been intentional, supports this theory. Perhaps less serious but more blatant errors include Joe's capture in Mottstown on Friday on page 298, and the account on page 306 of his capture on Saturday. As the story goes on, Friday is treated as if it had disappeared from the week. On page 298 Hines is described (by the omniscient narrator) as having come to Mottstown thirty years before and having been home only once a month for the first five years, since he held some kind of position in Memphis. On page 334 Mrs. Hines tells how, five years after Joe's birth, she and Hines came to Mottstown, and Hines "never went back to Memphis to work any more."

Light in August has been described in a variety of ways. It has been called naturalistic, realistic, comic, and tragic, but it refuses to remain constantly any one of these. Naturalistic generally means similar in attitude to the works of Frank Norris, Jack London, and Theodore Dreiser, which emphasize man's enslavement to conditions of heredity and environment and to his own natural appetites, and which see him doomed in the struggle to rise above them. It is possible to make out a case for Joe Christmas as an example of a naturalistic hero, but to do so requires that the reader ignore much of the rest of the book. A good deal of the novel is certainly realistically presented, but beneath this realism lurks a romantic chiaroscuro of both description and characterization. The events of Joanna's murder and Joe's terrible death are near to tragedy, but they are interlaced with extraordinarily comic anticlimaxes. There is the spectacle of the greedy Burch, yelping and eager as a foolish dog, urging on the search for Christmas. There is the scene in which the members of the posse burst into a cabin where Joe is supposedly hiding and discover only one astonished and terrified field rat. There is the comic sophistry of the scene in which Bryon, riding away from Jefferson forever, disputes with himself on the reality of his suffering: "All right. You say you suffer. All right. But in the first place, all we got is your naked word for it. And in the second place, you just say that you are Byron Bunch. And in the third place, you are just the one that calls yourself Byron Bunch today, now, this minute. . ." (372). And there is, of course, the bawdy comedy of the final chapter, which strongly suggests lewd satyr plays that traditionally followed Greek tragedy. But, as the antinomies of the content, broadly suggested in Lena and Joe, are never fully reconciled, so the tragic and comic aspects of the book form a dialectic of irony. And this irony itself is a kind of dialectic, a double vision which holds up the literal and shows it to contain its opposite.

The structure of the novel is circular, or perhaps cyclical, beginning and ending with the travels of Lena Grove. The action involving Hightower forms a smaller but concentric circle, within which are contained both the action in the present and the story of Joe Christmas. The circle is also the primary thematic symbol. It appears as the urn across which Lena metaphorically moves forever and without progress in "identical and anonymous and deliberate wagons" (6), and the unattainable and imperfect urns associated, respectively, with Hightower and Joe. It is the circular street in which Joe has traveled for thirty years. It metaphorically surrounds Joanna's house, from which paths used by the Negroes radiate like spokes on a wheel. It is the sand-clogged wheel of Hightower's consciousness, and the halo into which that wheel is transformed. As a symbol of wholeness, completion, perfection, eternity, it stands in ironic contrast to the real world of birth and death, time and change, action and suffering. But the symbol contains within itself its own opposite, and can stand as well for emptiness, futility, nothingness. Similarly, the circles of *Light in August* embrace as well as contrast: the book becomes a metaphorical color wheel of light and dark, good and evil, male and female, life and death, and all the other antinomies with which human life is faced. In the novel, as in the finite, experiential world of all human reality, the antinomies are separate, contradictory, exclusive. But from our perspective as readers these metaphoric colors sometimes whirl and blend into pure white light, and we can sense in the totality of the fictional experience some timeless and never quite articulable apprehension of the meaning of life.

Record and Reality

EDWARD W. SAID

DESPITE THE EXTRAVAGANT RANGE of its differing national and social origins, the cast of Conrad's *Nostromo* [1]— the most massive of his works—is bound together by two inner affinities. The first is that everyone in the novel has an unflagging interest in the fortunes of Costaguana. For the most part this interest takes the form of a private vision of those fortunes in which the individual enjoys an advantageous partnership with them. Charles Gould, for example, considers the good of Costaguana synonymous with the good of his work in the San Tomé mine. The second affinity is that nearly every individual in the vast novel seems extremely anxious about both keeping and leaving a personal "record" of his thought and action. This anxiety seems to be based upon an extraordinary preoccupation with the past, as if the past, left to itself, given only ordinary attention and no official recording, were somehow unthinkable.

After the first few pages of impersonal geography and history the reader is handed into Costaguana along the way cleared by Captain Mitchell, the English sea captain, who has lived a life of rather unthinking courage. For him, life in Costaguana has

[1] Published by Harper & Brothers, London and New York, 1904. Much of the work on this study was made possible by a grant from the Council for Research in the Humanities at Columbia University. Page numbers enclosed in parentheses are references to *Nostromo*, with an introduction by Robert Penn Warren, Modern Library, Random House, New York, 1951.

been a series of excitingly adventurous episodes to which he has given the proud name "historical events." When he later informs his audience that, like a much-lived, much-traveled Aeneas, he too was a part of these events (*quarum magna pars fui*), the sizable distance that separates his ingenuous record from the reality appears even wider. His loquacious and insistent recollection of the past takes for its theme the high adventure of life in Costaguana, though the dominant variation on that theme is the inherent rascality of the "foreign" mind. Mitchell's unfortunate run-in with the sanguine Sotillo—in which Mitchell emerges clearly the victor—emphasizes the disparity between Englishman and native, and because of this disparity the record of his activities recited by Mitchell moves even further away from the truth. He has little sense of the complexity with which his artless narrative has been coping.

In no characterization does Mitchell's narrative miss the mark as widely as in his portrait of Nostromo. But in this Mitchell is as wrong as everyone else. That the admirable capataz de cargadores has sacrificed his honor to a desire for a spotless, enviable reputation is a matter known only to Nostromo. Only he understands the meaning of the remark made by Dr. Monygham in a moment of passionate irritation with the *hombres finos* who have apparently robbed him of his enviable reputation. (He will later find out that he still has the reputation and with it an immensely onerous burden.) "The capataz is destroyed," he says now. " . . . There is no capataz" (487). As Sulaco grows in prestige and wealth many years later, so also does Nostromo grow in eminence within the new republic. Yet he lives *outside* his fame, which to our eyes seems a thing apart from him. The man and his reputation have become completely distinct from one another. To Sulaco though, Nostromo's carefully engineered record of heroism *is* Nostromo, and Sulacoan independence is believed to have been gained because of him.

The more modern and civilized citizens of Costaguana are no less sanguine about the record they want left. Their subtle intelligences allow them, however, a scarcely more accurate sense of history. More nervous, more sophisticated and introspective, their "records"—kept by them in various ways—are hardly more than poignant abstractions for which little use is evident. Martin Decoud, the originator, if not the executor, of Sulacoan independence, finds time in the midst of a fierce bombardment to write his sister a letter that may never reach her.

> In the most sceptical heart there lurks at such moments, when the chances of existence are involved, a desire to leave a correct impression of the feelings, like a light by which the action may be seen when personality is gone, gone where no light of investigation can ever reach the truth which every death takes out of the world. Therefore, instead of looking for something to eat or trying to snatch an hour or so of sleep, Decoud was filling the pages of a large note-book with a letter to his sister. (255)

No matter how urgently recorded and felt, feelings like this are regrettably private and counterweighing them in the novel is Don José Avellanos's enduring record, in which the country's elder statesman leaves a public narrative of Costaguanan political life. His book, *Fifty Years of Misrule,* is written out of disinterested political wisdom; Decoud's letter to his sister, and his subsequent activity on behalf of Sulacoan integrity, are motivated by his lover's illusion.

Neither, if judged by their practical effects on Costaguanan history, can compare with the record left by Charles Gould, writ large in the incredibly influential history of the San Tomé silver mine. Holroyd, who thinks of himself as leaving a record of his Christian altruism; Sir John, the British railroad builder who crisscrosses the land with steel rails that signify progress and expansion; and Gould, their reticent minion in Sulaco—these three work for the mine together under the auspices of Costaguana's major *idée bien reçue:* material interests. In the minds of their agents these interests give rise to so dehumanized a set of goals that spiritual life petrifies into a slavish round of work done for the mine. The record of this work is, of course, kept in the history of the mine's grand success.[2]

[2] Charles Gould's dedication to the rebirth and the progress of the mine is a perverted and, I think, intended analogy to the history of Christian

To this maliciously successful record, Giorgio Viola's touching faith in "liberal" politics provides a sad and hopeless foil. His dedication to an irrelevant ideal—irrelevant because Costaguana is so dominated by silver interests—makes him, in Sulaco, a relic to whose ponderous silence and majestic bearing the city is vaguely deferential. His one decisive action, which is the accidental murder of Nostromo, is a ceremony inspired by an ancestral record of "honor" and by Garibaldian ethics. Inadvertently, Viola mars the record of Nostromo's perfection; this is the climax to what Douglas Hewitt calls Conrad's deflating of Nostromo.[3]

Conrad's own publicly available record of the novel's composition, written many years after *Nostromo*'s completion in 1904, is his "Author's Note."[4] It is very much like all of his other "Notes": engaging, affable, and relaxed. One is given, for example, only a *sense* of the trouble the novel caused him in the phrase "the most anxiously meditated of [my] longer novels" (1). Yet a random sampling of the letters written by Conrad to his intimates while composing the novel reveals a struggle with difficulties of the most radical sort. "Anxious meditation," next to these throes of work, is an innocuous euphemism. Early in 1903, some weeks after he had begun the novel, he wrote H. G. Wells a letter that concluded with the following remarks: "I, my dear Wells, am absolutely out of my mind with the worry and apprehension of my work. I go as one would cycle over a precipice along a 14-inch plank. If I falter I am lost."[5] In May he wrote Edward Garnett,

faith in the world. Like Christianity, the mine's power over its devotees begins with the fabled resurrection of a dead enterprise, proceeds to the inspiration of heretical struggles for the control of its emerging force, and culminates with the establishment of an institutionalized faith in silver. The perversion occurs at the outset: whereas Christianity promises a free and quickened life, the mine requires the spiritual enslavement of its followers, for only as shackled fetishists can they be kept serviceable to the mine.

[3] Douglas Hewitt, *Conrad: A Reassessment,* Bowes and Bowes, Cambridge, 1952, p. 50.

[4] It is difficult, if not impossible, to date the "Author's Note" exactly. It is certain, however, that Conrad wrote one for *Nostromo* between 1919 and 1922, most probably toward the end of 1919.

[5] Gerard Jean Aubry, *Joseph Conrad, Life and Letters,* Doubleday, Garden City, 1927, Volume I, p. 311.

his "literary confessor," [6] that *Nostromo* was not yet a quarter written. "I am indeed appalled at myself when I think what rotten contemptible bosh it must and shall be. By Jove I am too tired and with a heart worn too threadbare to be honest." [7] Conrad's honesty with his friend A. H. Davray was sufficient, on August 22, to describe a terrible state of affairs produced by stupor of mind, a disgust of his pen, and a terror of the inkpot. With half of the novel now written he had embarked upon a terrible journey from which he could expect no relief. "Solitude is taking me over: it is absorbing me. I see nothing, I read nothing. It is like being in a tomb which is at the same time a hell where one must write, write, write." [8] On the same day he described himself to John Galsworthy as "a mental and moral outcast," always "deeper in the mire." [9] As the year wore on, the writing of *Nostromo* became more and more of a physical task: he wrote Wells on November 30 as if the book were threatening him with a physical catastrophe.

Things are bad with me—there's no disguising the fact. Not only is the scribbling awfully in arrears but there's no "spring" in me to grapple with it effectually. Formerly in my sea life, a difficulty nerved me to the effort; now I perceive it is not so. However, don't imagine I've given up, but there is an uncomfortable sense of losing my footing in deep waters. . . .

I say so because for me, writing—*the only possible writing* —is just simply the conversion of nervous force into phrases. With you too, I am sure, tho' in your case it is the disciplined intelligence which gives the signal—the impulse. For me it is a matter of chance, stupid chance. But the fact remains that when the nervous force is exhausted the phrases don't come— and no tension of will can help.[10]

[6] Edward Garnett, *Letters from Joseph Conrad, 1895–1924,* The Bobbs-Merrill Company, Indianapolis, 1928, p. 184.

[7] *Ibid.,* p. 187.

[8] "La solitude me gagne: elle m'absorbe. Je ne vois rien, je ne lis rien. C'est comme une espèce de tombe, qui serait en même temps un enfer, ou il faut écrire, écrire, écrire." Joseph Conrad, *Lettres Françaises,* edited by Gerard Jean Aubry, Gallimard, Paris, 1930, p. 50. Translations of letters from this volume are mine.

[9] *Life and Letters,* I, p. 317.   [10] *Ibid.,* p. 321.

On December 5 he had reached the 567th page of the novel, and, at that moment, writing to A. K. Waliszewski, he felt it necessary to observe about himself that he had become "an Englishman . . . and [that] *homo duplex* had more than one meaning." [11] The letter was written at a time when Conrad knew that appeals to the publishers asking for their sympathy for his overworked capacities, for his terrific spiritual problems with his work, would neither earn their pity, nor an extension to their deadlines. In 1902 he had weathered a severe crisis with William Blackwood, his publisher.[12] Now, at work on the most troublesome project of all, Conrad realized that the shortest way to the world's affections was a show of cheer; he hoped that a stiff upper lip would make him more understandable to his adopted countrymen. The horrors of composition continued of course, but he developed a rather mannered outward composure. He literally created a genial, outward Conrad, his *persona*, to whom struggles with his work were unknown except as manifestations of an underground second self over whom he had no control. As Conrad continued in later years before his successfully won-over public, the underground man disappeared; an evasive and charming author, who produced the "Author's Notes," remained instead. So amiable a personage could not discuss such embarrassments as, for example, the loss of spiritual footing; difficulties like that were better left to an ignored, hidden past. Thus the personal *record* of an author presented to his public was as different from the realities that the record concealed as Captain Mitchell's "historical events" are different from the real events. (Mitchell, of course, *is* ignorant of what really happened; Conrad was not, obviously). The sense of being a *homo duplex* in more than one way that Conrad spoke of to Waliszewski refers, I think, to the conscious doubleness of his life at the time that he was working on *Nostromo*. If for no other reason than a desire to forget what was

[11] "Je suis devenu anglais . . . *homo duplex* a plus d'un sens." *Lettres Françaises*, p. 60.
[12] I have discussed this crisis (which had its origins in 1898) and its implications for Conrad's development in a soon-to-be published doctoral dissertation, "The Letters and the Shorter Fiction of Joseph Conrad," done at Harvard in 1964. See especially pp. 75–96.

extremely unpleasant to him, he postured outwardly as if every-thing were fine, and—because he seemed to have little choice—he continued his hellish efforts to finish his novel.

By the early part of 1904 he was again writing Wells, this time assuring him that "no one's position is too absurd to be argued with. An enlightened egoism is as valid as an enlightened altruism—neither more nor less." [13] The meaning of this assertion is that he had arrived at a point where two opposing positions, or realities, seemed to have equal validity. Was this not another way of saying that his real struggles with *Nostromo* on the one hand, and his public image on the other, were each making acute claims on him? Each demanded from him a sort of ultimate recognition. Two equally articulate individualities fighting within the same single existence led him close to virtual madness; on April 5, 1904, he announced to David Meldrum that he was "verging on insanity." [14] That he managed to go on with what he used to call "that dread thing" is, I think, something of a miracle. He suffered many bouts of debilitating illness, his wife was also frequently ill, and as his letters to William Rothenstein show he was almost al-ways in financial straits. Writing the painter on June 27, he said:

> I dare do nothing. Either my soul or my liver is very sick. If it is the liver then the cold shall make it worse. Even here I go about shuddering when a cloud passes over the sun. And I am tired, tired, as if I had lived a hundred years. Reverting to the matter of that salvage you are conducting to preserve a rather rotten old hulk (but full of the best intentions)—I think [here follows some detailed advice and requests about some money Rothenstein was arranging to get for Conrad] . . . It is late—and tomorrow is another dread day. C. Graham has been here for the Sunday and we talked much of you. He is in very good form and very friendly but the episode of his visit has not refreshed me as much as I expected. I am not myself and shall

---

[13] *Life and Letters*, I, p. 329.

[14] Conrad, *Joseph Conrad: Letters to William Blackwood and David S. Meldrum*, edited with introduction, notes and appendices by William Blackburn, Duke University Press, Durham, 1958, p. 180.

not be myself till I am born again until after Nostromo is finished.[15]

The agony was terminated a short time later: *Nostromo* was finished on August 30, 1904. Eight years later he wrote André Gide of the novel in terms that expressed a combination of incredulity and alienation, for by 1912 the composition of *Nostromo* had become a problematic experience he could no longer stand to remember in exact detail. "It's a black oven [*un four noir*], you know. I, I have a kind of tenderness for that enormous machine. But it doesn't work; that is true. There is something that prevents it from working. I don't quite know what. All in all, even with all my tenderness, I myself cannot stand to read it." [16] Because Gide was one of Conrad's closer friends the letter has none of that impersonal whimsy of which Conrad was capable in his "Author's Notes." Nevertheless it is quite apparent that a disengagement has occurred in Conrad's mind between the actual process of composing the novel and his manner of recalling the experience some years later. Perhaps the manner of the later recollection was only a convenient way of narrating a messy affair; after all, who inclines to specific details, when details—unpleasant ones with neither shape nor focus—are all that one remembers?

There is an interesting parallel to be drawn between the characters of *Nostromo* and Conrad himself. In each case the individual has performed or witnessed problematic, jumbled action, from which a descriptive record of it is distilled. So restless is this action, so engrossing its complications, that, at the time it occurs, the individual is totally immersed in it. When the action is later recalled it has become "history," which in the novel at least is usually a comparatively thin record, a summary definition of the

---

[15] Conrad, "Letters to William Rothenstein, 1903–1921," unpublished manuscript letters at Houghton Library, Harvard University, letter 5.

[16] "C'est un four noir, vous savez. Moi j'ai une espèce de tendresse pour cette enorme machine. Mais elle ne marche pas; c'est vrai. Il y a quelque chose qui empêche. Je ne sais pas quoi. Du reste avec toute ma tendresse, moi même je ne peux pas supporter la lecture." *Lettres Françaises*, p. 120.

past. In their recollection of the past the characters of *Nostromo* are also affected by their idealism, which, to judge by its force, borders on vanity. Nostromo's ideal of what a brave man should be forces him to hide the secret of his scandalous theft; to his fellow citizens he pretends that the silver has sunk to the bottom of the Golfo Placido so that they may continue to believe that his "record" of behavior is still unimpeachable. There is little doubt that his interest in the silver is quite subordinate to his concern about his reputation. But the novel's task is to represent the actuality, the record of it by an individual, and the individual himself as he is mediating between actuality and record. All three of these things add up to *Nostromo*'s dense fabric.

So strong a plan of representation derives, I think, from Conrad's habit of viewing his life as an uneasy compromise between two conflicting modes of existence. Because it reflects Conrad's radical uncertainty about himself and also the tension he so often felt between opposed positions on any given matter, it is a complex habit. The first mode is to experience reality as an unfolding process, as action-being-made, as always "becoming." To experience all of this is to feel oneself in the midst of reality. The second mode is to feel reality as a hard quantity, very much "there" and definable. To experience this is to view reality retrospectively, since only in looking back upon what has already occurred can one master the unceasing movement of action-being-made. Yet because mastery inevitably means control, the retrospective view modifies, and even contradicts, the richly complex dynamics of a specific action. In *Nostromo* the two modes are of course the conflict between immersion in action and the retrospective definition (record) of that action, and as readers we are expected to note the often startling disparities between action and record that such a conflict produces.

We are also expected to ask whether a correspondence between the record and the action is ever to be hoped for. Presumably such a correspondence is possible for most people and in some situations, yet it is never even momentarily allowed in *Nostromo* except, as we shall see in a moment, in Emilia Gould's mind. The rest of the time the characters who carry out the retrospection are distorting actuality almost beyond recognition. That is why nearly every character seems curiously myopic about Costaguanan politics. No one wants to see what is really happening. Instead everyone sees what he would like to *believe* happened. The result of this myopia in Costaguana gives *Nostromo* one of its principal subjects.

The reconcilation between action and record is performed by Mrs. Gould, the only character in the novel with really accurate vision. She has the capacity both for understanding action as it happens, and for being aware of the psychological traps men create for themselves as they cast a congratulatory glance back over their activity and plan new action. It is, after all, because the retrospective inaccuracy of a personal record breeds inaccurate, wrongheaded self-assessments that Charles Gould is so pathetic a figure in the novel. A life-long education in the pathetic mismanagement of a life comes to Emilia during the course of her marriage to him. She watches him slowly drawn away from her by the attractive personal challenge he finds in the mine. The more successfully he copes with the challenge the more he is claimed by material interests. For his success is measured in the enlarging scope of his material interests: he is Charles Gould first, and then he becomes *el rey de Sulaco*. But Emilia can admire the king at the same time that she knows the other Charles, a poor slave who sacrifices himself to the delusion that silver, his silver, can be humane. The more he is a king, the less able is he to know what a slave he really is.

Emilia's ability to see accurately, and at the same time charitably to accept people for what they are, is unique in the novel so that every one of the men is attracted to her. Dr. Monygham sees her as a good fairy who is seated in a charmed circle at the Casa Gould. Decoud quite naturally gravitates toward her quiet house and honors her even as he loves Antonia Avellanos. It is left to Nostromo—perhaps because he has dared the most—to pay her the supreme compliment, which is to reveal his dishonoring secret to her. During that wonderfully described, hushed moment toward the end of the novel, the uncomfortable vacillation between what Nostromo is and what he has made others believe about himself is revealed to Mrs. Gould. The spell he has cast on Sulaco is broken, and he is exposed as a thief. Because the Republic of Sulaco has been founded on his daring ride over the mountains for royalist help ("he carried all our lives in his hands" [539]), it also is exposed as a state based on a sham reputation. Here is a portion of the scene:

> "Nostromo," Mrs. Gould whispered, bending very low, "I, too, have hated the idea of that silver from the bottom of my heart."
>
> "Marvellous!—that one of you should hate the wealth that you know so well how to take from the hands of the poor. The world rests upon the poor, as old Giorgio says. You have been always good to the poor. But there is something accursed in wealth. Señora, shall I tell you where the treasure is? To you alone. . . . Shining! Incorruptible!"
>
> A pained voluntary reluctance lingered in his tone, in his eyes, plain to the woman with the genius of sympathetic intuition. She averted her glance from the miserable subjection of the dying man, appalled, wishing to hear no more of the silver.
>
> "No, capataz," she said. "No one misses it now. Let it be lost forever." (624–25)

The intense poignancy of the scene is all the more effective if we remember the agonies of Conrad's creative life. It is not difficult to imagine him wishing for some relief from the deception of the pose he was forced to assume. Nevertheless he must have known that his entire creative existence could remain viable only so long as he maintained his masquerade as a cheery writer of tough adventure yarns. He could never confess himself to anyone, but he could do it vicariously in nearly every one of his stories. For all of his heroes hide some shameful secret, and each of them dreams of the day when he can be cleared before those he loves best. Yet Conrad's severity of vision enables Mrs. Gould to express understanding and assurance without granting either one or the other to anyone else in the novel. Busy Sulaco has become so prosperous that its shabby past can no longer embarrass it. It stands above its complicated history, secure in the unambiguous record of its rags-to-riches adventure. Only Mrs. Gould knows Sulaco for what it is, but she can never make her knowledge effective. Her moment of greatest understanding and illumination is also her moment of least practical influence. Yet she knows that it is possible for the integrity and courage of one person to sustain the life of a nation. So, as Nostromo had once saved Sulaco with his daring ride (although he had already dishonored himself), now she preserves Sulaco's record by withholding a secret certain to dishonor the country. The tragic fact, of course, is that her courageous act is nugatory by the standards of modern politics; of what use is it to possess a morally harmful secret about a whole country? From what sort of real, tangible threat has she saved Sulaco? The magnificence of the moment does not entirely depend upon our admiration for Mrs. Gould, but also upon Conrad's justly cynical depiction of her as a frail, politically powerless woman. One can picture her proclaiming her secret in order to arouse the conscience of Sulaco—and being diplomatically hushed by Don Juste, the elegant parliamentarian.

The Silver

As in so many of Conrad's other works, *Nostromo* pits the sea and the land against each other as if they represented opposing values; unlike most of his "typical" works, however, *Nostromo* concerns itself mainly with land affairs. Yet the sea is a power of which Costaguana is very much aware: it lies off the republic's coast, a vast, inexpressibly strong, and unchanging desert, very different in its eternal brooding from the petty self-seeking of land life. The sea swallows up Martin Decoud with its huge indifference to his human littleness, and, in his final yielding to it, he seems drawn to its unlimited power like a man seeking union with the infinite.

Decoud's death very convincingly dramatizes the difference between land and sea. The land, in *Nostromo*, has concentrated its values into silver, which, when put to the test of the open sea off Costaguana, fails Decoud miserably. Yet silver gradually assumes a greater and still greater influence in the lives of Costaguanans. By the end of the novel it has practically become the *raison d'être* of the independent Republic of Sulaco. Decoud goes as far as to call the silver-producing mine "the greatest fact in the whole of South America" (237). The silver enslaves everyone in the novel except Mrs. Gould, for whom silver's valuable solidity and hardness are not attractions. The trouble is that silver seems to provoke visions of concrete power and achievement in the minds of its devotees. Men almost want to model their lives into perfect, hard blocks of silver; yet they do not realize that such lives will be stunted and selfish. The silver craze displaces normal human judgment so completely as to divert the broad course of human activity into a narrow stream that resembles molten silver flowing into an ingot mold. This prisonlike activity is the record of Costaguana suffering under the influence of "material interests," a general dementia of which silver fetishism is a particular branch.

To have put all of this into the book is not a simple-minded social novelist's trick to shock readers into an appreciation of the value of spiritual interests, or for that matter of "sea" interests. *Nostromo* has little to do with advocating other interests over material ones. It accepts material interests as facts and not as fantasies to be wished away. The novel does, however, use Costaguana's passion for these interests in order to trace a pattern, ostensibly social, historical, and economic, which makes pertinent reference to human psychology, and to a kind of inscape of Conrad's mind. Thus *Nostromo* is a novel about public, political history that is reduced, over the course of several hundred pages, to a condition of mind, an inner state. It is like a *trompe l'oeil* painting of a city that upon closer inspection turns out to be an anatomical drawing of the brain.

Like all great novels *Nostromo* has an almost inviolable objective impersonality, but unlike all other great novels *Nostromo* has both the objective impersonality *and* a very subjective personality of its own that criticizes and undermines the objective edifice. It it necessary, I think, to say all of this as emphatically as possible because it has become customary to speak of *Nostromo* as belonging to the same class of fiction as *War and Peace*, not only in its size but also in its manner and conception.[17] In sheer size, of course, the two novels are similar, but beyond that comparing them is not valuable. *Nostromo* aspires to no authority on matters of history and sociology, and neither does it create a normative world that resembles our own. Rather, it is the result of a strangely idiomatic vision (something which *War and Peace* is able to conceal definitively) that obviously derives from the almost incredibly peculiar life and vision of its author. Finally, *Nostromo* is most assuredly not the product of a great established literature. Even though it is written in English, its author was not an Englishman but a Polish *émigré* who was educated in France. Because its origins as a novel were so devious, *Nostromo* bears little real relation to novels in either French, English, or Russian. It is most profitable to compare the novel with novels written in the more insecure, individualistic and nervous American tradition. *Nostromo's* closest counterpart anywhere—at least in strangeness of idiom and intention—is *Moby Dick*.

There are certain clues planted in *Nostromo* that incline one to view the novel as a solid, objective edifice undermined and haunted by a private vision, and, since these clues need to be connected with each other and with what we have been saying about the silver, they will need detailed description. The most immediate fact in the novel is Costaguana, somewhere on the coast of South America, a country whose history reflects the type of continent of which it is a part. The heritage of South America is, "as the great Liberator Bolívar had said in the bitterness of his spirit, [that] 'America is ungovernable. Those who worked for her independence have ploughed the sea'" (206). In this struggle for independence the "ancestral Goulds," whose presence in Costaguana was so "indelible" (52), participate very actively. They have been there for three generations, prospering as merchants, revolutionists, and liberators; they have been well known and respected. Until the era of Charles Gould, however, no Gould could command the respect and influence that earns the

---

[17] The comparison is made in Jocelyn Baines, *Joseph Conrad: A Critical Biography*, Weidenfeld and Nicolson, London, 1959, p. 297.

mine's latest owner the title *el rey de Sulaco*. The background of this title is what, in the Gould chronicle, concerns the novel most.

Unlike his ancestors Charles has come to Costaguana after many years of life abroad; in this he is similar to the majority of characters in the novel. Each of them has a period of expatriation from Costaguana, on the one hand because of exile, or, on the other, because of foreign birth. In the first group are Decoud, Montero, and Don José; in the second Nostromo, the Violas, Dr. Monygham, and Mitchell. During the course of the novel each of these characters earns his citizenship in Costaguana either by an act or by a process of naturalization. Charles Gould's naturalization is accomplished under urgent pressures. He grows up as a homeless Englishman in Europe who is helplessly tied to a desperately angry father. Thousands of miles separate the boy and his father, and the boy grows into manhood with a need for attachment and purpose. Gould senior has been given the mine concession against his will as payment for a loan, and since the mine is sterile he wastes his life in frustration. Charles, however, becomes more interested in the mine at the same time that his father is slowly being killed by it (63). What to the father had been a bitter waste of effort is, for the son, a challenge to his moral strength: not only will the mine vindicate his father's tenacity, but it will also be the instrument of Costaguana's betterment. At this point Charles cannot see that his own ambitions and the country's improvement are almost the same thing. In young Emilia he finds a worthy companion and steward of his hopes, and he marries her immediately after receiving news of his father's death. In the following passage Conrad characterizes them at the time of their marriage:

> These two young people remembered the life which had ended wretchedly just when their own lives had come together in that splendor of hopeful love, which to the most sensible minds appears like a triumph of good over all the evils of the earth. A vague idea of rehabilitation entered the plan of their life. That it was so vague as to elude the support of argument made it only the stronger. It had presented itself to them at the instant when the woman's instinct of devotion and the man's

instinct of activity receive from the strongest of illusions their most powerful impulse. The very prohibition imposed the necessity of success. It was as if they had been morally bound to make good their vigorous view of life against the unnatural error of weariness and despair. (81–82)

When transplanted from Europe to Costaguana "a vigorous view of life" and an "idea of rehabilitation" are implicit modern defiances of Bolívar's bitter maxim. Charles can be defiant because he is young and, as any reader of Conrad's "Youth" will remember, youth has a facility for romanticizing unpleasant realities. Charles also has a severe sense of rectitude; he is like an architect who sees that a building is "off" because of some defect in construction, and cannot resist correcting it. Yet the mine represents more to him than the fulfillment of a moral imperative. Once he realizes that "the mine had been the cause of an absurd moral disaster" and that "its working must be made a serious and moral success" (64), Charles begins to respond to the attractions of action considered for its own sake. He thinks that doing something is always better than doing nothing, particularly as the lesson his father's plight has taught him is the unhappiness of inactivity. Charles's plan is to build the mine, to rework it, and so to plough the sea of which Bolívar had spoken. Furthermore the project for the mine is Charles's way of disproving his father—and God— neither of whom had seen anything of worth in Costaguana.

> And he asked his wife whether she remembered a passage in one of his father's last letters where Mr. Gould had expressed the conviction that "God looked wrathfully at these countries, or else He would let some ray of hope fall through a rift in the appalling darkness of intrigue, bloodshed, and crime that hung over the Queen of Continents."
> Mrs. Gould had not forgotten. "You read it to me, Charley," she murmured. "It was a striking pronouncement. How deeply your father must have felt its terrible sadness!"
> "He did not like to be robbed. It exasperated him," said Charles Gould. "But the image will serve well enough. What is wanted here is law, good faith, order, security. Any one can declaim about these things, but I pin my faith to material interests. Only let the material interests once get a firm footing,

and they are bound to impose the conditions on which alone they can continue to exist. That's how your money-making is justified here in the face of lawlessness and disorder. It is justified because the security which it demands must be shared with an oppressed people. A better justice will come afterwards. That's your ray of hope." His arm pressed her slight form closer to his side for a moment. "And who knows whether in that sense even the San Tomé mine may not become that little rift in the darkness which poor father despaired of ever seeing?"

She glanced up at him with admiration. He was competent; he had given a vast shape to the vagueness of her unselfish ambitions. (92–93)

Charles embarks upon his mission in the country; his mind preserves "it's steady poise as if sheltered in the passionless stability of private and public decencies at home in Europe" (53). He believes in work, in honesty, in self-possessed conduct, in steadfastness. Like the other characters in the novel he believes that if he abides by his program (which he believes will be his record for the future) and acts according to it, then the results foreseen by the program *will* come about. The more he believes and then acts on his belief, the more tenaciously he clings to his beliefs; and the less able is he to *think* critically about what he is doing and why he is doing it. Man, Conrad reminds us, "is a desperately conservative creature" (61). Gould's conservatism—as anyone's might be—is of the kind that banishes thought from his existence, on the grounds that thought might bring ideas capable of damaging what is being conserved. In time Charles is victimized by an endless vicious circle of activity as completely as his father was by the futility of South America. "Action is consolatory. It is the enemy of thought and the friend of flattering illusions. Only in the conduct of our action can we find the sense of mastery over the Fates. For his action, the mine was obviously the only field" (72).

It seems to Gould that instead of life being, as Marlow had put it eloquently in *Heart of Darkness*, "a mysterious arrangement of merciless logic for a futile purpose," [18] life is the satisfac-

[18] Conrad, *Complete Works*, Doubleday, Garden City, 1925, Vol. XVI, p. 150.

tory realization of an easily understandable logic. Take the most chaotic place on earth, believe something strongly enough, apply it to that place—and you are able to make order out of chaos, because underneath everything there is a benign order. The discernment of that order, alas, is woefully subjective, but no one seems aware of so disastrous a snag. Even as wise a man as Don José Avellanos believes this. The title of his book reminds one that for all of those fifty years of misrule there could have been a right rule. Old Giorgio Viola intuits the right rules merely by looking at his treasured portrait of Garibaldi; Decoud at first lives his life according to the rules of a boulevardier; and Captain Mitchell stubbornly applies the ramrod-stiff code of the parvenu English gentleman among the "natives." Each of them insists that his view of the world is the right one. It is a familiar rationale. More than likely Conrad may have discovered its abstract pattern in Schopenhauer, who, as Galsworthy informs us, had been a great favorite of Conrad's.[19] For what is an uncritical, sustained belief in order but an egoism based on the assumption that "the world is my idea?" The purpose of this egoism is a sense of mastery over life, and its origin perhaps the fear that life may not be worth living after all.

As always, Emilia Gould is different from the others; or, if she is not different at bottom, her character is less overtly venal. As a young girl she seems to have been so sure of her competency in living as to expect an equal competency in anyone she would love. "[Charles] had struck her imagination from the first by his unsentimentalism, by that very quietude of mind which she had erected in her throat for a sign of perfect competency in the business of living" (54). When she becomes the first lady of Sulaco, who is "gifted in the art of human intercourse" (50), we are given superficial evidence of her competency in the business of living; a more profound sign of that competency is her realization that it is only Charles who can give "a vast shape . . . to the vagueness of her unselfish ambitions" (93). Another person, an incompetent one, might have stood in his way; *she* dedicates herself—with *noblesse oblige*—to the furtherance of his ambitions. Society in

[19] John Galsworthy, *Castles in Spain*, Heinemann, London, 1928, p. 91.

Sulaco is hers; whereas her husband conquers the land financially and politically, she conquers it socially.

> A woman with a masculine mind is not a being of superior efficiency; she is simply a phenomenon of imperfect differentiation—interestingly barren and without importance. Doña Emilia's intelligence being feminine led her to achieve the conquest of Sulaco, simply by lighting the way for her unselfishness and sympathy. She could converse charmingly, but she was not talkative. The wisdom of the heart having no concern with the erection or demolition of theories any more than with the defence of prejudices, has no random words at its command. The words it pronounces have the value of acts of integrity, tolerance, and compassion. A woman's true tenderness, like the true virility of man, is expressed in action of a conquering kind. (73–74)

Conrad leaves us in little doubt that the "action of a conquering kind" (which we shall discuss a little later), is undertaken by the Goulds because they have committed themselves to the world they have created, which is the world in which their "unselfish ambitions" are given concreteness and form. At the moment that Emilia accepts her husband on that unhappy day in Italy many years ago, Conrad writes: "And immediately the future hostess of all the Europeans in Sulaco had the physical experience of the earth falling away from under her. It vanished completely, even to the very sound of the bell" (69). Charles's world becomes hers, and the history of their married life becomes the history of the mine (73). The mere business of living is transformed by them into watching over a vested interest. It is their world and they become unthinkable without it: life turns into a perpetually renewed act of attachment. (Curiously enough, Conrad's manner of describing the Goulds' life as constantly renewed attachment parallels the description of existence by modern phenomenology, the philosophical science of experience.) The norm of Charles's existence is the constant saving of the country from the savagery of its inhabitants (53–54). Every intellectual and spiritual value that usually complicates human life (skepticism, self-criticism) is put aside. Instead, all values derive from the silver ingots that have become life's goal. To the

Goulds, and indeed to everyone in Costaguana, the silver is not merely the object of a simple concupiscence; if it were that it would have been easy, as Conrad's predecessors in Victorian England had done, to rail at the obvious corruptions brought on by the cash nexus. No, the silver has "a justificative conception, as though it were not a mere fact, but something far-reaching and impalpable, like the true expression of an emotion or the emergency of a principle" (118). It follows that "the San Tomé mine was to become an institution, a rallying-point for everything in the province that needed order and stability to live. Security seemed to flow upon this land from the mountain-range" (122).

With "his shoulders alone sustain[ing] the whole weight of the 'Imperium in Imperio'" (164), Gould is to Costaguana as Shakespeare's Prospero is to his island. The management of the mine, the constant visits to it, the dynamite he plants in it are evidence of his commanding executive spirit toward the mine. He is able to radiate magical influence into every corner of Sulacoan life; the Casa Gould is Sulaco's version of Prospero's cave. But just as Prospero has sacrificed his own dukedom for the scholar's robes, so also has Gould sacrificed his proper estate, his humanity, for the mine. Emilia Gould is her husband's only concession to humanity, for, as he once tells her, the best of his feelings are in her keeping (79). Such a remark makes it possible, I think, to speak of the death of Gould's soul, if we mean by soul that entity in man which is most concerned with human feeling and activity. The engrossing work that Gould performs for the mine's sake has claimed his attention so thoroughly (particularly as it is work requiring a minimum of human feeling) that his soul has become supererogatory, and simply ceases to exist. As evidence of this death one ought to consider, for example, that for a character so apparently powerful in Sulaco he radiates an extraordinary passivity, especially when he is compared with his wife and with the three energetic characters in the novel—Decoud, Nostromo, Monygham—who also undergo a death of the soul.

Gould dies into the mine's service but is never reborn out of it. Rather than ennobling him it debases him, and he "lives" on a purely mechanical level as a dehumanized organizer, the arch-foreman of an endless mechanical process. There is something of the same depressing effect that Gould's activity produces in D. H. Lawrence's description of Gerald Crich who, in *Women in Love*, totally organizes his family's coal mine into what for Lawrence becomes a monument to death-in-life. Decoud's agony on the *Isabel* is that he suffers a death whose cause is the crushing of his soul by a solitude that he nobly resists. Even if Decoud's struggles against the overwhelming power of silent immensities do not save him, he has nevertheless remained vital right up to the end: his recollections of Antonia and his ironic musings on his predicament are proofs of his human activity. Gould of course survives human solitude only because he concedes his human problems and works uniquely for an inhuman process. Nostromo dies a metaphoric death on the Golfo Placido, but he is reborn a thief and scoundrel. Monygham too has died when, under the torture devised by Guzman Bento, he betrays himself completely. Yet he later chooses a myth—Mrs. Gould—and lives again, using it to prop his existence. Emilia, who is frequently described as a fairy, is something of a magic triumph for all that is best in humanity. Is it not magic, in so threatening and dehumanized a world, for her soul to retain its identity so that she is herself, alive and human, at every point in the novel?

Her resilient consistency of character is remarkable because *Nostromo* is so concerned, even obsessed with rapid changes, with inaugurations of new states. There are constant changes from one political status to the next, from one emotional mood to another, from one personal confrontation to another. The paradox is that all these bewildering changes occur for one unchanging reason: the silver. In his own life, Gould typifies the change made for the silver's sake: while his feelings are in someone else's keeping he has become the mine's wholly devoted steward. Since, in so becoming, he has given the country one firm, unimpeachable, unchanging value—the silver—and has himself become as constant as the mine, it remains for everyone else to adjust to these constant values. Each person believes himself to have made a perfect adjustment, and yet each of these adjustments provokes discord. The reason for this is quite apparent: to everyone, the best adjustment is the final possession of the mine. No wonder that immediately after the mine is established in Costaguana a whole series of revolutions takes place. Only when Gould decides to intervene on the side of the Blanco party is order restored; Gould and the Blancos bring Ribiera, who "was their own creature" (41), to power.

The extent of "revolutions," of inaugurations into new states, in Sulaco is further complicated and enriched by Conrad's subtle, yet functional adumbration of the South American setting. He shows, for example, the relation between the atmosphere of the New World and the art of declamation (91), which presses for continual changes in the emotional and political *status quo*. Also, he understands the effect of Old World Caesarism upon the emerging political mentality of the New World. The brilliantly accurate account of the Monterist revolt is a result of Conrad's grasp of this phenomenon. Most remarkably, he catches the climate of ungovernable excess that dominates life in Sulaco once the critical break from the values that the silver has dislodged—a break for which the Goulds are perhaps responsible—has been made.

Conrad's representation of life in Sulaco is always so convincing in its dramatic and social versimilitude that one tends to forget that he is depicting a world based upon unreality. The mine's service is extremely demanding, and it is long, but it is not, as one might think, simply "normal": the illusion of normality is all the more remarkable when Conrad extends it to cover all phases of life in Costaguana. Yet to have considered the implications of the action, as we have done, is to see the entire foreground of the novel undergoing a prolonged revelation of horror, a revelation initiated at the beginning of the mine's influence and ending with Nostromo's death. In order to make this a little clearer, the distinction made earlier in this essay between action and record is useful. To read *Nostromo* as if its intensely articulated surface were all there was to it (and, I hasten to add, the richly documented surface is designed to give the illusion of all the truth one needs to know) is to read a record very much like the ones created by different characters in the novel. This is another way of saying that *Nostromo* is masquerading as an ordinary political or historical novel. The *real* action, on the other hand, is psychological and concerns man's overambitious intention to create his own world because the world as he finds it is somehow intolerable: this action underlies the historical and political events in *Nostromo*. The horror occurs in the gradual, prolonged discovery that the world created by man is just as intolerable as the world he has attempted to supersede. So vast a conclusion needs political and historical substantiation; hence *Nostromo*'s bias for connecting individuals to history, and history to the cruel designs of life.

The example of Charles Gould is instructive. In his decision to take up his father's work in the mine he is given very little real choice. Can one believe that he could have done anything else except return to Costaguana and make a moral success of the mine that had killed his father?

> Two big lamps with unpolished glass globes bathed in a soft and abundant light the four white walls of the room, with a glass case of arms, the brass hilt of Henry Gould's cavalry sabre on its square of velvet, and the water-color sketch of the San Tomé gorge. And Mrs. Gould, gazing at the last in its black wooden frame, sighed out:
> "Ah, if we had left it alone, Charles!"
> "No," Charles Gould said, moodily; 'it was impossible to leave it alone."
> "Perhaps it was impossible," Mrs. Gould admitted slowly.
> (231)

Because he is a man, and because life has faced him with an impasse ("forget about the mine that has killed your father and do something else") he must resort to action. What begins for him as a sort of sophisticated avenging of his father turns, before he is aware of it, into a desire to master life. Like many of Conrad's other protagonists Gould is decoyed by life into an impossible course of action. The difference between Kurtz and Gould is that Kurtz pronounces on the machinery of existence: "The horror, the horror." Gould is silent: he goes on with his work.

The major similarity between Kurtz's experience in Africa

and Gould's in South America is to be found in the atmosphere which, conducive to extremes of thought and emotions (perhaps because it is "foreign"), stimulates the protagonist to further efforts at mastery. The so called New World of South America is Conrad's manner of identifying the whole modern world which, because of its addiction to extreme forms of action, persuades morally convinced people of the necessity for action of a mastering, conquering kind. The articulate Decoud muses on the character of the New World: "There is a curse of futility upon our character: Don Quixote and Sancho Panza, chivalry and materialism, high-sounding sentiments and a supine morality, violent efforts for an ideal and a sullen acquiescence in every form of corruption" (189). Left to themselves Quixote and Sancho might destroy each other in a crazed war. But, as Decoud says, behind this deeply divided character are "the natural treasures of Costaguana." They "are of importance to the progressive Europe represented by this youth" (189). So Gould, the representative of progressive Europe, seeks to possess that treasure because it means revenge for his father's death, the imposition of order on the New World, and the chance to dominate.

Gould is convinced that what he does is right. Once again the prescient Decoud comments indirectly. "It seemed to him that every conviction, as soon as it became effective, turned into that form of dementia the gods send upon those they wish to destroy" (221). The real horror of this thought becomes apparent when one reflects on the impossibility of life without conviction. Life is action: action is based upon conviction: conviction is dementia: life is dementia. Decoud himself proves this. Raillery to him is a way of life: he scoffs at everything, and he accepts nothing. Yet he leaves Sulaco on a crazy errand with the silver because he is a man capable of a lover's illusion (which is a form of conviction whose aim is domination). As he dies, the illusion becomes less and less applicable to the terrifying solitude that underlies the life without action to which he is committed on the *Isabel*. His more successful companion, Nostromo, is another example of the process repeated. Decoud dies, but Nostromo emerges from the darkness as a thoroughgoing cheat. In the end Nostromo is also destroyed, and we are left asking the same question about life that Conrad himself is asking: is there any other pattern in life? In Sulaco there is an unreal prosperity based on Gouldism and Nostromo's exploit. On the Golfo Placido, what is there but solitude and death?

After Nostromo returns from the sea, and after he rides over the mountains to save Sulaco, we are reintroduced to Sulaco, once again by Captain Mitchell. If his first guided tour of the city (which had occupied the early part of the novel) had been inaccurate, the second one is nothing but well-intentioned propaganda. As if to underline the irony in Mitchell's views on Sulaco's new-found prosperity, Conrad has him take a hypothetical visitor on a tour of all the main "places of interest"; the point is that monuments, as Nietzsche once observed, provide one with the most insufficient and inaccurate sort of history. And so the chronicle of Sulaco goes. It flourishes in its monumental prosperity, with its silver exports reaching every corner of the world. "The most famous and desperate affair" (582) of one man's life has produced the very richest rewards. The reader is caught up in the jocular warmth of a wealthy country, jealous of its prestige and power, a partner among civilized nations. No one in Sulaco, except for Mrs. Gould, has second thoughts about the origins of Sulaco's power and wealth: no one remembers Costaguana, no one really cares about Decoud's death, no one worries much about the meaning of Sulaco's independence. This, of course, is the way of political life, and Conrad realistically portrays it.

But we must remember that Sulaco is a created state and as such represents the triumph of Gould's work, which had been to create his own world, to rule it, to possess it completely. Just as the silver had come to symbolize an objectified, justificative value, so too does Sulaco represent the objectified wish of one man. Yet, in defying life's intractability, Gould had escaped to a world of his own making; however, that world finally makes a prisoner of him. His wife, alone, is able silently to articulate her awareness of the horrible perfection that this plan has attained.

> She saw the San Tomé mountain hanging over the Campo, over the whole land, hated, wealthy, more soulless than any

tyrant, more pitiless and autocratic than the worst government, ready to crush innumerable lives in the expansion of its greatness. He did not see it. He could not see it. It was not his fault. He was perfect, perfect. . . . But she saw clearly the San Tomé mine possessing, consuming, burning up the life of the last of the Costaguana Goulds; mastering the energetic spirit of the son as it had mastered the lamentable weakness of the father. A terrible success for the last of the Goulds. . . . An immense desolation, the dread of her own continued life, descended upon the first lady of Sulaco. With a prophetic vision she saw herself surviving alone the degradation of her young ideal of life, of love, of work—all alone in the Treasure House of the World. The profound, blind, suffering expression of a painful dream settled on her face with its closed eyes. In the indistinct voice of an unlucky sleeper, lying passive in the toils of a merciless nightmare, she stammered out aimlessly the words:
"Material interests." (582–83)

Even though she, like most of Conrad's women characters, is content to endure silently, it is necessary for the critic to discover what is common both to so eloquently expressed a sense of horror as hers and to Conrad's urgent passion to incarnate this horror so painstakingly in fiction. To this discovery—which is a discovery of Conrad's vision of life's machinery—we must now turn.

The Machinery

In her comprehending silence at the end of the novel— which is set ironically against Giorgio Viola's uncomprehending and murderous silence—Mrs. Gould achieves a whole and balanced view of the past, the present, and the future. She has this catholic view because "it had come into her mind that for life to be large and full it must contain the care of the past and of the future in every passing moment of the present" (582). This is the wholeness of vision for which Nostromo's winding narrative stream has been seeking ever since the novel's murky, disorienting early pages. In the confusion caused by its uncertain focus Nostromo is like many of Conrad's other tales in which the course of the narrative stream is unclear. Because of that we are never really certain about the time. The present, for example, seems most reluctant to take the center stage and hold it, unless it is dragged to our attention and kept there by as willing a volunteer as Mitchell, the simple-minded Marlow type whose job is to set things moving, perhaps because he feels himself "in the thick of history" (150). No sooner does he start his narrative and add a few reflections of his own, than he is pushed aside, almost in dissatisfaction, by an overwhelming rush of qualifying recollections. Within the first eighty-five pages of the novel we pass from a general description of Costaguana to Ribiera's rescue, to the Viola family, to Nostromo's part in the rescue, to the dinner party on the eve of the railroad's inauguration, to Sir John's trip, to Henry Gould's presidentship under Bento, to tea at Don José's house, to the history of the mine, to the courtship of Charles and Emilia Gould. All of this is a prelude to the story of the slow establishment of the mine in Sulaco, which is the burden of Part I of *Nostromo*. Part II is concentrated around two long scenes: the one between Decoud and Antonia at the Casa Gould, and the rescue of the silver by Decoud and Nostromo. Finally, in Part III, the novel takes up the defeat of the Monterist revolt and the new era in Sulaco's history. During this time Nostromo himself is killed. Interspersed are the stories of Dr. Monygham, Hernandez, Father Corbelàn, Hirsch, and Sotillo; there are also some important interludes provided by scenes between the Goulds and scenes at the new parliament. In all of this there is no strict chronological order.

The roundabout, rather than the straightforward, linear narrative had been, of course, the manner subscribed to and practiced by Conrad and Ford Madox Ford, his erstwhile collaborator. They argued that it allowed them the maximum in psychological realism since one does not know an event all at once; instead, knowledge of events comes to the mind in small pieces that are gradually put together. Life itself is too diffusely complex, they felt, for the concentrated, packaged actuality presented by earlier novelists. In *Nostromo*, however, the narrative's reluctance to show its exact position in the present is perhaps the result of a more interesting and functional hesitation. The "cool purity" of

Higuerota (the tall mountain which "seemed to hold itself aloof from a hot earth" [29] and from Sulaco at its foot) makes humanity—inconsistent, weak, wavering—ashamed. Higuerota holds Sulaco in its gaze as if it were the eye of God, turned away from the Golfo Placido and now brooding over Sulaco. The mountain is a transcendent, constantly felt power in the novel; in its awesome monolithic strength the mountain's distant presence is as unattainable an aspiration to the fragmented action of the novel as Mallarmé's *azur* is to his tortured soul. It may have been the contrast between Sulaco's atomized political life and Higuerota's abiding, concentrated presence that made Arnold Bennett, writing Conrad about *Nostromo* on November 22, 1912, exclaim: "The said mountain (is) . . . the principal personage in the story." [20] Bennett's remark is exaggerated of course, but the force of the mountain is unmistakable. One can imagine Conrad feeling the grand, Olympian presence of the mountain in the narrative; seeking a comparable human force in the panoramic action he is about to relate, he hesitates, explains, qualifies. From his own experience he knew, for example, that a master mariner commands the art of sailing with the same consistent domination that Higuerota has over Sulaco. In Sulaco's political life there is no such dominating individual. Life is too untidy, man too weak. The narrative's meanderings are a search for the superior man, who, like Nietzsche's *Übermensch*, compels history.

All of this is rather speculative. Is it not safer to remark that Higuerota's presence endows the novel with a sense of height and space and depth? There it stands, its solidity giving the novel a specific spatial perspective. Yet an examination of Conrad's many available letters to his closest personal friends reveals a despairing search in his own life for precisely the qualities Higuerota possesses: consistency, power, and unity. The mixed origins of his life, in his Polish birth, his French cultivation, and his English nationality, and his double career as a sailor turned man of letters, gave him an acute sense of his splintered individuality. In his let-

[20] Ed. Gerard Jean Aubry, *Twenty Letters to Joseph Conrad,* The First Edition Club, London, 1926.

ters written between 1890 and 1895 to Marguerite Poradowska, his aunt, he often appears in pursuit of a single workable identity for himself. The letters are ramblingly articulate and extremely self-concerned, but when he briefly finds himself, as he does on July 20, 1894, he is lucidly aware of a persistent doubleness to his "selfhood."

> But you are afraid of yourself; of the inseparable being forever at your side—master and slave, victim and executioner—who suffers and causes suffering. That's how it is! One must drag the ball and chain of one's selfhood to the end. It is the [price] one pays for the devilish and divine privilege of thought; so that in this life it is only the elect who are convicts—a glorious band which comprehends and groans but which treads the earth amidst a multitude of phantoms with maniacal gestures, with idiotic grimaces. Which would you be: idiot or convict? [21]

Later, to Garnett, he was to lament the absence of a starting point for his stories because his life seemed to have no clear starting point;[22] so confused was he about himself that he could find no terminal in either time or place for his mind to hold on to. Perhaps his most pathetic lament was made in a letter to Edward Noble, an apprentice writer, on July 17, 1895. "It is an individuality [Noble's]," he wrote, "that will stand wear and tear, that has resistance and power,—while I shall be used up in a short and miserable sputter of dim flame. It is so." [23] When he persevered in his hope that his individuality might achieve lasting strength, he worked himself into a rage of scorn at the folly of such a thought; individuality, he concluded, was a mere sham. He wrote Garnett of this on March 23, 1896:

> When one looks at life in its true aspect then everything loses much of its unpleasant importance and the atmosphere becomes cleared of what are only unimportant mists that drift past in imposing shapes. When once the truth is grasped that one's

[21] Conrad, *Letters of Joseph Conrad to Marguerite Poradowska, 1890–1920,* translated from the French and edited with introduction, notes, and appendices by John A. Gee and Paul J. Sturm, Yale University Press, New Haven, 1940, p. 72.
[22] Garnett, *Letters,* p. 59.   [23] *Life and Letters,* I, p. 176.

own personality is only a ridiculous and aimless masquerade of something hopelessly unknown the attainment of serenity is not very far off. Then there remains nothing but the surrender to one's impulses, the fidelity to passing emotions which is perhaps a nearer approach to truth than any other philosophy of life. And why not? If we are "ever becoming—never being" then I would be a fool if I tried to become this thing rather than that; for I know well that I never will be anything. I would rather grasp the solid satisfaction of my wrongheadedness and shake my fist at the idiotic mystery of Heaven.[24]

But to grasp the solid satisfaction of his wrong-headedness was not among his capabilities. He needed inner security of mind and character to sustain him, even in wrong-headedness, and his lonely battles with his fiction made it impossible to have security. To describe the progress of his work he wrote frequently to his friends of struggles in a black cave, of being in a terrible nightmare, of rowing across an ocean of ink without any goal in sight.[25] When, in "Typhoon," he was able to portray an unimaginative man single-mindedly standing up to nature's worst, he considered his fictional feat in the making of MacWhirr's character something of a compensation for the strength of character he himself did not have. On August 26, 1901, he wrote to William Blackwood about a book of naval experience written by Admiral William Kennedy; apparently the book contained a good deal in it that was reminiscent of Conrad's own "Typhoon."

> Now a book of that sort *is* the man—the man disclosed absolutely; and the contact of such a genuine personality is like an invigorating bath for one's mind jaded by infinite effort after literary expression, wearied by all the unrealities of a writing life, discouraged by a sunless, starless sort of mental solitude, having lost its reckoning in a grey sea of words, words, words; an unruly choppy sea running crosswise in all the endless shifts of thought. . . . A wrestle with wind and weather has a moral value like the primitive acts of faith on which may be built a doctrine of salvation and a rule of life.[26]

[24] Garnett, p. 46.   [25] *Life and Letters,* II, pp. 83–84; *ibid.,* p. 51
[26] Conrad, *Letters to Blackwood,* p. 133.

Having created in MacWhirr a character of consistency and strength, Conrad came to the unexpected conclusion that he should hold MacWhirr in emphatic disrespect. He reasoned that the invigoration provided by someone like MacWhirr did not compensate for whatever desirable virtue (skepticism, for instance) was lost when a "consistent" character was gained. He wrote of this rather shrewdly reasoned view to Galsworthy on November 11, 1901; it is easy to remark that Conrad's disrespect derived from his envy for what he did not possess.

> Say what you like, man lives in his eccentricities (so called) alone. They give a vigour to his personality which mere consistency can never do. One must explore deep and believe the incredible to find the new particles of truth floating in an ocean of insignificance. And before all one must divest oneself of every particle of respect for one's character. You are really most profound and attain the greatest art in handling the people you do not respect.[27]

So curious an amalgam of attitudes accounts, in Conrad's shorter fiction, for such diverse types as Kurtz and MacWhirr. Imagined as consistent characters they are puzzling to the reader because of Conrad's shifting point of view toward them. Are Kurtz and MacWhirr either noble or admirable? The difficulties of this question can be traced to the corner of deathlike inner emptiness in which for better or for worse their real individuality lies. Because of the extraordinary sense of inner lifelessness these apparently heroic characters exude, Conrad can be said to have a truly ambiguous conception of character. Although they are endowed with the consistency and courage that Conrad believed he did not have, these men also remind one of specters. The same can be said of Charles Gould and Nostromo. Each in his own way rescues the action of the novel from aimlessness; each dominates it momentarily as Higuerota dominates Sulaco. Thus in the first third of the novel there are two "rescues" of Costaguanan history: Nostromo's resuce of Ribiera, and Gould's rescue of the San Tomé mine. Gould is figuratively captured by the mine at the outset: because of his servitude, rather than despite it, he rises

[27] *Life and Letters,* I. p. 301.

in political importance, and in so rising he matches Higuerota's eminence on a mundane level. Yet his submission to the cause of silver is, as we said earlier, a sort of suicide. Perhaps this is Conrad's way of forcing us to believe that the consistency of character gained by Gould (which is institutionalized in his royal title) was not worth the sacrifice of his human "eccentricities."

Nostromo's is a different case. He is presented to the reader in the most flattering way as the dashing devil-may-care leader of Sulaco's dock workers. Yet from the beginning his existence is somewhat paradoxical, for he is, as Mitchell remarks, the leader of "an outcast lot of very mixed blood" (15), *and* he is also Nostromo, "our man," to all of Sulaco. The outcast and the man who is "one of us" will remain the two aspects of his formidable character that hold our interest, even though the second, popular aspect will grow like a cancer to envelop the other, freer, outcast one. (There may even be an intended connection between his name, our man, and the mine he serves in the later part of the book; the San Tomé silver can say confidently of him, he is *mine*.)

Nevertheless, in Part I he is allowed an extraordinary moment of beautiful, unspoiled freedom. To my mind it is the most splendid moment in any of Conrad's fiction and for the sheer excitement and immediacy of its effect it belongs next to Hemingway's superb description of Maera, the proudest and the most tragic of matadors, in *Death in the Afternoon*. Maera's pride, his unparalleled manly carriage were quite equal to his bravery and skill with the bulls.[28] Like Maera, Nostromo has, during that moment of real glory, an inner, authentic nobility that matches his dazzling appearance. Resplendent in his uniform, the mounted capataz is confronted by Paquita, his Sulacoan sweetheart; the lovers are surrounded by a crowd that is curious about Nostromo's every act. He is this crowd's man as a matador is the audience's man when he is fearless and free. The girl hurls a flower at Nostromo's face, and then she taunts him; he remains slow and careless. When she threatens to stab him for his indiffer-

[28] Ernest Hemingway, *Death in the Afternoon*, Jonathan Cape, London, 1963, pp. 78–83.

ence he leans down and picks her up, asking at the same time for a dagger. He lets her cut off all his silver buttons, and then he is finished. "The circle had broken up, and the lordly capataz de cargadores, the indispensable man, the tried and trusty Nostromo, the Mediterranean sailor come ashore casually to try his luck in Costaguana, rode slowly towards the harbor" (144). Is it not correct that a man with such "unapproachable style" and "finished splendor" (138) should command the destiny of Sulaco? Here is the complete hero for whom the novel has been searching.

The capataz's triumphs do not, however, go uncriticized. In the first place Conrad's style heaps too many flattering phrases upon him. This technique, which characterizes the style of the whole novel, is the excessive use of appositional phrases. Nostromo is not just the capataz but also "the indispensable man, the tried and trusty Nostromo"; Decoud is the boulevardier, the universal wit, the lover; Gould is the king of Sulaco, the hope of Costaguana, the perfect man—and so on. In its obsessiveness, in its constant ironic shocks, in its overdone jocularity and courtesy, the technique is Dickensian. The second criticism of Nostromo is furnished, very explicitly, by Teresa Viola, who cannot resign herself to the successes he gains because she thinks he is an unashamed kowtower to the English. Her constant objections to his behavior are like the mocking echo of the adulations he receives from everyone else. For the most part, however, she does pierce his perfect camouflage of style and splendor to glimpse the equally perfect vanity that drives him. What enables her to do this is the "intimacy of antagonism as close in its way as the intimacy of accord and affection" (280). Yet Nostromo tolerates her for her husband's sake. The old man has a "personal quality of conviction, something they called 'terribilità'" (35) that Nostromo deeply respects. Not that he hasn't as intense a conviction of his own; it is rather that Viola's conviction is more objective somehow than Nostromo's completely subjective, degenerate self-conviction. Perhaps because of this subjective self-conviction he is vulnerable to Teresa's attacks on him although she does not understand that for all his vanity Nostromo is as amoral (rather than unmoral) as any animal. It is not, as she believes, the "fine words" but the silver that corrupts him: it makes him a slave to his own unthinking vanity and acquisitiveness. The silver also makes his reputation a problem to him, for until his magnificent exploit in the Placido he manages to channel the two aspects of his character (the popular and the outcast) into a free, profitable, and rather picaresque existence.

It is because of his uninhibited vanity and his faith in himself that Nostromo distrusts Decoud's skepticism. Decoud appears to be "an idle boulevardier" whose "cosmopolitanism [was] in reality a mere barren indifferentism posing as intellectual superiority" (168). Worse yet, Decoud "had pushed the habit of universal raillery to a point where it blinded him to the genuine impulses of his own nature" (169). Only when he submits to "that note of passion and sorrow unknown on the more refined stage of European politics" (173), is Decoud able to accept himself and put a stop to the scoffing that alienates him from his inner self. In the rather attractive sentimentality of his love for Antonia Avellanos, Decoud begins to act like a rational patriot who welcomes the responsibility of serious action which is based, paradoxically enough, on a lover's illusion.

During all of this time Gould continues to be tenaciously committed to the mine he has rescued and rehabilitated. When Part II begins, Sulaco has itself been involved in Gould's commitment, since Sulaco's civic existence is completely dependent on the mine. Besides Gould only Nostromo occupies a position of comparable (though not equal) power in the city. When the threat of Monterist invasion faces the city the duty of tending the silver is divided, quite properly, between Gould and Nostromo: Gould will remain in Sulaco with his finger controlling a charge of dynamite buried in the mine, and Nostromo will take the silver ingots themselves out of the city. Decoud is chosen to go with Nostromo because it is generally believed that an educated, intelligent patriot is necessary to complement the foreign man of action.

Together the two men leave Sulaco in the middle of a very dark night. The episode is described with a compelling tension, one far more controlled in tone and contour than the journey Marlow takes into the heart of darkness. (Interestingly, the presence of Hirsch, the cowardly stowaway, gives the scene something of the same macabre absurdity to which Marlow, in his description of the Congo voyage, insistently draws attention.) There is no masking narrative voice as there had been in *Heart of Darkness*, and so the worst aspects of that voice—its breathless insistence, its ill-timed jocularity—are avoided. The greater effectiveness of the later passage, however, is as much due to the episode's relevance to Conrad's personal predicament as it is to his strengthened technical assurance. The setting of the difficult adventure could have been taken straight out of his anguished letters and perhaps even from this one which was written to Garnett in 1899.

> The more I write the less substance do I see in my work. The scales are falling off my eyes. It is tolerably awful. And I face it, I face it but the fright is growing on me. My fortitude is shaken by the view of the monster. It does not move; its eyes are baleful; it is as still as death itself—and it will devour me. Its share has eaten into my soul already deep, deep. I am alone with it in a chasm with perpendicular sides of black basalt. Never were sides so perpendicular and smooth, and high. Above, your anxious head against a bit of sky peers down—in vain—in vain. There's no rope long enough for that rescue.[29]

As the two men row out from the harbor both of them know that the importance of their task is completely transforming their existence. Sulaco's material interests drop away from Decoud, who is now "in the toils of an imaginative existence [;] and that strange work of pulling a lighter [which] seemed to belong naturally to the inception of a new state, [now] acquired an ideal meaning from his love for Antonia" (294). Yet in a short while he feels himself "on the verge of delirium" (295) produced by his overintense exertions in an unreal cause. This immediately recalls Conrad's own sentiments as he worked at the novel. Conrad's letter to Edmund Gosse on March 23, 1905, includes the declaration that "I have often suffered in connection with my work from a

[29] Garnett, p. 153.

sense of unreality, from intellectual doubt of the ground I stood upon." [30]

Nostromo has no sympathy with this sort of intellectual convolution. Because he is certain that only "sheer desperation will do for this affair" (306), he is inspired to strange extremes of vanity and bravery. Even Decoud, who has always known about Nostromo's vanity, is surprised by the qualities that now emerge in Nostromo's behavior. "The usual characteristic quietness of the man was gone. . . . Something unsuspected by every one had come to the surface" (313). This is Nostromo's bloodthirsty determination to live up to himself, a determination that sweeps aside all the barriers of class between the two men and compels Decoud into his service.

During this absolutely central episode in the novel the two men are intellectually and spiritually poles apart. Nostromo not only exults in the darkness but turns it into an advantage because he is so certain of himself; Decoud, on the other hand, suffers the immense handicap of self-doubt and feels himself in the grip of a growing sense of unreality. Yet he gradually becomes accustomed to the oppressive darkness. "It was part of a living world, since, pervading it, failure and death could be felt at your elbow" (314). Nostromo is the quintessential man of action who is working to secure his great reputation even more firmly; Decoud is a man of thought who suddenly discovers himself in a totally unfamiliar situation. Neither of the two men is *really* working for himself for, in their efforts on behalf of the silver, they both recognize and serve a common master.

> Each of them was as if utterly alone with his task. It did not occur to them to speak. There was nothing in common between them but the knowledge that the damaged lighter must be slowly but surely sinking. In that knowledge, which was like the crucial test of their desires, they seemed to have become completely estranged, as if they had discovered in the very shock of the collision that the loss of the lighter would not mean the same thing to them both. This common danger brought their differences in aim, in view, in character, and in position into

absolute prominence in the private vision of each. There was no bond of conviction, of common idea; they were merely two adventurers pursuing each his own adventure, involved in the same imminence of deadly peril. Therefore they had nothing to say to each other. But this peril, this only incontrovertible truth in which they shared, seemed to act as an inspiration to their mental and bodily powers. (328)

The authentic stresses of this scene derive, I think, from Conrad's obsessive notions about himself. The two adventurers are the double strain in Conrad's life which, as we noted earlier, he had come to believe made him a *homo duplex*. The atmosphere of deadly peril in which the two men find themselves as uncongenial partners represents the nightmare world that Conrad inhabited as he worked on his fiction. The analogies between Conrad and the two men extend even into the past histories of Nostromo and Decoud. The Genoese adventurer is a sailor whose desertion of his ship is kept rather noticeably in the background; throughout his career Conrad was fascinated with the idea of desertion, and so recurrent a theme is it that Gustave Morf, an early critic of Conrad, was able to base his integral reading of the fiction on the idea.[31] Moreover, Nostromo is a thoroughgoing man of action who has successfully moved his profession from sea to land; if this is still Conrad talking about one of the two men he was, Nostromo is an idealization of the sailor-turned-landlubber that Conrad himself had become. Yet the capataz is also an opportunist and an adventurer and that he is those things is one of the unavoidable results of being a professional man of action. It is significant that Conrad rather defensively anticipated the danger of being called an opportunistic adventurer himself, perhaps because he felt that at some point in his sea career he had been one. Interestingly, he once wrote a correspondent a somewhat petulant reminder that he was not a simple adventurer![32]

Decoud is Conrad's portrayal of himself as the confused

[31] Gustav Morf, *The Polish Heritage of Joseph Conrad*, Sampson Low, Marston, London, 1950.
[32] *Lettres Françaises*, p. 56.

intellectual for whom the ground he walks on is subject to doubt. His most serious moments (which occur during the long scene when he discusses his ideas with Antonia at the Casa Gould) echo the romantic, self-doubting tone of Conrad's letters to Marguerite Poradowska.

Before considering the real purpose of the mission undertaken by the two men it is necessary to consider Conrad's reasons for bringing Nostromo and Decoud together in the episode. If one recalls that *Nostromo* examines the problematic relation between action and historical record, then Decoud and Nostromo together represent the relation on a human level. It goes without saying, however, that the two men are sufficiently realized as characters to also represent *themselves* more than adequately. But in terms of the novel's total concerns, the masterful scene on the Golfo Placido takes up the issue between a true intellectual knowledge of action and the flattering distortions of a created record; between individuality as it really lives its problematic, difficult life in the world, and individuality as it believes and makes others believe it is; between a complicated inner dimension and a strategically simplified exterior; between Decoud's complex and passionate understanding of the wholly difficult realities of his situation and Nostromo's desire to make his reputation the dominant image in Sulaco's life; in short, between Conrad's authentic voice in his rich, confusing private writings and the voice he literally made up for his "Author's Notes."

The issue among all of these conflicting alternatives is forced by the crisis in Sulaco's history. What now happens to Sulaco is to be decided in the deportment of the two men. The analogy for the "objective" historical crisis in the city is, in Conrad's life, the state of extreme personal and artistic crisis he had found himself in by 1902. He felt that he was not producing well enough, he never had enough money, his whole existence seemed to be in the most unimaginable disarray (and of this his publishers were always willing to make a point); there seemed to be no alternative except to do something soon to change his predicament. Shortly after the crisis a new Conrad emerges who, as we noted elsewhere, publicly replaces the old tortured figure of the past twelve years.[33] This new *persona* is mirrored in the success Nostromo achieves because of Decoud's timely death. A smiling public man emerges whose place in the new Sulaco is based on a deliberate fraud. If Nostromo is partly an idealized apology for a life of action, he is also a shattering criticism of the public personality.

Gould's connection with all of this is interesting. His sustained immersion in his work at the mine typifies man's identification of life with work, or, as Conrad had put it in *Heart of Darkness,* the devotion with efficiency to an idea.[34] To this devotion, Nostromo and Decoud are irremediably tied even though they think that they are acting for their own reasons. In the same way that Gould is "run" by Holroyd, they are "run" by Gould; none of the men has any freedom. Each is the sustainer of another's vanity, Decoud of Nostromo's, Nostromo of Gould's, and Gould of Holroyd's. After Decoud's death, Gould muses that

> The only thing that was not changed was his position towards Mr. Holroyd. The head of the silver and steel interests had entered into Costaguana affairs with a sort of passion. Costaguana had become necessary to his existence; in the San Tomé mine he had found the imaginative satisfaction which other minds would get from drama, from art, or from a risky and fascinating sport. It was a special form of the great man's extravagance, sanctioned by a moral intention big enough to flatter his vanity. Even in this aberration of his genius he served the progress of the world. (421)

In immediate relation to the work he does, each man, according to the novel, believes himself free, and is believed by others to be free; from the point of view afforded the reader by the total action of the novel exactly the opposite becomes true. The king of Sulaco is as subjugated as the lowest peon working in the mine. In what way, one wonders, is Gould different from the Indians to whom the mine is a fetish (442)? Both the workers and their master are subservient to the mine, and if the grand

[33] See note 12.
[34] Conrad, *Complete Works,* Vol. XVI, pp. 50–51.

Englishman doesn't work with his hands, does it mean that his spiritual slavery is any less degrading? True, Gould has a position, but that is all he has. If Decoud and Nostromo on the Golfo Placido represent Conrad's double nature engaged in a struggle for freedom—and even though Nostromo is the actual victor we are left in little doubt that he has settled for a morally inferior way, particularly if the struggle can be taken as an attempt to discover the profoundest level of attainable human freedom from life's exigencies—Gould, ever at his post with one finger on the dynamite fuse, embodies the ever-continuing process of life at its most dishearteningly vain level. It is the level at which man insists upon creating his own world, and then desires at all costs to preserve the values of that world of his. Better to destroy that world than change it: *he* might change but *it* must not change. The rescue of the silver brings Nostromo and Decoud closer to Gould.

As the action sorts itself out in the Monterist revolt and in what follows after the revolt an extremely depressing truth is quite evident. Once rid of its confusions by such heroes as Gould and Nostromo, action or history-in-the-making has had a malignant plan of its own hidden within its seemingly chaotic surface. As the plan reveals itself a remarkable similarity turns up between the current of a person's life and the process of history. In a human life—Gould's, for example—it might appear possible to believe in the freedom of one's initiatives or in the freedom of one's action; at the same time, such freedom, viewed from a more accurate perspective, shows the same activity to be unfree. This pair of contradicting views is also true of the novel's total action. At the beginning of the novel the action seemed to be winding its confused way forward until a hero appeared who was able to dominate it; whereas we later discover that the action had merely been looking for a hero (Nostromo or Gould) to own, to use, to enslave.

It was no accident on Conrad's part so to have conceived the novel. The moral of such a conception is that the very fabric of life is manufactured by some devilish process whose purpose and logic is profoundly anti-human. The substance of this belief was expressed in a powerful letter to Robert Cunningham Graham.

> There is a,—let us say,—a machine. It evolved itself (I am severely scientific) out of a chaos of scraps of iron and behold!—it knits. I am horrified at the horrible work and stand appalled. I feel it ought to embroider,—but it goes on knitting. You come and say: "This is all right: it's only a question of the right kind of oil. Let us use this,—for instance,—celestial oil and the machine will embroider a most beautiful design in purple and gold." Will it? Alas, no! You cannot by any special lubrication make embroidery with a knitting machine. And the most withering thought is that the infamous thing has made itself: made itself without thought, without conscience, without foresight, without eyes, without heart. It is tragic accident,—and it has happened. You can't even smash it. In virtue of that truth one and immortal which lurks in the force that made it spring into existence it is what it is,—and it is indestructible!
>
> It knits us in and it knits us out. It has knitted time, space, pain, death, corruption, despair and all the illusions,—and nothing matters. I'll admit however that to look at the remorseless process is sometimes amusing.[35]

The idea is wholeheartedly despairing and eminently private. It endows *Nostromo*, I believe, with what Henry James, Conrad's admiring colleague and friend, would have called "a deep breathing economy and an organic form." [36] The remarkable achievement is that Conrad was able to project this esoteric vision of life into the public, solid, and real world of Costaguana. No wonder that the writing of the novel was such a strain on Conrad; to have been so fanatically true to his extremely pessimistic views about existence must have been painfully difficult to stand for long. If this is kept in mind as one reads the novel it is possible to feel the war going on between Conrad and the novel.

Readings of the novel that emphasize its purely political dimension weaken *Nostromo*'s greatest impact. The capataz's accession to the role of principal hero, for instance, is very discon-

---

[35] *Life and Letters*, I, p. 216.

[36] Henry James, *The Art of the Novel*, with an introduction by R. P. Blackmur, Scribner, New York, 1934, p. 84.

certing to strictly political interpretations. Why should so much time be given Captain Fidanza's private life? With its political course charted anew Sulaco ought to retain stage center and not have to play a supporting role to a semi-conventional story of covert passion and mistaken death. The fact is that Nostromo has become, toward the end of the novel, a miserably haunted creature because he has attempted to live outside the machinery of existence. He has not made the attempt by his own will but because a lucky accident has conferred great wealth upon him and forced him into the attempt. As he muddles on he is sufficiently interesting to Conrad to warrant the continuing special attention that is so obvious in the famous passage that describes Nostromo's "rebirth." The passage really reiterates his natural qualities for it is these qualities that will enable him to go on alone. He understands that he is thrust into an existence beyond that of conventional society and that the treasure, which is suddenly his, is the cause. But his growing attachment to the silver, and the sufferings he endures for it, make it plain that he is still the victim of life's anti-human machinery. Now he begins to feel a secret shame that intensifies the extent of his moral disgrace. This is the price exacted by life from one upon whom it has bestowed the status of "hero." Consequently, the idea of the treasure and secrecy become connected in his mind (551). When Viola is given keeping of the new lighthouse Nostromo believes this to be a calamitous event:

> He was struck with amazed dread at this turn of chance, that would kindle a far-reaching light upon the only secret spot of his life, whose very essence, value, reality, consisted in its reflection from the admiring eyes of men. All of it but that; and that was beyond common comprehension, something that stood between him and the power that hears and gives effect to the evil words of curses. It was dark. Not every man had such a darkness. And they were going to put a light there. A light. He saw it shining upon disgrace, poverty, contempt. Somebody was sure . . . Perhaps somebody had already . . . (586–87)

Yet he *is* an unusual man. Only he and Mrs. Gould finally know all that there is to be known of life's horror, he by experience, she by the knowledge he gives her of it. Perhaps Dr. Monygham could also have had this knowledge but he is too much under Mrs. Gould's spell to know it for himself. No, it is Nostromo alone—like Kurtz and Lord Jim—who knows the dread secret and feels its shame; the tragedy—which has something farcical about it (405)—is that he feels shame for a colossal secret for which the world seems to have no use. Even in this, life, the machinery, has tricked him. He must bear a burden of slavery to the silver that also belongs to Sulaco, although he alone is selected to feel the trouble of it. Society cuts him off from itself by making it impossible to reveal his secret to anyone. Had society shared in the knowledge of his dread secret it could have freed itself.

When he dies, Sulaco has time only for its material interests; no one except Mrs. Gould has been made any wiser by his death. Those who, like Viola and his wretched daughter, do care that Nostromo is dead, those live in a silent world of immense, empty spaces across which an incoherent cry, which symbolizes mankind's inarticulate sadness over itself, floats. The immobility that ends *Nostromo* is a sterile calm, as sterile as the future life of the childless Goulds, in which all action is finally concentrated into a cry of despair. No better ending for the novel could have been written. Existence has worked its worst and after that there is only an acceptance of what is everlastingly true: having shown that, the novelist's pen drops from an exhausted hand. The only relief is that which comes when one no longer contemplates life's machinery. But because Conrad was a possessed realist such relief was not possible; a short time after completing *Nostromo* he was to begin work on *The Secret Agent*.

Since *Nostromo* contains a highly passionate, almost religious, vision of life, it is fitting that Father Romàn—the one character in the novel who is schooled in the tradition of grand visions—expresses the outlines of the vision most convincingly.

. . . political atrocities . . . seemed to him fatal and unavoidable in the life of a state. The working of the usual public institutions presented itself to him most distinctly as a series of calamities overtaking private individuals and flowing logically from one another through hate, revenge, folly, and rapacity, as though they had been part of a divine dispensation. (443)

Romàn's interpretation is affected, of course, by the creed of which he is a priest. Thus the divinity he mentions does not contradict Conrad's representation of a "divine" machinery in life, but it errs on the side of optimism by assuming the divine to have a benign purpose. Similarly, Romàn envisions a logic to the complications caused by human weakness: he does not, as Conrad *does,* see logic—equally relentless and disastrous—in the "divine dispensation," in the machinery that manufactures human life. The major qualification enjoined by *Nostromo* upon Romàn's vision is that such weaknesses as hate, revenge, and folly do not alone carry calamity through time. For human courage, idealism, and hope, like human weakness, are also aspects of being human and being active as a human individual. Man's fault, in other words, is that he is alive, for in being alive he nurtures and sustains weaknesses that turn into strengths, and strengths that turn into weaknesses. Every moment of life is filled with activity and that activity issues from human beings whose motives are invariably tarnished by their "humanity."

Even if *Nostromo's* meaning is not pleasant it cannot be accused of revolting one with its disgust for life. There is no disgust, as there is, for example, in Swift, because Conrad's position is that of a man wholly in life, a man who has been decoyed into life and must remain there. Any attempt made to leave life in the way that Nostromo attempts results first in unbearable pressures and secondly in death. So uncompromising an assertion about one's relation to life makes Gulliver's homecoming disgust for the English Yahoos seem romantic if only because Gulliver has had one ennobling experience (his sojourn among the Houyhnhnms) to cherish. For all its realistic horrors Swift's examination of humanity is fantastically romantic; Conrad's coldly realistic. Between them, Swift and Conrad define the possibilities—at least until Beckett, who combines them—for incriminating us as human beings. Swift turns away finally to hope for a better time and place; Conrad burrows further into life, re-creates it, is fascinated and tormented by it.

Because *Nostromo* is, in the best or moral sense, a realistic novel, there is good reason for considering it to have made one of the most profoundly negative statements in the English novel. The near-contemporary work of D. H. Lawrence and even of Joyce, in which an admixture of earth identifications, myths, archetypes, passionate life forces, and dream visions perpetually appears, makes comparatively affirmative statements. One has the feeling that for Lawrence and Joyce life is not only worth living but also worth celebrating. For Conrad the very harsh solidity of the world and hence of life in that world, is something to jar one continually into efforts to master it, and, failing in the efforts at mastery, to let it incriminate itself. If Charles Gould, and indeed all of Sulaco—like the rest of mankind—have fallen in love with their own creations (442), Conrad's precept, his undying lesson in the writing of *Nostromo*, was not to have fallen in love with *his* creation. The ultimate greatness of the novel is that life, through Conrad, wrote it, but that Conrad, life's harried agent, had enough strength finally to withhold consent to it. The lesson is one of self-abnegation. In a world such as ours, in which cataclysmic horror seems a breath away, it is easy enough to forget the horror, or to reject everything and live in an unreal world of our own fanciful making. Only the true artist and the man of immensely honest intellect can portray the world realistically and give that portrayal its freedom. To have been imprisoned by life —as Conrad was—is the human condition; the condition of art, which is *Nostromo*, is the *noblesse oblige* that gives life its freedom, and in so doing allows others to know life for what it is.

The Novel of Ideas

GEORGES I. BRACHFELD

The work of art is the exaggeration of an idea.[1]

The Counterfeiters, by André Gide, portrays an author, Edouard, who is writing a novel entitled *The Counterfeiters* and who comments on this novel in his diary and in conversations. Gide also kept a diary, the *Journal of the "Counterfeiters,"* [2] in which he recorded "inch by inch" his progress on the work. Moreover, both before and after this period (from 1914 until long after June 8, 1925, when he completed the book), Gide jotted a number of notes on the novel in his regular journal. Thus, like an object placed between several mirrors facing one another at varying angles, *The Counterfeiters* confronts the serious reader with an intricate interplay of reflections.

Though it may appear as an exercise in intellectual narcissism, *The Counterfeiters* was intended by its author to be a "pure" novel. The reader will search in vain in its pages for plots that have a beginning and an end, for characters who linger long enough to be liked or known, for plans and aspirations that reach fulfillment or failure through logical progression, for love that falls within recognizable patterns, for a universe in

[1] *The Journals of André Gide*, tr. by Justin O'Brien, Alfred A. Knopf, New York, 1949, Vol. I, p. 76. In subsequent references, the *Journals* are indicated by "J" and the volume number.

[2] André Gide, *The Counterfeiters with Journal of "The Counterfeiters"* (the novel translated by Dorothy Bussy, the journal by Justin O'Brien), Alfred A. Knopf, New York, 1959. In subsequent citations, the novel is indicated by "C," the journal by "JC."

which both God and Satan, not the Prince of Shadows alone, vie for the soul of man. It was not the writer's intention to create that kind of logical, satisfying reality. It would have been easy, he mused in his *Journal*, "to get the approval of the majority by writing *Les Faux-Monnayeurs* in the accepted fashion of novels, describing persons and places, analyzing emotions, explaining situations, spreading out on the surface everything I hide between the lines, and protecting the reader's sloth!" [3]

The complexity of this "pure" novel is further increased by Gide's contradictory desire, within a narrow framework of self-imposed strictures, to "pour everything into it without reservation." [4] He wished to fill it with all his thoughts on matters ethical and aesthetic, to convey all his aspirations, social as well as personal, to transmute his frustrations into art, to leave nothing unsaid that he felt he still had to say, to repeat that which had not been sufficiently heard, as if this work were to be his last major pronouncement, "the only novel and final book" [5] that he would write.

He had a great deal to say, as a witness of his times and as a man whose soul was torn by personal tragedy. Born in 1869, André Gide was fifty years old when he began writing his book. The years of his adult life had been a time of reappraisal for our whole civilization as new forms of art sought to express man's new awareness, and new ideologies proposed massive answers to man's perennial anguish. Gide had closely observed the striking progress taking place in the visual arts, which, it has been said, brought in a short span of time more radical changes than the evolution of the previous five centuries. All forms of art aspired toward purity. Strouvilhou, one of the most paradoxical characters in *The Counterfeiters*, voiced Gide's own opinion when he exclaimed: "I have often wondered by what miracle painting has gone so far ahead, and how it happens that literature has let itself be outdistanced. In painting to-day, just see how the '*motif*,' as it used to be called, has fallen into discredit. . . ." [6] The same Strouvilhou parodies the Dadaists when he alludes to squads of young poets aspiring to wreck the hackneyed constructions of

[3] *J*, III, 65.   [4] *JC*, 384.   [5] *Ibid.*   [6] *C*, 307–308.

their elders. Beginning in 1916, as a protest against a civilization that had brought upon the world the horrendous war then engulfing it, the proponents of *dada* clamored against accepted, conventional values in art and literature, and in favor of boundless spontaneity. They bestowed their admiration on Gide's *Lafcadio's Adventures*, but he remained aloof from what he called *"une entreprise de démolition."* In the early 1920's, *dada* fused into surrealism, which, following Freud's explorations of man's subconscious mind, strove to express the hidden reality of our psyche. A political analyst thus described the climate of the times: "Artistic convention, ethical conformism, and the tyranny of money were denounced at one and the same time. The Christian order as much as the capitalist order were under attack." [7] Not long after Nietzsche had proclaimed that "God is dead" new ideologies rose from the ambient ruins, Communism in Sovietland, Fascism in Italy. It was against the background of this world in upheaval that André Gide loosed the characters of his novel.

At this mid-point in his career André Gide had also reached a critical moment in his own life. At the crux of his emotional crisis was his relationship with his cousin Madeleine, whom he had married in 1895. Since their childhood, he had loved her with the purest, most ethereal love. After their marriage, he rationalized his attraction to boys by dissociating love and pleasure. Now, and perhaps for the first time in his life, he was in love with an adolescent, who is identified as M. in his *Journal*. In 1918, as he left with M. on a trip to England, Madeleine, in a fit of despondency on learning of her husband's hitherto secret deviation, burned all his letters to her, in a gesture echoed in the novel by Mme. de La Pérouse's destruction of her husband's letters from his brother.[8] Gide wept for a week, and forever remained disconsolate at the loss of this life-long correspondence to which he had confided the best of himself, and which, he believed, would have exonerated him before posterity. Now that Madeleine knew, he no longer needed to hide the secret of his flesh. All through his

[7] Raymond Aron, *L'Opium des Intellectuels*, Calmann-Lévy, Paris, 1949, p. 55 (my translation).
[8] *C*, 232.

life, while writing his works, he had constrained himself to silence on this subject for fear of hurting her. After this dramatic event, André Gide published *Corydon*, a treatise in defense of homosexuality; *If It Die* . . . , memoirs written with the intention of exposing and justifying his deviation; and *The Counterfeiters*, in which a mother prefers for her son the love of a man.

The break with his past was marked also by the new direction of his works and thoughts. Before 1919, Gide had written several short novels which he called *récits* or "tales," because of the limpidity of their texture and the unilinear simplicity of their plots. They are acts of confession, but also cautionary tales. Through events and in settings drawn from Gide's reminiscences of his own life, the protagonists strive toward unattainable absolutes. In *The Immoralist*, Michel, who closely resembles Gide, after sacrificing his wife in his quest for fulfillment, finds a vacuous freedom at the limit of self-dispossession. In *Strait Is the Gate*, Alissa, whose model is Madeleine, abandons her fiancé in her search for God and meets with sterile despair at the limit of self-sacrifice. Both tales were Gide's aesthetically disguised efforts at persuading Madeleine that they could not go through life in separate ways. But she clung devoutly to the Protestantism of their past, while he sought increasing freedom through the new code of ethics that he elaborated. This was the freedom to live according to his God-given nature, and to strive toward harmonious happiness. *The Pastoral Symphony*, written when Gide was already in love with M., protrays a Protestant pastor, married and the father of several children, enamored of a young girl. Not less willing than Gide to transgress the moral dicta of his religion, and with the writer's own propensity toward a tendentious interpretation of the Gospels, the pastor deludes himself into thinking that Christ's admonitions to love justify his adulterous love. The pastor's self-induced blindness attests, however, to Gide's own lucidity: after he had come close to converting to Catholicism, reading with new insight during the dark years of the war the fervent words of the Gospels, he chose to remain free of all orthodoxies. If this decision suggests a premonition of the break with his wife, it also suggests Gide's awareness that his love for M. was incompatible with his carefully wrought theory of the separation of love and pleasure. Gide's path after 1919 took him farther and farther away from Madeleine. These three *récits* had been inspired by her, or motivated by the need to convince her. The novel, Gide declared, was written for M., "to win his attention and his esteem." [9] He considered his fictional work until this date as "negative," its moral message being one of restraint and moderation. Now that he had broken all bonds with the past, he wished to finish his novel and seek new horizons. He sold some landed property and his library, and left with M. for the Congo. There, opening his eyes on the misery about him, he gave free rein to his concern with the social question that led him in the thirties to a flirtation with Communism.

Certain events in Gide's life which throw additional light on the themes developed in the novel may be summarized in a few words. As in a Racinian tragedy, most of them took place within his soul. Born in Paris to wealthy bourgeois parents, Gide was raised within the strict dictates of a puritancial Calvinism and of the narrow conventions of his class. His father died when he was eleven years old, and his ethereal love for his cousin Madeleine and the constant surveillance of an authoritarian mother imbued with stern moral principles predisposed him to a tortured and prolonged adolescence. An only child, isolated from friends and instructed mostly by private tutors, he became an introspective young man who was soon attracted to the rarefied atmosphere of the groups of symbolist poets; but he revolted at the age of twenty-four against the strictures of both Church and conventional morality and against the Symbolists' contempt for life. He sought and found escape in Africa, to which he often returned in his later years in search of purity and freedom from convention. On his return from Africa, he married Madeleine in a gesture which reveals his essential faithfulness to his past. For some years thereafter his life was that of a writer whose appeals to freedom and authenticity, in lyrical outbursts such as *The Fruits of the Earth,* reached a very small public. Through ironical works also little read, he elaborated critically his new code of

[9] *J*, III, 15.

ethics. Fame finally came to him in 1909, when *Strait Is the Gate* appeared, but it soon turned to notoriety with the publication of *Lafcadio's Adventures* in 1914. During the war years, as he devoted himself to philanthropic work, his soul was torn between appeals from God and Satan. The dramatic events of the postwar years have been mentioned. Violent attacks, especially from Catholic writers, brought him wider fame. While these critics accused him of being a perverter of youth, others acclaimed him as a moral liberator. Soon after his return from the Congo he publicly declared his sympathy for Communism, but he revolted later against this new orthodoxy. The serenity he achieved during the last years of his life was that of a man at peace with himself, the bearer of a message of guarded optimism about the fate of humanity. He received the Nobel prize in 1947 and died in 1951.

All through his life, the author of *The Counterfeiters* pursued his quest for authenticity and inner harmony. He often stated this essential preoccupation, in words such as these: "The only drama that really interests me and that I should always be willing to depict anew, is the debate of the individual with whatever keeps him from being authentic, with whatever is opposed to his integrity, to his integration. Most often the obstacle is within him. And all the rest is merely accidental." [10] In alluding to the conflict between authenticity and whatever stands in its way, Gide was not echoing the Pascalian view that man, because of his limited faculties, faintness of heart, self-love, and delusions, and in general because of his debased nature, is incapable of reaching truth, or even of wishing to attain it. On the contrary, Gide's attitude was optimistic. He predicated man's ability to know and be himself on a constant tension of will power guided by critical sense, somewhat in the Cartesian or Cornelian tradition. Broadening his particular case into a universal axiom, in the classical manner, he generalized his revolt into a liberating code of ethics for all men.

Foremost among the obstacles that confronted the young Puritan at the threshold of manhood was the inhibiting action of the Church. Searching for self-fulfillment on his return from the first voyage to Africa, Gide read into the Gospels a message of

[10] *J,* III, 116.

revolt against the Church and the family. He projected writing a book he would have titled *Christianity against Christ*. Instead, under the heading "Christian Ethics," [11] He confided to his *Journal* for 1896 his new interpretation of the Bible. Christianity, he felt, could still contribute to man's progress and liberation, but only if divested of the limiting action of the Church: ". . . first Catholicism, then Protestantism, after having been expansive formulas, long ago became restrictive formulas; hard sheaths and shells in which the mind is cramped." He summoned Christ's own words in justification of the new code of ethics to which he aspired: "No matter how much I read and reread the Gospels, I do not find a single word of Christ that strengthens, or even authorizes, the family and marriage. On the other hand, I find some that negate them." Christ then appeared to him as a revolutionary figure, "finally negating the institution of the family (and that will serve as authority for suppressing it), taking man himself out of his environment for a personal career and teaching by his example and his voice not to have any possessions on the earth or any place to lay one's head. Ah, my whole soul longs for that 'nomadic state' in which man, without hearth or home, will no more localize his duty or his affection than his happiness on such creatures." Once the family is denied, love knows no bounds, so Gide proclaimed: "endless broadening of the object of love as soon as the family is negated."

Gradually, as his convictions became more assertive, Gide depersonalized God and humanized Christ, relegating the Creator to the role of a supreme force of nature devoid of any moral or providential character, and attributing to his Son, whom he then likened to Prometheus, the function of a superior individual sacrificing himself for the good of humanity. The family fared no better in his mind. Hypocritical fathers, unfaithful wives, and rebellious children, vying in an atmosphere at times reeking with incest or unavoidable shame, constitute the families of his fictional microcosm. In each of these families, be it in a Christian, Biblical, or mythological context, religion provides authorizations for the most damnable actions and attitudes. It is no wonder then

[11] *J*, I, 77–79.

that the purest heroes of Gide's creation, those who appear to be destined for the most harmonious development of themselves, are for the most part bastards. They are not hampered by heredity, so he would have us believe; having no model to imitate, they may strive genuinely to be themselves; the promise of their life is in direct ratio to the obscurity of their birth. A condition for the highest manifestation of the individual, which Gide stated in opposition to Maurice Barrès's exaltation of God, family, and fatherland, is *le déracinement*, uprooting. Uprooted by their birth, the chosen heroes of Gide's fiction have a clear path toward self-fulfillment. Ironically, most of the protagonists thus endowed with this gift of freedom eventually fail, for their lack of Gide's own critical sense and will power. In summary, the new generation may fulfill its promise if it rejects the taboos of an obsolete religion and the thwarting bonds of family and country, to seek the highest manifestation in self-sacrifice. With the necessary qualifications, this program is implemented by Bernard in *The Counterfeiters.*

At the root of Gide's revolt against his Church and his society was the realization of his anomalous sexual tendencies. At odds with a social system which tolerated no deviation from normality, and unwilling to live in contempt of moral laws, he elaborated a new code of ethics according to which homosexuality, far from deserving condemnation, is even preferable to heterosexuality. These thoughts found expression in *Corydon,* published secretly at first and only in a handful of copies, then given to the public in 1924 in a considerably enlarged edition. Fully aware of the shame and punishment that his friend Oscar Wilde had suffered in England only a generation before, André Gide, after concealing for many years the secret of his flesh, committed an outstanding act of courage: he confessed his inversion, championed the rights of homosexuals, and then went on to present homosexual love as the norm in *The Counterfeiters.*

In a less controversial area, he had already spoken in defense of criminals. Before taking this precise orientation, his interest had been exclusively psychological. He wondered about the relationship of cause to effect in man's actions and whether it is true, as

La Rochefoucauld propounded in his *Maxims*, that the acts outwardly most disinterested reveal, on examination, self-interested motivations. Could man, by a supreme act of freedom, escape the laws of determinism? Is man capable of a distinterested act, nay, of a gratuitous action? Many readers of Gide's *Prometheus Ill-Bound* and *Lafcadio's Adventures* were deluded into believing that these books described unmotivated actions, pure effects without causes, not detecting the irony surrounding each of the gratuitous actions. Whether it is Zeus's diabolically planned gesture in the mythological work, or Lafcadio's senseless murder of Fleurissoire during a moment of boredom and dejection, the act gives rise to infinite consequences. It would then appear that the lack of causes is compensated by the multiplicity of effects. But a closer analysis discloses a motivation on the part of each protagonist: a desire for diabolical tampering with human destiny on the part of God's ironical counterpart or a rebellious assertion of freedom by a young man ostracized from the society he wished to enter. There are no gratuitous actions, and rare are the disinterested acts through which man sacrifices himself for others in a selfless assertion of his limited freedom.

Basic to Gide's interest in the hypothetical gratuitous action is also his preoccupation with the extent of man's freedom. In novels that may be construed in this context as moral experiments, he imparted an insatiable thirst for freedom into two heroes he created somewhat in his own image, Michel who resembles him closely, and Lafcadio whom he patterned after his idea of the young man he might have wished to be. Both fail piteously to achieve their goals. Through the destiny he foisted upon them, Gide verified the axiomatic truth that freedom is defined by its limitations. The example of Bernard will further illustrate this aphorism.

In a fervent quest for authenticity and freedom, André Gide revolted ardently against all that stood in his path. Like the Prodigal Son in his poetic retelling of the parable, he escaped from the House—a symbolic shortcut for Church and family, comfort and conformity—to seek in the desert his authentic self and the wonder of other truths. He left behind, with God the Father and a mother radiating love, an older brother whose self-assigned function was to translate divine law into dogma. The Prodigal returned, however, as in the Biblical parable, his mind filled with immense visions, but his heart weary and yearning for the warmth of the House. There, a younger brother also dreamed of escape, and left at dawn in search of his own truth. Gide himself never left the House completely. This is why he married his devout cousin, and also why so many of his Catholic friends, foremost among them Charles Du Bos, Paul Claudel, and François Mauriac, believed for a long time that he was on the point of returning to the Christian faith. He did not convert, but he never eradicated the lingering marks left upon him by his sojourn in the symbolic House. Thus, even at the height of his commitment to Communism he exalted individual values in the belief that the Christian and Communist ideals are not imcompatible. His lifelong concern with social questions, though deliberately repressed until the completion of *The Counterfeiters,* may be traced to his belief in the duty of Christian charity and the responsibility to others incumbent upon persons of wealth—a belief which had been inculcated in him by his mother during the pious years of his adolescence. Several times in his writings, Gide recounted the story of the S.S. *Bourgogne* shipwreck, the same story that Lilian in the novel told Vincent to justify her lack of scruples. For the author, however, the lifeboat from which desperate swimmers were cruelly rejected stood for the privileged status of the few, whose wealth was based on the misery of the many. He wished that all might be saved. Moreover, the otherworldliness of the deeply religious attitude of his adolescence remained with Gide and prevented him from ever fully believing in a concrete reality. He recognized the source of this incapacity: "That original Christian upbringing, irremediably, *detached* me from this world, inculcating in me, not so much a disgust for this earth, as rather a disbelief in its reality." [12] The author of *The Counterfeiters* placed the crucial question of the novelist's attitude toward reality at the very core of his novel.

It is also from the Gospels that Gide drew the guiding

[12] *J,* III, 57.

aphorism of his life, "For whosoever shall save his life shall lose it; but whosoever shall lose this life, the same shall find it." This apparent paradox becomes luminous when it is understood that the two lives in question are not the same, one being the life of the flesh on earth, the other the eternal life of the soul. In a secular context, as Gide saw it, one is the insincere life oriented toward the acquisition of immediate advantages, whereas the other is devoted to the pursuit of higher goals at the expense of quick rewards. In *The Counterfeiters,* Vincent, like the legendary Faust, surrendered his soul to Satan in exchange for material gains, or, in other words, wasted his life for the sake of material pleasures. This aphorism also applies on the aesthetic level, for, according to Gide, aesthetics is the ethics of the artist. What matters to the true artist is his enduring art—his soul—not an immediately successful, sensational work that bears within it the seeds of decay, such as that which Passavant was writing in the novel. Moreover, in an act of abnegation which is a supreme affirmation, the writer must, in the manner of the French classicists or of Gustave Flaubert, efface himself before his work. Whatever his endeavor, man achieves the highest manifestation of himself through that which transcends him, as the work of art transcends the artist. Very early in his life, Gide expressed this in a succinct formula: "We must manifest." [13]

The writer in search of his authentic self transferred his preoccupation into the creatures of his fictional microcosm. At the risk of oversimplification, they may be divided into two broad families of minds: the Gidian and the non-Gidian. Those are Gidian who seek their true nature, whose essential quality is sincerity, whose inescapable need is to "be" rather than to "appear." Non-Gidian are those who live a counterfeit life, who conform to conventional morality and religion, who strive to "appear" rather than to "be." Gide's ethic is based on a distinction, not between good and evil, but between authentic and false. Many may start, like Michel and Lafcadio, in the Apollonian path of enlightened search for freedom and authenticity, but they fail or abdicate because of a flaw in their critical sense or a weakness in their will.

[13] See *J,* I, 74–75.

Rare are those who, like Bernard, achieve a Gidian integrity before the last word of the book permanently fixes their posture. Others, from the moment of their inception in the writer's mind, are doomed to Gidian reprobation, as they clothe their weaknesses or self-interest in a complacent hypocrisy, for none of these can bear to be openly insincere. Their need for moral sanction is Gide's own, with this difference: social acceptance suffices them, whereas, more exactingly, he seeks his own approval. Still others, in a more restricted group illustrated by Strouvilhou in the novel, dare to be openly insincere: they are the true amoralists in Gide's imaginary world. The sincere character must go counter to the accepted morality of a society whose structure is based on insincere values. He must oppose religious beliefs which lull the mind to questions unanswerable by reason alone. According to the beliefs he rejects, he then falls prey to the very symbol of rebellion, Satan.

Ironically, Gide himself pretended to believe in the devil in order to explain his ethics. At first, the young André paid scant attention to the Evil One, accepting without question the notion of the Adversary who vied with God for the soul of Job. For the young Calvinist, he was merely an agent of God's anger or, according to a romantic interpretation, a champion of nature and of man's instincts against the prohibitions of the Church. As the mature writer reflected on the years of his emancipation, he ascribed his early aspirations toward a fuller life to the action of the Demon who, he wrote, "made himself classical with me, when it was necessary to catch me, and because he knew that I could never willingly assimilate to evil a certain happy equilibrium." [14] It was only in 1914 that the myth of the Prince of Shadows began taking a distinct hold of Gide's imagination. Then, after a young friend had told him he believed in the devil before believing in God, Gide noted in his Journal: "I told him that what kept me from believing in the devil was that I wasn't quite sure of hating him." [15] Gide must have been amused by the ambiguity of this thought. The germ of an ambiguous myth was then planted in his mind, a fertile soil indeed, which blossomed to its

[14] *J*, II, 146.   [15] *J*, II, 84.

fullest growth in 1916. Then, against the stark background of the war, he went through a period of inner trouble and dejection. He confided to the pages of a green booklet, included in his *Journal* under the title *Numquid et tu?* . . . , the struggle in his soul between God and the devil, or rather between God and what Pascal calls *la concupiscence,* that is to say all that detracts from God's grace. Nevertheless, in spite of past moments of weakness when his "resistance" to the belief in Satan seemed to decrease, Gide repeatedly claimed that he did not believe in the devil, as in this statement of 1946: "As for me I consider the devil a pure invention; exactly as God himself. I do not believe in him: but I pretend to believe in him and readily indulge in this game." [16] His dalliance with Satan was an intellectual game, which prompted a friend to say that he was cheating with the devil. This game was rendered even more intriguing by the elusive nature of the dark Angel, about whom Baudelaire had made a cunning remark Gide liked to quote: "The devil's most effective ruse is to convince you that he does not exist." Above all, Gide found in the Evil One an explanatory myth. In the dialogue the writer entertained or imagined with his detractors, it became clear to him that his actions and attitudes were attributed by them to the devil's sway over his soul. If Madeleine had been completely aware of her husband's aberrance, she too might have relied on this explanation. As soon as he himself postulated the existence of the devil, or, in other words, when he adopted the view opposite his own in the dialogue, then a new explanation of his whole life became clear to him. When the truth was revealed to his wife in 1919, and the dialogue between them had ceased, the concept of the devil as an explanation had ceased to be personally useful. It could then enter the domain of fiction, Gide's ideal receptacle for discarded obsessions. In *The Counterfeiters,* the devil moves incognito, lurking behind his chosen servants in pursuit of souls to swallow.

One might even suspect that Satan himself guided the pen that wrought this complex and tragic chronicle. This is tanta-

[16] André Gide, *Préfaces, Ides et Calendes,* Neuchâtel et Paris, 1948, p. 141 (my translation).

mount to saying that Gide himself—a god before the unborn creatures of his fictional microcosm—chose to play the part of the devil, maliciously tampering with traditional aesthetic dicta and reversing accepted moral values. He opened wide a Pandora's box of evils clothed in moral trappings. Like false coins in their thin veneer of gold, they looked authentic, but did not ring true. The world he thus created is not the reality of the conventional novel, where cause and effect are logically related, where character and environment interact to foster necessary events. Gide, somewhat in the manner of La Rochefoucauld, raised the veil of hypocrisy that saves appearances, to reveal the true nature of man. Like the seventeenth-century moralist, he knew that a certain energy drives men to great actions, be they evil, as in the case of Strouvilhou, or beneficial, as Bernard intended them. This energy, bent on upsetting the accepted order of things, may be ascribed by well-thinking people, firmly entrenched in their privileges, to the action of the devil. Gide, who did not believe in the devil, placed in the soul of his heroes the Greek daimon of ancient myth, an inner divinity propelling men to their destiny, beneficial angel, or destructive demon, as the hero chose.

Reflecting Gide's essential preoccupation, the pervading theme of the novel is authenticity. As a young writer meditating on his art he had said: "The symbol is the thing around which a book is composed." [17] The symbol at the center of this novel is the false coin. This false coin, however, appears only incidentally at the center of the novel and briefly thereafter. Obviously, the yellow glass token, like the clothes in Carlyle's *Sartor Resartus,* is merely a pretext, in this case a pretext for symbolic variations on monetary themes. "Ideas of exchange, of depreciation, of inflation, etc., gradually invaded his book." [18] Gide tells us of Edouard's unwritten *Counterfeiters.* In Gide's book, the symbol is webbed into a parable, a simple tale fraught with a universal moral lesson and affording broad interpretations. People and events in *The Counterfeiters* are exemplifications of this parable.

On the surface, *The Counterfeiters* appears as the retelling of Bernard's revolt against his family and eventual return to it. It

[17] See *J,* I, 76.   [18] *C,* 176.

is again the story of the Prodigal Son, with a significant twist. As in Homer's long epic, in which a crucial episode of Achilles' life is the core around which the poet recreates the society and events of a fabulous period, Bernard's simple tale of revolt and submission is placed within a context that gives it meaning and affords a critical view of French society shortly before World War I. Without pursuing an analogy to which Gide himself invited us by revealing his desire to give his novel an epic quality, let it be noted that in both works the depiction of individual fates suggests universal comments on man.

Whereas what we may call the parable of the False Coin proposes a key to the interpretation of the psychological content of the novel, the parable of the Prodigal Son, as Gide reconstructed it in the earlier dramatic prose poem, may then serve as a guide to its framework. Bernard's escape from the House opens this chronicle and his return closes it. He is the adolescent who breaks away from the security of his family home in search of self. He leaves behind two brothers. Charles, the elder, firmly entrenched in the comfort and hypocrisy of the House, is ironically cast as a lawyer—had not the older brother, in Gide's rewriting of the parable, claimed to be the sole interpreter of God the Father's vague dicta? The younger brother, Caloub, appears on the last page to be ready to scale the symbolic wall, doubtless with some assistance from Edouard.

The House, from which all adolescents yearn to escape, is presented as a vipers' nest of shame, hypocrisy, and conformity. All families in Gide's fiction are thus portrayed as harboring shameful secrets beneath the glossy surface of respectability. In Bernard's outwardly respectable family, the mother is an unrepentant adulteress. Parenthetically, it is obvious that Gide's preference goes to the rebellious adolescent and to the woman who dared break with conventions in order to love sincerely—he rewarded her with a pure hero—rather than with the solid citizens, Profitendieu and Charles. The Molinier family appear as a pale reflection of the Profitendieus. Here, it is the father who is adulterous, abetted by his wife, intent on saving face; the younger brother is a member of a gang of delinquents; and the older

/ 167

brother, Vincent, who has fled from the House, finds at the limit of the desert—or of self—not God, but Satan. The symmetry is completed by Olivier, Bernard's weaker counterpart, whose faintness of heart tragically thwarts his forward surge. The most flagrant case of family hypocrisy is that of the Vedel-Azaïs clan, ruled by a naïve and puritanical old patriarch. There, the two adolescents, each in his own pathetic way, revolt against the stifling hypocrisy imposed upon them, while their mother seeks Icarus-like escape in flights of pseudo-Lamartinian poetry, and their father clings to beliefs now apparently meaningless to him in order to assure the family a subsistence. Alexandre, the almost forgotten older brother, found refuge from it all in the jungles of Equatorial Africa. A glimpse at the Passavant family, insights into the embroiled events in the La Pérouse family, reveal the same pattern of hypocrisy and disunity beneath the mantle of honorability. The family is to Gide the major obstacle to the adolescent on his road to fulfillment.

The adolescent is the object of Gide's predilection. Opening his eyes in a first awareness on the world about him, the youth is yet uncommitted, free as he never again will be. Better yet if, like Bernard, he is a bastard and therefore, according to Gide's poetic license with logic, unmarked by the determinism of heredity; he may then realize all the potentialities of his being, unhampered by authority or convention, and launch his soul on an uncharted course. The child—the author of *If It Die* . . . considered his own childhood as the most obscure period of his life, and children as amoral beings—the child is characterized by his latency, by his gratuitousness: that is to say by a propensity toward extreme attitudes and dangerous actions, as if they were a matter of play, without heed to the consequences. His sudden awareness of the seriousness of life is epitomized by the inner cry of the schoolboys as the pistol Boris held shattered his temple: "But I didn't know it was loaded!" This explosion tragically bridges for him the gap between illusion and reality. He enters adolescence when, from aimless play, he espouses revolt and seeks escape from his family. The adolescent, in a state of revolt, seeks a new context, new heroes to imitate. It is not yet too late for him, but all depends on his ability to choose the right mentor—Passavant or Edouard?—or better yet, to find within himself a model to emulate.

Beyond adolescence Gide believed that our choice has been made, our postures have become fixed. We repeat the gesture that we first made sincerely, even when it has lost its meaning; we perpetuate a lie, in faithfulness to a credo once held, and because this is the way that others see us. We dare not disrupt this resemblance to ourselves. Edouard's attempt at avoiding this straitjacket in a vain clinging to adolescence is but another fixed posture. The dilemma of choice may be resolved, however, as Bernard's example purports to show. From the child to the adolescent to the young adult André Gide thus presents in his novel a study of the individual's personal evolution.

Moving on to the next generation, he focuses his gaze on the couple. There, all attitudes appear as frozen, and life together continues at two different levels, appearance and reality. This dichotomy is inescapable: love itself, which may have presided over the original union, is founded on a sort of lie. Gide endorsed Stendhal's profound analysis of the process of crystallization, whereby we endow the loved one with the gifts and qualities for which we love him. In simpler terms, love is founded on an illusion, and it is a near constant of Gide's fiction that women are the victims, men the objects, of this illusion, as if the writer could not overcome a feeling of guilt with respect to his own marriage. When the veils are withdrawn, and reality gradually replaces illusion, a reverse process takes place, that of decrystallization. Faced with an unbearable reality, the wife may reject the sham, as Madame Profitendieu did only too briefly, or organize the family life around it. Life then becomes a succession of hypocritical acts. This is the life not only of the Profitendieus, but also of the Moliniers and of the old couple La Pérouse. Are we to conclude that enduring love is impossible? Certainly Laura's and Douviers's marriage of convenience, soon floundering into adultery, clearly eliminates reason as the basis of a true and lasting union. The spontaneous love affair between Laura and Vincent fares no better, nor does the stormy infatuation between Vincent and Lilian Griffith, which leads to intense hatred. Laura, again, might have found happiness with Edouard, whom she has not ceased loving, were it not that his sexual deviation precluded this union. In this particular instance, Edouard, like Michel of *The Immoralist* and Jérôme of *Strait Is the Gate* before him, bears witness to Gide's disbelief that heroes resembling him may ever achieve marital happiness. The only profound and somewhat lasting love in the pages of this novel is that of Bernard for Laura, an ethereal feeling devoid of carnal desire and demanding no reciprocity. The flesh may find its satisfactions elsewhere, as in the few furtive embraces with Sarah, but without affective commitment. The example of Olivier and Edouard suggests that only homosexual love brings total fulfillment, albeit also transitory, and that it is preferable to heterosexual love. This conclusion is reinforced by Pauline Molinier's open preference for Edouard's ambiguous tutelage for her son Olivier. Marriage as an institution, whether founded on love or reason, crumbles before Gide's disabused portrayals. Love itself may stand, either as a disembodied ideal or in short-lived exaltations, optimally between man and boy. All else is pretense.

Religion, this higher form of love, is also pretense. It is under the aegis of religion, in the Vedel-Azaïs family, that hypocrisy stifles the personality of its members. Here, as in a demonstration *ad absurdum*, Gide has heaped damning distortions. Hypocrisy appears as a form of blindness, unconscious in its purest state, as in the case of old Azaïs, or deliberately self-induced, as one is made to suspect is the case of the pastor Vedel. Azaïs, impervious to reality, sees in the pernicious association of young schoolboys a pure effort toward goodness. Vedel closes his eyes to the doubts that besiege him in order to pursue his functions mechanically. In a tragically ironic contrast Rachel, the sacrificial lamb of these Puritans, grows physically blind. In *The Pastoral Symphony*, which at first he had wished to title, ambiguously, *The Blind One*, Gide had already written about the peculiar kind of blindness induced by total hypocrisy. He described this phenomenon in this paradoxical comment on *The Counterfeiters:* "The true hypocrite is the one who ceases to perceive his deception, the one who lies with sincerity." [19] The total hypocrite has lost contact with reality. At an intermediate state of blindness, Vedel shields himself from reality, denying it in a self-interested faithfulness to a former self. Armand induces in himself a reverse sort of blindness: in a sterile, self-destructive revolt he is suppressing all that is good in him, and declares emphatically his hate for virtue. Characteristically, Armand's extreme reaction occurs in one who had been destined for the Christian ministry. La Pérouse, in a strange delusion borne of despair, is convinced that God has tricked him. He echoes by his accusation Gide's own conviction that Christ's most authentic words were the cry he uttered on the cross: "My God, my God, why hast thou forsaken me?" In the universe Gide created in this novel, at the heart of which religion manifests itself as falsification, God is either absent or portrayed as a counterfeiter.

Molded by men, institutions reflect men's hypocrisy. The sincere adolescent seeking a cause to which he may devote his energies recoils before the sham of political groupings in which regimented youths serve hollow slogans, or the excesses of literati striving to strike poses or indulging, like Passavant, in devious literary machinations. Bernard, faced with Laura's suffering, has opened his eyes on earthly reality. He has learned that the unbounded freedom he sought can find meaning only in its limitations. After an anguished night of inner struggle he has conquered his angel, which he also calls a demon, and which must be identified as the Greek daimonic force within us. Now, he will return home, take employment, and modestly attempt to be of service, as an individual. He is the only personage in this novel capable of grappling with reality.

Reality appears as the touchstone of sincerity and character. The ability to perceive it and cope with it, instead of covering or distorting it, is the condition of Gidian salvation. From the pathological to the hypocritical to the demoniacal, all save Bernard fail the test of reality. This failure is not merely that of the older generation. Boris's psychological disturbances are traced by the Freudian psychologist Madame Sophroniska to the child's at-

[19] *JC*, 393–94.

tempts at evading an abhorrent reality. The remedy she proposes is a clear look at reality. Vincent, consorting with Lilian Griffith or delivering his brother to Passavant, Olivier out of spite accepting the latter's invitation, the children playing Ghéridanisol's ruthless game, all turn their eyes away from reality and are severely punished for it. The demoniacal characters alone tamper lucidly with reality and escape the consequences. Lilian Griffith, Passavant, Strouvilhou, and Ghéridanisol, all servants of the devil, arrayed here in descending hierarchical order, have this distinctive trait: they feel no need to provide a moral disguise for their actions. Unlike Gide himself and the many characters he created in his own image, they need no moral justification in their own eyes, they are truly amoral. In a Gidian sense, they are "false hypocrites" or, paradoxically, sincere individuals. As Satan's agents, eluding the symbolism of the parable of the False Coins, they act as behind-the-scenes manipulators, pulling the levers that propel the plot. The other actors conform effortlessly to the role assigned them in the parable: Douviers inflates his manliness, Armand devaluates his personality, Olivier in his relationship with Passavant deludes himself into accepting the false as true, many falsify their true beliefs in a generalized depreciation of authenticity, all reacting athwart reality.

According to Gide himself, the multiplicity of principal characters in *The Counterfeiters* caused him great difficulty in its composition. It presents a like obstacle to a summarization of its plot. Indeed, each of the more than twenty highly individualized personae, endowed with a singular destiny, generates his own plot. All being Gidian creatures, their fates conform, however, to the same general movement: they are swept by a centrifugal force which projects them away from their homes or from themselves. Escape from home characterizes revolt; separation from self is a sign of submission achieved through a compromise between what one is and what one pretends to be. The only hero who submits without self-distortion is Bernard. This is why Bernard's progress through the events of this novel, proposing a positive lesson, imposes itself as one of its main plots. Another character eludes classification, as he seems to transcend any reduction to the norm: Edouard. But Edouard, in spite of his lucidity and of his efforts to do so, does not escape the stigma of inauthenticity. It appears in his case that blindness to reality is a cause, rather than a consequence, of his hypocrisy. Thus, although his stated objective for the novel he proposes to write is to show the struggle between reality and what the novelist strives to make of it, he is unable to assimilate any rash intrusion of the real event into his fictional construction, whether it be the sudden irruption of a "real" false coin or the unexpected murder-suicide of Boris. His hypocrisy, to be sure, manifests itself at an aesthetic level, as he shirks the uncompromising honesty that he professes. It is true also that, at times, he experiences the difficulty of "being," especially under the impudently pragmatic look of Bernard. What distinguishes Edouard is his awareness of sham and his effort to denounce and overcome it. He too is subject to the centrifugal force that sweeps the other characters, but, in a paradoxical way, he maintains himself in a constant state of self-dispersion, a state of tension between the limits of his being. Laura describes him thus: "He is never the same for long together. He is attached to nothing, but nothing is more attractive than his elusiveness. He is perpetually forming, unforming, reforming himself. One thinks one has grasped him . . . Proteus! He takes the shape of what he loves. . . ." [20] The reader may be tempted, the more so if he has read some pages of Gide's *Journals,* to equate Gide and Edouard, the creator and his creation. Edouard rejoins in this respect Michel of *The Immoralist.* There, André Gide transposed into fiction events and places from his own life and, experimenting on a virtually living part of himself, endowed his hero with one of his essential drives. But, implacably, he doomed him to failure, vitiating his character with a tragic flaw which, upon analysis, may be reduced to a delusion about reality and its exigencies as Michel destroys himself in a vain quest for absolute freedom. Among the most obvious similarities between Gide and Edouard are their puritanical background, their sexual deviation, and their disbelief in reality. Both attempt to write a novel portraying an author writing the same

[20] *C,* 186.

novel. But Edouard does not realize that the novel he envisions is impossible of writing, whereas Gide, ironically aware of it, writes the story of Edouard's failure. That is the second main plot of *The Counterfeiters*. Whereas the plot generated by Bernard centers on ethical questions, the core of Edouard's plot is in the aesthetic domain. The two intertwine like point and counterpoint in a Bach fugue.

The ethical and the aesthetic questions, content and form, reality and its fictional projection, are variations on the same theme: Gide's quest for authenticity in his art, his effort to write a "pure" novel. Of this effort, he made one of the main subjects of his novel. Wary of absolutes, he created a protagonist imbued with his own extreme aspirations and, as in all previous similar cases in his fiction, doomed him to failure. Gide stands in relation to Edouard like an artist painting his self-portrait. The artist on the canvas is doing the same thing, but the lines on his painting remain blurred. The play within the play, as in *Hamlet,* gives the dramatist an opportunity for self-conscious disquisitions on his art. Gide's reflection on the art of the novel as noted in the *Journal of "The Counterfeiters,"* to which may be added, with some caution, Edouard's notations, guide the reader in his grasp of the aesthetics of *The Counterfeiters*.

A fundamental decision that the novelist made bears on his relationship to his characters. Would he, like Stendhal or Balzac before him, and most other novelists, adopt the omniscient, omnipotent attitude implicit in a third-person relation? Would he choose, on the contrary, a loquacious hero, such as Lafcadio, to tell the story in the first person, thus assuring a form of objectivity through this subjective narrator? Or would he yield to the temptation of the diary, recently used with such subtlety in *The Pastoral Symphony,* in which the reader reconstructs reality by applying the corrective of his own critical mind to the biased views of the writer? Recognizing that the intricacy of his projected construction precluded simple solutions, Gide decided on a compromise. He used the third person, but with self-imposed limitations: rather than reading his characters' minds, he surmises what they are thinking and at times interprets their words and actions, in a constant dialogue with the reader. He wishes to give the impression that each character, acting according to his own nature, independently as it were, is observed rather than determined by his creator. He is most often overheard and his words repeated by the novelist, which explains the length and multiplicity of the dialogues. The diary form is also used, increasingly as the novel progresses, thanks at first to Bernard's indiscretion— which becomes Gide's own indiscretion as he later fails to provide a reason for opening the pages of Edouard's private notebooks. It is as though Gide invited his readers to observe with him the comportment of his characters, addressing us directly in an occasional first person as he comments on it, and remaining somewhat detached, rejecting any complicity in their misdeeds. Indeed, he must have fancied himself playing a hidden part in the novel, that of a devil rather amused by the chaos he had wrought.

The characters are known by their deeds and words, as if they were on a stage and we the spectators. What A says to B, or of B, is revealing of both A and B. The truth about a character is at the point of convergence of several viewpoints, including the author's and the reader's. Likewise, events grow in significance, or reality, as they are retold by different speakers. A case in point is the manner of presentation of the love affair between Laura and Vincent, through partial disclosures by Olivier first and then by the author, with the fuller tale retold by Lilian as she has heard it from Vincent. In the retellings, Olivier reveals his romanticism and timorousness, Bernard his pragmatism and daring, George his precociously fabricated personality, Vincent his vanishing decency, and Lilian her cynicism and inner fire. By this process of multifaceted exposure, somewhat akin to cubist art, the reader is guided on a circular tour of reality. Similarly, the association to which George belongs presents to each character a different aspect of its reality, conforming to his own bias. For Strouvilhou and his young henchman it is a ruthless means of compromising notable families in order safely to ply their counterfeiting trade; for the young members, it is an exciting game; for Azaïs, a virtuous group; for the magistrates, a gang of juvenile delinquents. The reader, privileged to know all the facts available, forms his

/ 175

own opinion, no doubt colored by his own bias. Thus it is that Gide's deliberate refusal to judge or draw conclusions invites the reader's collaboration.

Gide solved the dilemma of the novelist baffled by the elusiveness of reality by presenting reality as an elusive thing which conforms, as it were, to the idiosyncrasies of the beholder. Unlike the visual poet Théophile Gautier, who asserted that "The artist is a man for whom the outer world exists," Gide claimed that the artist "is he who does not believe, not completely, in the reality (in the *single* reality, at least) of the outer world." [21] For Gide, ideas, not people, are endowed with integral reality. It is as if ideas first imposed their existence on his mind, and then sought manifestation through characters. Or it may be said that the characters in his novel appeared to him first as embodiments of ideas. Thus, at the origin, there were not characters imposing their personalities, or events their necessity, but artistic and moral concepts seeking expression. A few examples may suffice: Gide created Edouard so that he might reveal the novelist's predicament, Passavant so that he might revile an easy and false solution to it, Bernard and the other adolescents in order to examine the several forms of their revolt, Pauline Molinier to exemplify the process of decrystallization, families and clergymen so that he might uncover their hypocrisy, Vincent in order to depict the Faustian surrender of the soul to the devil in exchange for worldly satisfactions, amoral characters to disclose the covered action of the devil. Thus Gide constructed what Edouard calls "a novel of ideas." The naming of some of his protagonists also discloses the priority Gide gave idea over character: Profitendieu, he who draws profit from God; Passavant, he who gets ahead, or places himself ahead; Strouvilhou, readily rhyming with *filou,* swindler; Lilian Griffith, an extension of Lilith, the she-devil of Talmudic lore; Bercail, calling forth *bergeries,* pastoral poetry; Mouton, sheep; all snugly fit their bearers, as in a philosophical tale by Voltaire.

Edouard as well as Gide knew, however, that what distinguished a "novel of ideas" [22] from a "thesis novel" is that in the

[21] *J,* III, 114.   [22] *C,* 175.

former ideas are manifested through characters. Ideas have reality, characters lend them life. If characters are not to remain allegorical figures, they must be given a convincing context: a place in society, a past and a family, friends and preoccupations, all the complex fabric of life. Gide would have Edouard recoil before the difficulty, and his own predilection for the bastard as a hero is in part predicted on the latter's lack of a past and family. In spite of the writer's effort to portray the density of life in the relationships of his characters, it must be noted that, except on rare occasions among friends, they do not communicate at any depth with one another. Each fulfills his destiny in isolation. As characters require a context, so the acts they generate require motivation. This necessity interferes with the writer's avowed desire merely to watch their evolutions, as he intervenes to reveal past data, bemoaning the fact that his novel "is taking shape in reverse." [23] Perhaps one of the functions of Edouard's diary is to disclose needed background information, thus relieving Gide himself of the traditional task of providing motives.

The unavoidable necessity in the novel to localize the heroes and their actions at a given historical time also detracted, Gide felt, from the universality of the ideas he wished to express. Racine achieved in his tragedies a stylization unencumbered by a slavish imitation of reality—what Nietzsche called a "formidable erosion of the contours"—by choosing legendary protagonists abstracted from material contingencies, evolving in a remote and indistinct past and in a "palace at will." In a sense, the Racinian heroes gained in universality what they lacked in realistic precision. In their case, realism was transferred from the outer to the inner man. Impelled by the exigencies of his medium, Gide set his novel shortly before the First World War. A close examination of some clues in an attempt to date this chronicle with greater precision is self-defeating. The most precise indication is that Alfred Jarry's play, *Ubu Roi*, has just been booed by the Parisian public.[24] That was in 1896. But the mention of a Montrachet wine of 1904 vintage [25] and of Passavant's luxurious limousine suggests a later date. Since Jarry, the only "real" person in the novel, died in

[23] *JC*, 398.   [24] *C*, 274.   [25] *C*, 312.

1907, that year seems to set an outside limit. It is idle to speculate on this question, for Gide, deliberately or inadvertently, mixed the cards.

The novel's duration is less than four months, from a Wednesday in July to mid-October next, but events related by Edouard in his diary take us back to October of the preceding year. In the first part of the book, time is nearly at a standstill, as a multitude of events and encounters accumulate in less than twenty-four hours: here, the novelist cut a "slice of life" not in length, as the naturalists had done, but in depth. The historical context of his novel is presented in such terms that except for the presence of the gold pieces and for some incidental indications, one could well imagine the action taking place in our days. André Gide was writing for the future.

After breathing an idea into each of his characters, placing them in a lifelike context and at a given time and place, Gide endowed them with free will. Their freedom of choice places the responsibility for their acts on them, not on the author, so he would have us believe. He merely observes them as they follow their tortuous paths. The fact that he drew from newspaper reports some details about the operations of a ring of counterfeiters and about the suicide of a schoolboy does not contradict this claim. These incidents were incorporated into the novel, with essential adaptations, because they fit the writer's purpose, not as a guiding plot. The ideas to be manifested take precedence over the plot, as they do over the characters. The passing of counterfeit gold pieces is merely a pretext in the book, the basis for a significant parable. Boris's suicide detained Gide's attention more markedly, not only because of its episodic interest, but also as an instance of indiscriminate play and the consequences ensuing from it. Only Ghéridanisol among the schoolboys knew the expected result of their morbid game. But this minor servant of Satan, who engineered the crime without motivation, alone eluded personal consequences. This sudden jolt given by reality brought George back to his mother, and perhaps shook Gontran out of his isolation, although he was only a spectator. It appears that, in the whole of Gide's fiction, Ghéridanisol's well-disguised murder is the only purely gratuitous action. What the Zeus of *Prometheus Ill-Bound* and Lafcadio in *Lafcadio's Adventures* attempted to do without success, only this minor devil achieved, precisely because he is a devil. Thus in a sense ends Gide's dalliance with the abstract notion of a gratuitous action. The last one to appear in his fiction is performed by a soulless lackey of Satan. Since Gide did not accept the existence of the devil, this is his ambiguous manner of stating his disbelief in the possibility of a gratuitous action.

Most characters in the novel are only glimpsed, as the novelist briefly focuses his light upon them, and then they disappear, often without a trace. Even a highly individualized hero like Armand projects his distorted shadow only momentarily against the troubled background and then is withdrawn from the reader's gaze. Likewise, embryos of possible plots appear briefly and vanish into oblivion. A faint refraction, as with Vincent, sometimes teases the curiosity of the reader. That is the image of life, which does not resemble the traditional novelist's neat constructions. Similarly, in this novel which pretends not to improve on life, many events simply fail to occur: an instant sooner, Olivier would have found Edouard, and their destinies would have changed. Words not spoken, as between Olivier and Edouard, gestures not made, as when Olivier failed to open the door behind which Laura was weeping, determine our fates as much as positive actions. It seems that it is Olivier especially who thus misses his destiny. In Gide's novel, as in life, cards were dealt out wrongly. But it is Gide who, deliberately, mixed the cards. Therein lies one aspect of his irony.

Gide's irony, overt or covert, pervades the whole novel. It is not enough to lend his heroes one of his tendencies, inflate it, then castigate them for their hybris. Gide mixed the cards at all levels. We have no difficulty in recognizing him in the words and actions of Bernard or Edouard, in spite of the obvious differences. But it is baffling to hear Passavant or Strouvilhou express some of his own opinions, the former condemning the symbolists' detachment from life, the latter denouncing inauthenticity in art and literature, both, however, with an exaggeration that separates them from him. It is also a form of irony, on the part of a self-conscious writer such as Gide, to mar his carefully wrought plots with coincidences difficult to accept, such as Strouvilhou's unexplained presence at Saas-Fée and the even less understandable surrender of Boris's talisman to him by Sophroniska, or Edouard's witnessing of a theft by his own nephew. Life itself, however, is replete with such inconsistencies. Another form of irony is evidenced in the author's attitude toward his reader. After bringing the reader to suspend his disbelief, he destroys the illusion by a sudden personal intervention, as if to warn him that the interest in the novel is to be sought not in the episodes or in the emotions, but in the clash of ideas.

Style, according to Gide's precept for this book, is to present no surface interest. The only excerpt from Edouard's book shown to us [26] sets off ironically and incongruously the difference in this respect between Gide and Edouard. The stilted prose, the artificial dialogue, the moralizing tone and the ridiculous names give humorous evidence of Edouard's inability to write the book he projects. As Edouard moralizes about the event, his error may be due to his reluctance to present reality simply and objectively, which is exactly what Gide had done with this incident, transposing quite faithfully into *The Counterfeiters* [27] what he had noted in the *Journal of "The Counterfeiters."* [28] Gide's rendition of this episode in Edouard's diary in simple, direct terms has the quality of an anthology piece, as do other passages, such as Gontran's funeral watch over his father or the taut retelling of Boris's death.

In writing *The Counterfeiters*, André Gide performed a masterful act of self-restraint. Through its wealth of ideas, characters, and events, the attentive reader becomes aware of what has been left unformulated and unfinished, and he accepts the author's invitation to fill in the silences and prolong the events, as if he had witnessed life itself. Edouard, Gide's ambiguous projection into the novel, raises questions to which Gide's book is an answer. Is that answer satisfying? The student of literature finds in it a subtle and dramatic analysis of the process of literary creation. To the moralist, beyond the depiction of moral decay, it proposes the

[26] *C*, 335–37.   [27] *C*, 77–78.   [28] *JC*, 387–88.

luminous example of Bernard, the undaunted young man to whom the future belongs. By his quality of reserve, the universality of the questions raised, and his concern with man, André Gide rejoins the classical tradition of seventeenth-century France. *The Counterfeiters* is one of those books that raise essential questions for each generation of readers, the answer to which is in themselves.

The Examined Life

CARL S. SINGER

ANYONE WHO still feels obligated to offer an opinion on the much discussed case of the Court *vs.* Joseph K. is well advised to begin with a declaration of impartiality. Anyone, that is, who has remained convinced of the sense and legitimacy of treating *The Trial* as a work of art. In general, of course, the critic is not required to disavow explicitly all commitment to non-aesthetic doctrine; but with reference to Kafka—in view of the already awesome accumulation of interpretation contributed by established psychologists, theologians, etc.—the critic must call attention to the fact that he is voluntarily confining himself to literary questions, if only to remind himself of his amateur status in all other matters. The anguish and distress implied in the titles of many books on Kafka—*The Kafka Problem, Kafka and the Labyrinthic* are typically unsettling examples—have both generated and thrived on just such amateurism. But there is little point in further taxing those whom Kafka has driven to a frenzy of overextension. Instead I think it will prove valuable to investigate the causes of the frenzy, the qualities of Kafka's work and of *The Trial* in particular, that are disruptive of the calm prerequisite of critical detachment.

Undeniably, there is much in *The Trial* that is so unfamiliar as to disorient even the most determined literary approach. We cannot fasten upon Kafka's method of character development, for the simple reason that none of his characters are "developed" —what we see and hear of them is not intended to give us the comforting sense of acquaintance by an eventual yielding of essence. Again, we cannot discern in *The Trial* the workings of a plot, or even note a specific arrangement of events that leads to the hero's undoing, because the arrest that opens the book occasions, precisely, the cessation of purposeful activity on the part of Joseph K.: his subsequent undertakings are not so much in vain as irrelevant. Finally, to close this series of subtractions provisionally, what are we to make of the milieu of *The Trial?* Here also Kafka thwarts standard critical procedure, though by giving not too little but rather too much. The description of K.'s city has the oppressive density of a movie viewed a few feet from the screen: minor, seemingly random details present themselves with an unwarranted insistence while the picture as a whole remains blurred. The more intently we peer, the less distinct becomes the composition of the background. Speculation on "the significance" of the unpredictable stream of objects that catch K.'s eye—dust in the attic court chambers, wash hanging on a clothes line—tends to be, consequently, somewhat embarrassing. In short, Kafka's apparent disregard for the conventions of the novel results in a considerable formal inaccessibility. And this, I believe, accounts for the liberties taken by many of his interpreters, who, often with the best of intentions, entirely neglect the matter of style. The attempt to establish and appreciate Kafka's own novelistic conventions must, however, be made, since it is likely to disclose more of his elusive meaning than that which survives in the various doctrinaire translations of his writings.

Since there is no magic key to Kafka's work, we must be content to operate with prosaic tools. The critical concept of "point of view" is the most effective one at our disposal. The shape reality assumes depends on who is looking at it, and when the shape is as confused as in *The Trial,* the only reasonable course is to determine whose eyes (what sort of eyes) are responsible for the confusion. And in this particular at least *The Trial* poses no problems whatsoever, for Kafka's employment of point of view is remarkably pure and straightforward. A single pair of eyes fixes reality in *The Trial*—and they belong not to the author but to Joseph K.; as we read we are aware only of what is registering upon his consciousness. Thus Kafka's narrative technique aims at, and doubtless achieves, the opposite of omniscience: there is only K.'s eternal ignorance, the recital of his failures to obtain information. The author totally absents himself; he supplies no commentary to K.'s thoughts and actions, nor does he reveal the motives and judgments of the other participants in the proceedings. It is this unrelieved immediacy of presentation that compels us to participate in what is commonly referred to as K.'s *Angst*.

The recognition that we are in the midst of Joseph K.'s world admittedly does little to order the chaos of *The Trial*. The question becomes, what manner of man is it whose imagination peoples the attics of dilapidated tenements with examining magistrates? Lukács suggests that Western writers, in response to the total lack of purpose and direction in their culture, have gotten into the habit of considering psychopaths and idiots the best-qualified witnesses of life; and Kafka is for him the foremost exponent of this habit.[1] The claim, despite its unduly harsh wording, is not easily refuted. Certainly K. is forever thinking of those bright days when, in his capacity as a high bank official, he acted with spectacular cunning and dispatch. Yet the K. we see "in action" is incapacitated—unable to defend his position in court and office alike. But whether or not K.'s fate after the arrest should be labeled pathological is not, for our purposes, an issue of primary importance; we have to come to terms with the vision of reality that Kafka transmits in the testimony of his incapacitated witness. Only then can we assess its validity.

Characters Without Definition

I have said that Kafka refuses to develop his characters, that no matter how much we come to know of them, we never get to know them. This apparent anti-technique is really the substitution of one technique for another: Kafka subordinates characterization to point of view. Joseph K. not only cannot compete with

[1] George Lukács, *Wider den missverstandenen Realismus*, Classen Verlag, Hamburg, 1958, p. 31.

Balzac and Dickens in cataloguing human types, he simply cannot catalogue at all. Not that he doesn't try. In fact, although he worries a good deal about the possibility of a premature judgment giving a disastrous conclusion to his own endeavors, he doesn't scruple to pass immediate judgment on others. Invariably, however, people refuse to conform to his first impressions of them, they force him to change his mind—and to keep on changing it—with their every gesture, almost their every word. And, since we have no way of bringing this fluctuation of opinion to a standstill, we are necessarily as baffled by these "characters" as K. himself. None of K.'s conjectures are shown to be blatantly false —for this would give us a resting point. The trouble is rather that the individual traits he seizes upon are never exhaustive but simply elements of a series—a series which K. cannot integrate. Unable to discover the continuum which defines personality, K. finds that the most casual of meetings are apt to turn into nightmares.

To measure the effects of this aspect of K.'s incapacitation, we should first consider a character whom K., before his arrest, had always thought totally unmystifying—the Uncle. Sensing a certain bustle outside his office, K. recalls the manner of this long-awaited visitor with the ease of a man accustomed to handling his fellows in a superior, condescending fashion.

> He had often pictured him just as he appeared now, his back slightly bent, his dented straw hat in his left hand, stretching out his right hand from afar and thrusting it with inconsiderate haste across the desk, knocking over everything in sight. His uncle was always in a hurry, for he was plagued by the unhappy idea of accomplishing, during his regularly only day-long visits to the city, everything he had planned, without at the same time neglecting whatever offered itself by chance in the way of conversations or business deals or enjoyments. . . . "The ghost from the country," K. usually called him. (Chap. 6, p. 112) [2]

[2] The translations of the passages quoted are my own; therefore, the page references are to the standard German edition of *The Trial: Der Prozess*, Dritte Ausgabe, Fischer Verlag, Lizenzgausgabe von Schocken Books, New York, 1946.

There is a satisfying, near Dickensian precision about this portrait. We smile at this bumptious harassed provincial; here at last is someone who need not be taken seriously. But K. soon realizes that the old caricature no longer really contains the Uncle's character. Inexplicably, the "ghost from the country" seems to be an initiate in the very matters his cosmopolitan nephew is at a loss to understand—to K.'s dismay, and our own astonishment, he becomes a person to be reckoned with. There can be no doubt that the Uncle remains a perfect clown of social ineptitude; yet all the while that K. is trying to laugh, his uncle's questions and revelations, shouted out for all the world to hear, are making him shudder. In a final effort to silence this booming harangue, K. announces with affected coolness that his case has nothing to do with the regular courts, isn't connected with his work in the bank, and really is of no importance whatsoever. But the Uncle knows better:

> "That's bad," said the Uncle. "What?" K. said and stared at his uncle. "I mean that it's bad," repeated the Uncle. . . . "I thought," said K., "that you would attach even less importance to this whole business than I do, and now you are taking it so seriously." "Joseph," cried the Uncle . . . "you are completely changed, you always had such a keen mind, and it's abandoning you?—now of all times. Do you want to lose your case? Do you know what that would mean? It would simply finish you. And the whole family would be pulled down with you, at the very least our name would be dragged through the mud. Joseph, pull yourself together. Your indifference is driving me crazy. Looking at you I'm almost tempted to believe the old saying: to have such a case is the same thing as losing it." (Chap. 6, pp. 117–18)

K.'s startled exclamations, the matter-of-fact tone of the Uncle's remarks (his proverb, a truly staggering specimen of folk wisdom, leaves no room for argument)—these are notes typical of all the conversations in *The Trial*. The people K. comes in contact with always manage to overwhelm him by their self-assurance; they know what they're about and K. does not. His notions that they are silly, flighty, infirm, humble, or stupid are well founded but of no value to him when he tries to anticipate what they will say or do. Of course, as readers we have what would appear to be a great advantage over Joseph K., who is perhaps too busy or upset to figure things out. We can close the book whenever we wish and attempt to decide once and for all whether, for instance, the Uncle is really an officious country bumpkin or instead a knowledgeable counselor whose advice should be heeded. But we quickly see that no amount of reflection solves the problem. We have only K.'s contradictory impressions to go on, and there is no evidence in the text to show which of them is right, or even more right. Opening the book again, we may be struck by the Uncle's suggestion that K. consult Advocate Huld; but whether this is worthwhile advice or merely foolish boasting of not-at-all-powerful connections depends upon whether or not Huld can be of any use to K., and this, in turn, depends upon whether Huld really intends to defend K., or simply hopes to use such a famous case to boost his reputation, or perhaps actually means to betray K.'s interests in return for special favors from the Court, and all this, in turn, depends upon whether or not Huld's activity can have any effect one way or the other, since the Court does not officially countenance the mediation of lawyers in the first place, and so on. But to perform such an analysis is the same thing as becoming Joseph K. (my apologies to the Uncle). Suffice it to say that we have no means of correcting or steadying K.'s evaluation of his uncle, just as, for the most part, we cannot claim to understand *The Trial* better than K.

K.'s women constitute still greater torments—despite, or rather because of, the degree of intimacy he achieves with them. People simply have a way of exploding in K.'s face, and, naturally, the closer the contact the more devastating becomes the shock. Thus the bank executive, running true to form, even finds himself routed by the wiles of a scrubwoman. In fact, K.'s abortive affair with the court attendant's wife is so exemplary a demonstration of the "Kafkaesque" that it will be well to linger awhile on its vicissitudes. The woman first comes to K.'s attention as the object of that clamorous sexual assault which gave a disastrous ending to

K.'s first hearing. Understandably little disposed in her favor, K. is quite surprised to learn that she considers herself a respectable married woman. But she is convincing in her reply to K.'s sarcasm, and he is soon ready to accept her version of the regrettable disturbance. " 'Are you alluding to the incident in the last assembly through which I disturbed your speech?' the woman asked. . . . 'It wasn't to your disadvantage that your speech was interrupted. It was judged very unfavorably afterwards.' 'That may be,' said K. to change the subject, 'but that doesn't excuse you.' 'I am excused before all who know me,' the woman said. 'The one who attacked me on that occasion has been persecuting me for a long time' " (Chap. 3, p. 65). A few minutes later, however, this unfortunate but faithful wife again surprises K. by remarking on the exceptional beauty of his eyes and inviting him to take a good look at her legs (under the pretext of showing what nice stockings the examining magistrate has given her). K.'s reaction is eminently reasonable: "So that's what it's all about, K. thought. She's offering herself to me. She's corrupt like all of them here. She's had enough of the Court officials, which is certainly understandable, and so she greets any stranger that happens along with compliments about his eyes" (Chap. 3, p. 68).

But when she freely talks of the examining magistrate's nascent passion for her and promises to use her influence over him in K.'s behalf, K. is, of course, again mollified. To be sure, he doesn't have much of a chance to savor the idea of commanding a fifth column, for his new-found helpmate shows no inclination to act in accordance with her new role. At the appearance of the law student who had "attacked" her at the hearing, she darts away from K. with a speed that is, at the very least, disconcerting, and announces: "I have to go with him now . . ." (Chap. 3, p. 72). Yet, without allowing him any time to express his surprise, she blithely, if incomprehensibly, continues: "But I'll come back right away and then I'll go away with you, if you'll take me. I'll be happy if I can get away from here for as long as possible. The best thing, of course, would be to get away for good" (Chap. 3, p. 72). Stunned, then gladdened by these assurances of devotion, K. manages to adjust his sights once again: if she means to abscond with him, there is no sense in her going to the judge first; indeed what sweeter revenge could there be than to leave the judge waiting—forever. Accordingly, K. sets off to free the woman from the clutches of the law student, whose loud kisses he now construes as positive evidence of the persecution she had complained of before. But now the scrubwoman stupefies K. with one more surprise: she isn't resisting the student's embrace at all. " 'You don't want to be freed!' K. screamed, and placed his hand on the shoulder of the law student who snapped at it with his teeth. 'No!' cried the woman and pushed K. back with both hands. 'No, no, anything but that, what are you thinking of! That would be my ruin. Leave him alone, oh please, just leave him alone. He's only following the orders of the examining magistrate. He's carrying me to him.' 'I don't care where he's going and I don't ever want to see you again either,' K. said . . ." (Chap. 3, pp. 74–75). And K., trembling with rage and disappointment, watches the happy couple until they scamper out of sight.

In following the burlesque *péripéties* of this romance, we recognize the characteristic form of the frustration experiences that abound in Kafka's work. But what, exactly, is the cause of this frustration? Clearly, not so much the hero's failure to effect his designs as his failure to discover what his designs should be. For to discover what may reasonably be expected and asked of other people, one must first have some idea of what these people are really like, and, as we have seen, K. is forced to discard one such idea after another. And if he regards his rejection as the "first unequivocable defeat" (Chap. 3, p. 75) he has suffered at the hands of the Court, we must admit that we cannot conceive how he might have avoided this defeat. The court attendant's wife is, after all, an incredibly trying character. Just how trying becomes palpable in a rehearsal of the stages of K.'s confusion. Was he right in his original distrust of her? Not if she really was the helpless victim of the law student's ardors. Was he then right in his later sympathy for her? Not if she really is prone to random promiscuity. Was he then foolish in taking her offer of help seriously? Not if she really is tired of the court officials. Was he then right in fighting for her? Not if she really is at the examining magistrate's beck and call. And so on. K. has been vanquished by a collection of characters who all call themselves the scrub-woman, a collection which is disparate and, apparently, inexhaustible. "The woman waved to K. as he looked after her, and sought to show by moving her shoulders up and down that she wasn't responsible for this abduction, although her movements did not evince a great deal of regret. K. stared at her as if she were a stranger, without expression. He didn't want to betray either that he was disappointed or, on the other hand, that he would easily be able to get over his disappointment" (Chap. 3, p. 76). This last sentence, defying the law of the excluded middle, eloquently circumscribes K.'s position. In the attempt to meet all contingencies—to do justice to all the contradictions he cannot resolve—K. inevitably becomes absurd. As he himself realizes, only by staying at home, only by renouncing all designs, could he possibly have preserved his dignity. Ultimate passivity, death, is the sole conclusion the logic of *The Trial* permits.

At this stage in the proceedings, however, K. still consoles himself with thoughts of those segments of his life upon which the Court is powerless to intrude. He imagines how badly this despicable law student would fare in his own domain, for example, in a confrontation with K.'s once-a-week beloved Elsa. Actually, Elsa invariably occurs to him in the midst of his self-immolating adventures with the women who know of his case; small wonder, since she is dependably, payably one-faced, while the others seem to be veritable functionaries of the Court in their delight at dumbfounding him through protean elusiveness. Even Leni, who by virtue of her lust presents herself in a comparatively monolithic fashion, turns out to be a person of treacherous depth. She leads K. away from his would-be lawyer with the challenge, "Must you always be thinking of your case?" (Chap. 6, p. 132). She changes direction in her next admonishment: " '... don't be so adamant. After all, one can't defend oneself against this court; one simply has to make a confession. Just make your confession the first opportunity you have' " (Chap. 6, p. 132). And she comes full circle in a comment she makes on another occasion: " 'You haven't been to see us in so long, even the lawyer has been asking after you. Don't neglect your case!" (Chap. 8, p. 205). But behind these mere inconsistencies of speech is the riddle itself of her oppressively militant desire for K. At first she fairly compels K. to regard himself as the unique object of a glorious passion, though after a while, especially in the light of Lawyer Huld's none-too-delicate hints, she emerges as a curiously selective nymphomaniac who asks of her men only that they be "accused." (Whether Huld is hinting at the truth or instead trying to humiliate K. is another insoluble question.) And finally there is Fräulein Bürstner, the perennially fascinating "little typist." Later on I shall deal closely with her role in the plot of *The Trial*. For now, as far as her character is concerned, I think it can be said that K. experiences her first as a vaguely loose seductress, then as a woman mindful of her reputation and strict in matters of morality, and, ultimately, as the lame, everyday Miss Montag (German for Monday). In short, the women are bewildering. And yet the distress they bring K. into does not really differ in kind from that which he feels in his encounters with his uncle, lawyer, etc.: all are open characters, people who worry K. because he cannot define them.

Elsa and the assistant manager are the only conventional characters in *The Trial*, for they alone submit to the control of K.'s reason. Then again, they are both representatives of the business world, which is ordered by reason. But with his arrest K. has become aware of, and captivated by, another world, one which is so little amenable to reason that a bank executive's perceptions of it resemble those of "an idiot." I use Lukács' term, but with reservations, since I think most of us would admit to being, at least now and then, almost as idiotic as K. in our nonofficial contacts with other people. Only when reading "for pleasure" do we expect that isolated gestures and chance speeches will prove to be reliable indicators of character; in real life we recognize that the deeper our involvement with a particular person is, the more laborious and protracted the process of definition and understanding is apt to become. But, by confining us to the insights of his emphatically nonomniscient hero, Kafka makes of us the unaccustomed demand that we apply the same process to characters in a book, i.e., he evokes the pains and embarrassments associated with reality instead of affording us the pleasures of fiction. The demand itself is perhaps not entirely without literary precedent; it is rather in consistently denying us the chance to satisfy it that Kafka's technique is truly unparalleled. Ortega y Gasset writes of Dostoyevsky:

> Not only does he refuse clearly to define his figures beforehand, but as their behavior varies from stage to stage they display one facet after another and thus seem to be shaped and assembled step by step before our eyes. Instead of stylizing the characters Dostoyevsky is pleased to have their ambiguity appear as unmitigatedly as in real life, and the reader, proceeding by trial and error, apprehensive all the time of making a mistake, must work out as best he can the actual character of these fickle creatures. . . . Dostoyevsky is a "realist" not because he uses the material of life, but because he uses the form of life.[3]

The similarity is apparent. Nevertheless, Kafka goes further; his work is distinguished by an excess of rigor. For Dostoyevsky allows us to "work out" his characters at least as well as we might in real life, while Kafka—or his witness Joseph K.—involves us in a process of definition that is not merely protracted but instead endless. Admittedly, this comparison still leaves us the option of dismissing Kafka's evocation of reality as enforced idiocy. We have, however, yet to consider the extenuating circumstances in Joseph K.'s case, the causes of his singular incapacitation, in a word, the significance of his arrest. If the trial which has so reduced him is relevant to our own condition, it is difficult, and certainly dishonorable, to discredit his testimony by declaring him mentally incompetent.

The Plot of Arrest

It is often said that K.'s vision of reality is the product of a guilty conscience. The formula is inviting but rather vague, especially since we share K.'s ignorance of the law he has broken. Pronouncements on his guilt are at best conjectures. On the other hand, we do know that K. comes to accept the idea of being tried

[3] *"Notes on the Novel,"* in *The Dehumanization of Art,* Anchor Books, Doubleday, New York, pp. 72–73.

and thus exposes himself to proceedings which, it seems fair to assume, are the effective agent of the transformation of his consciousness. Accordingly, I prefer to speak of K.'s vision as the product, or equivalent, of his punishment for some indeterminate crime of which he can never clear himself. I subscribe, that is, to the prison chaplain's remark that "The judgment doesn't come all at once, the proceedings gradually turn into the judgment" (Chap. 9, p. 253). K.'s trial is itself his punishment. But what exactly are the "proceedings"; in what exactly does the fearful burden that obliterates K.'s reason consist? On the surface of things—precious little. There are, after all, only three instances in the novel of direct and official intervention by the Court: the first, K.'s arrest—which turns out to be a largely pro forma affair since K. is subsequently allowed to do whatever he wishes; the second, K.'s first and only hearing—at which K. does virtually all the talking and so does not seem to suffer anything; the third, K.'s execution—which stands in no apparent causal relation to what has gone before. In fact, up to the very moment of his execution there is no earthly reason for K. to take the trial seriously; he repeatedly calls it a "joke," a "nothing," and not a single thing that happens forces him to change his mind. But, of course, without realizing it, he does change his mind, or rather makes up his mind as soon as he is arrested to treat the trial as a matter of life and death. "It astonished K.—at least, following the train of thought of the guards it astonished him—that they had driven him into his room and had left him alone here, where he certainly had manifold opportunities to kill himself" (Chap. 1, p. 17). Surely an incongruously grave reaction, no matter how inauspicious a beginning the arrest has given to his thirtieth birthday. Despite his show of composure, K. has been terrified by his arrest. Evidently he senses from the outset that he has been plunged into an existence so taxing as to be an education and argument for death. After K. has been informed that he is on trial there is, in effect, no need for the Court to intervene. It all but withdraws from the case with a mock declaration of *nolo contendere*, indicating that there is indeed nothing to fight about, since it is expected that the defendant will have the good sense to condemn himself.

Perhaps all that deters K. from suicide is his intermittent refusal to recognize that he is on trial. As for the most part the Court doesn't meddle in his affairs in any obvious way, he is at a loss to figure out just what has gone wrong with his life and is supported by the hope for a return to normality. Here, however, Kafka cannot blind us to his hero's confusion. With the book's end we realize that the peculiarities of K.'s post-arrest existence derive not from a momentary malaise but from a "sickness unto death." And, in comparing his life with our own, we have already discovered one of these fatal peculiarities, the fact that K. can no longer come to a conclusion about the character of anyone he meets. This, I think, discloses a good deal of the meaning of the arrest. K.'s thought processes have been arrested or, what amounts to the same thing, directed toward an infinite goal. Conclusions are no longer possible. And on at least one occasion K. himself senses that this is precisely what has occured: that somehow his being on trial has compelled him to engage in an infinite examination of his life, an examination which he can work at until he dies and still never complete.

> Thoughts of his trial no longer left him in peace. He had often considered the possibility of drawing up a written defense and handing it in to the Court. In this document he intended to present a brief description of his life and a commentary on every event that was at all significant, setting forth the reasons he had acted the way he had, and indicating whether these actions according to his present opinion were reprehensible or praiseworthy and the grounds on which he based his present opinion. (Chap. 7, p. 137)
> . . . the affidavit simply had to be drawn up. If he couldn't find any time for it in the office, which was quite probable, he'd just have to work on it in the nighttime when he was at home. And if even his nights didn't suffice, he'd have to take a leave of absence. . . . The plan would, to be sure, amount to a practically endless piece of work. Without having an unusually anxious temperament one could still easily come to the belief that it would be impossible ever to complete it . . . because in his ignorance of the actual accusation and, beyond that, of all its possible ramifications he would have to recall to his

memory his entire life in its smallest details and events, present
it and examine it from all sides. And besides, what a sorry task
this would be. It would perhaps be fitting to occupy him after
he had been pensioned and his mind grown childish, perhaps
then it could help him to while away the long days. But now
when K. needed all his attention for his work, when every hour
went so quickly because he was still moving upwards and already threatened the position of the assistant manager, and
when he wanted to enjoy the short evenings and nights as a
young man, just now he had to go to work on the composition of
his affidavit. Again K.'s thoughts broke off in complaints. (Chap.
7, pp. 154–55)

It is difficult to interrupt Kafka, especially when he is busy forging the chains of necessity and despair by which he pulls his hero
to death. Fortunately, K.'s musings end of themselves—significantly enough not with a conclusion, but with complaints and exhaustion. At any rate, this passage is perhaps the clearest exposition of K.'s baleful dilemma, as well as of the debilitating frenzy
it has driven him into. It is no wonder that he never gets around
to writing this affidavit: apparently the sort of examination required would, rather than inform his life, preclude all further en-
joyable living. Instead he roams about the city looking for outside
help, only to find that even in talks with his "advisors" examination conditions are in full force, that here too nothing can be
determined. So it is that existence becomes a trial. A trial without
end since, as K. realizes, even finishing the affidavit—if that were
possible—would be just a beginning.

> Wouldn't a careful defense mean—and anything else was
> pointless—wouldn't a careful defense mean the necessity of re-
> moving himself from everything else as far as possible . . . and
> how could he succeed in that at the bank. It wasn't simply a
> matter of the affidavit, for which a leave of absence might per-
> haps have sufficed—although requesting a leave of absence just
> at this moment would have been very daring in itself—it was
> a matter of an entire trial, whose length was incalculable. What
> an obstacle had suddenly been thrown in K.'s path. (Chap. 7,
> p. 160)

Whatever K. does throughout the book—little as it is—can best be considered an inevitably unsuccessful detour around this "obstacle."

This then is the substance of the arrest: K.'s career, all forward motion, has been checked by a fall into the bottomless pit of self-analysis and self-justification invariably associated with an earnest *apologia pro vita sua.* The predicament of Kafka's stunned thirty-year-old is reminiscent of an even more celebrated *crise du trente:* "In the middle of the journey of our life I came to myself within a dark wood where the straight way was lost. Ah, how hard a thing it is to tell of that wood, savage and harsh and dense. . . . So bitter is it that death is hardly more." But K., of course, never emerges from hell and so cannot be expected to "give some account of the good" to be found there. For him there is only the torture and the shame: ". . . it was as if the shame were going to outlive him" (Chap. 10, p. 272). Not even the execution, the humiliating "outcome" of the proceedings, releases K. from his examination. On the one hand, his former life—his total involvement in the politics of commercial success, his dispassionately hygienic relationship with Elsa, his lack of commitment to anyone other than himself—collapses under the scrutiny implied by the arrest; on the other, the scrutiny itself robs him of the peace of mind necessary for the establishment of a new life. In depicting the impressions of a person thus scrutinized Kafka has constructed a world where space is either dizzying extension or total constriction, where the flow of time only makes itself felt as an increase in exhaustion. "The unexamined life is worthless": Kafka agrees, merely proposing the codicil that examination excludes life.

The principle out of which this construction develops is, as I have said, point of view. K.'s view is not passive; he confounds— no doubt less happily than most of us—outside reality with projections from within. The process itself is recognizably human, sufficiently so as to obviate most of the clinical commentary. Since K. refuses to stay put in his room, he is tried on the street. From the morning of his thirtieth birthday on he conceives of himself as being on display, exposed to countless more or less brutal observers who are only too pleased to carry on the examination for him. He suffers most intensely from this exposure on those occasions when he feels the trial full upon him, whenever, that is, he is unable to distract himself with work at the bank or spurious machinations "against the Court." Accordingly, in the moment of arrest, having been overtaken by the proceedings while in bed, he posits the densest cluster of examiners to be found anywhere in the book. In answer to his impatient ring for breakfast there appear the two guards (in the German, *Wächter*, related to the English verb to watch), next his landlady peeks in to see what is going on, then an inspector summons him, and finally the three men accompanying the inspector reveal themselves to be K.'s colleagues—spies imported from the bank. Evidently the Court is taking no chances. But even before these official confrontations, officers of the arrest have already announced themselves, enforcing the examination the moment K. opens his eyes. "K. waited a little while [for the maid to bring the breakfast], glanced from his pillow at the old lady who lived opposite him and who was observing him with a curiosity quite unusual for her, then however, at once disconcerted and hungry, he rang" (Chap. 1, p. 9). She is soon joined by two equally inquisitive companions, and this gallery of spectators pursues K. from room to room (and finally out onto the street) with insupportably unabashed stares.

> Through the open window he again caught sight of the old woman, who with truly senile curiosity had stepped to the opposite window, in order to follow all the further developments. (Chap. 1, p. 11)

> . . . across the way he saw the old woman, who had dragged to the window an even older man, whom she was holding around the waist. (Chap. 1, p. 16)

> The two old ones again posted themselves at the next window, but their party had been increased, for behind them, towering above them, stood a man with his shirt unbuttoned on his chest who was pressing and twirling his reddish goatee. (Chap. 1, p. 19)

> Across the way the group was still at the window, and seemed only now that K. had stepped forward a little disturbed

in the peace of their view. The old ones wanted to move away, but the man behind them calmed them. "And just look at those spectators," K. cried to the Inspector and pointed them out with his finger. "Get away from there," he called over to them. And the trio did immediately move back a few steps, the old ones even went behind the man, who covered them with his broad body. . . . But they didn't disappear entirely; instead they only seemed to be waiting for the moment when they could approach the window again unnoticed. "Oppressive, inconsiderate people!" K. said as he turned around. (Chap. 1, p. 23)

In this manner unwanted but inescapable observation becomes the leitmotif of the arrest, setting the composition of *The Trial* in crescendos of discomfort.

We note that K. makes a certain show of indignation at being so closely watched, but his remonstrances remain half-hearted. Evidently he has more than an inkling of what this arrest is all about. He flirts with the idea of suicide and even tells the inspector that, while he has been surprised by the Court's invasion of his privacy, he is "by no means very surprised." In principle he consents to the proceedings—a fact which Kafka demonstrates with the clarity of the burlesque in K.'s reaction to the guards' insistence that he don a black jacket.

"Let me alone, damn it," cried K., who had already been pushed back to his clothes closet; "if you fall upon me in bed you can't expect to find me in formal attire . . . ridiculous formalities!" he was still muttering as he nevertheless picked up a jacket from the chair and held it out for a while with both hands, as if he were submitting it to the judgment of the guards. They shook their heads. "It has to be a black jacket," they said. K. threw the jacket to the floor and said—he didn't know himself in what sense he was saying it—"This isn't the capital hearing yet, you know." The guards smiled but repeated their "It has to be a black jacket." "If that will speed up the matter it's all right with me," K. said. . . . Secretly, however, he believed that he had really managed to accelerate the whole business by making the guards forget to force him to take a bath. He watched to see if they still might remember, but, naturally, it never even occurred to them. . . . (Chap. 1, pp. 18–19)

In anticipating the possibility that the inspector may not content himself with an analysis of externals, K. emphatically places himself at the head of the Court. That he runs to unscheduled hearings is as little a mystery as, say, Raskolnikov's inadvertent pursuit of Porfiry.

Unfortunately he has nothing to confess, at least—since his life is apparently his crime—nothing in particular. No one could finish the examination K. has begun, and yet it could only be of value as a finite preparation for a new life. Thus the promise is at once its own denial. The torment arising from this paradox comes clear in K.'s midnight meeting with Fräulein Bürstner, which Kafka includes in the first chapter as a corollary to the arrest. For K.'s awakening interest in the typist, a movement of his soul certainly more profound than that which results in the weekly trips to Elsa, is doubtless among the efficient causes of the examination. However, K. cannot satisfy his examiners; the regenerating interest involves him in an annihilating condemnation. Fräulein Bürstner encourages him to display himself but slams the door in his face in response to what she sees: K. is hooted off the stage before his show has fairly begun.

The first mention made of the typist establishes her central position in the proceedings initiated by K.'s court. The inspector has stationed himself in her room. And again, to judge from the tenor of his thoughts, K. is "by no means very surprised."

> This room was, as K. well knew, occupied by Fräulein Bürstner, a typist, who customarily went to work very early and returned late, and with whom K. had scarcely exchanged more than the civilities. Now her night table had been moved from beside her bed into the center of the room and served as the table of inquiry behind which the Inspector was sitting. . . . Three young men [the colleagues from the bank] stood in a corner of the room and were looking at Fräulein Bürstner's photographs. . . . On the handle of the open window there hung a white blouse. (Chap. 1, p. 19)

The phrase "as K. well knew" argues a type of concern not usually directed toward casual acquaintances; moreover, K.'s fascination with the furnishings of the room—the bed, the table, pictures, and blouse—pre-empts his attention from the inspector, veils his eyes to the identity of the three young men. And, as might be expected, on his return from the bank he postpones a visit with Elsa and waits up half the night in the hope of apologizing to Fräulein Bürstner for the "disorder" he has brought her room into, despite his fatigue, despite his landlady's assurance that she has already removed every sign of the disorder. But, for reasons he will not admit to himself, K. attaches enormous value to a confession to the typist and is not to be deterred. As it turns out, she is not at all adverse to a friendly chat with the bank executive, and even takes great pleasure in her role as examiner.

> "You see," said K., "you don't have much experience in legal matters." "No, that's true," Fräulein Bürstner said, "and I have often regretted it, for I should like to know everything, and legal matters interest me especially. The Court does have a strange fascination, don't you think? But I am sure to increase my knowledge in this field, for I am joining the clerical staff of a law office next month. . . . But if I am to become your advisor I will have to know what your case is all about." (Chap. 1, p. 38)

K. proceeds to set up the arrest scene, naturally taking the part of the inspector, and shouts "Joseph K." so loudly that he wakes the landlady's nephew, who knocks on Fräulein Bürstner's wall. Once again K. has created a "disorder." And now the easy-going typist reacts sternly; ordering him out of her room, she contemptuously denies K. the chance to expiate his guilt: "I can bear the responsibility for everything that happens in my room, and, to be sure, before all" (Chap. 1, p. 41). Of course, as we recall from the events of the morning, this is precisely what K. cannot do. Aglow with innocence she illumines K.'s guilt—and leaves him lost in it. K. essays a few desperate caresses, but is firmly pushed out of the room. This is almost the last we see of Fräulein Bürstner. Having informed him of his guilt, she becomes, like the Court, inaccessible to his pleas of defense, by retreating behind—or, for all intents and purposes, turning into—Fräulein Montag. K. believes that he catches sight of her on the evening of his execution, and the belief suffices to make him go along quietly to his death. "K.

wasn't at all concerned whether it really was Fräulein Bürstner, he simply became immediately conscious of the pointlessness of his resistance . . . he directed them [the assassins] towards the path the woman was taking, not that he had any desire to catch up with her, not that he had any desire to see her for as long as possible, but simply so as not to forget the warning that she meant for him" (Chap. 10, p. 268). The warning is that he will never be acquitted and so had best stop trying to defend himself.

In illustrating "the pointlessness of resistance" *The Trial* becomes the chronicle of one year of senseless activity. Do what he may, K. cannot alter the verdict; he loses his case, as the proverb goes, in having it. The plot of *The Trial*, therefore, is a single event: the arrest. The examined life is a condition, not a process. It is true that K. refuses to acknowledge his imprisonment in this static existence and gladly climbs endless flights of stairs to create for himself the illusion of motion. But since the stairs naturally lead to the ubiquitous chancelleries of the examining magistrates, K. might as well have been sitting in a cell blackening reams with the introduction to his *apologia*. In short, wherever K. goes he brings the tedium of his perpetually unfinished task with him. That he prefers to run rather than sit is, I suppose, understandable—after all, he prides himself on being a practical man, better versed in manipulation than reflection. Infinity, however, does not admit of progress: beyond the numbers of the chapters, there is nothing sequential about K.'s experience. The episodes are—each one in its own right—perfectly convincing demonstrations of futility, and as such interchangeable. If we do sense, nevertheless, a certain irreversibility in the proceedings, this is due not to anything that happens but instead to K.'s steadily mounting fatigue. So arises the fearful symmetry of the arrest and the execution—the correspondence of dates, the matching pairs of guards and assassins, the two disheartening encounters with Fräulein Bürstner: nothing has changed except that K. has grown tired, too tired to dismiss the idea of suicide. The only "function" of the intervening chapters is to embody his exhaustion, in uniform installments.

This is not to say that they do not make for interesting and even peculiarly suspenseful reading. For it is a quixotic spirit of enterprise that propels K. through his days of disappointment, and we, lacking the admonitions of any clear-sighted commentator, do not see the windmills until the hero feels their battering blows. Indeed a good part of Kafka's art consists in the construction of campaigns which commence with all signs pointing to an imminent victory, gradually lose momentum, and finally come to the abrupt stop of total defeat. K. must succeed, cannot at any rate lose, and is nonetheless routed. As an example: how can we resist K.'s surge of confidence at the beginning of his first hearing, the thrill of his certainty that he is about to scatter this dusty court of feeble old men to the winds? K. assumes, with every conceivable justification in his and, therefore, our eyes, that at the very worst no more than half of the Court is under the examining magistrate's control, that the men on the right side of the room constitute a rebellious party eagerly awaiting that dignitary's downfall. K. has only to announce his presence in a defiant tone to earn their enthusiastic applause. The examining magistrate squirms and acts with affected calm:

> "You are a house painter?" "No," said K., "rather the first manager of a great bank." This answer was greeted by the members of the party on the right with a laughter so hearty that K. found himself laughing along with them. The people rocked back and forth with their hands pressed to their knees, shaking as with violent coughing spasms. Even a few people in the gallery laughed. The examining magistrate had already become quite angry and, since he was probably powerless against the people on the main floor, tried to take revenge by threatening those in the gallery. . . . (Chap. 2, p. 54)

The Court does not even seem to have apprehended the right man. And yet the judge does not apologize, the session is not adjourned, the trial goes on! This in itself is enough to give us pause. Clearly, K. has become enmeshed in truly maniacal proceedings; what he says is bound to be irrelevant. But K. still thinks there is something to be gained from arguing (he already has attracted a large group of supporters; perhaps he really will be able to convince the entire court), and, listening to his incisive, classically organized speech, we cannot but have the highest of hopes for him. " 'I have no wish to impress you with a beautiful speech . . . and I probably couldn't even if I wanted to. The Honorable Examining Magistrate is no doubt a much better speaker. That is, after all, part of his vocation. All that I wish is simply an open discussion of an open grievance. Listen . . .' " (Chap. 2, p. 57). Employing Mark Antony's ever effective rhetorical device, K. exhibits fine, invincible form. The examining magistrate hides his head in his notebook, and K. goes on to describe with withering contempt the manner of his arrest, the corrupt guards, the arrogant inspector, the inexcusable invasion of Fräulein Bürstner's room, etc. That he has in fact won over the entire assembly, the faction of the left as well as the right, seems certain: "There was immediate silence, so completely did K. dominate the assembly. The men were no longer shouting at each other, they had even stopped applauding to show their approval, but they all seemed either already convinced or very close to it" (Chap. 2, p. 60).

Of course, in *The Trial* things are rarely what they seem. There occurs now a peripety so gross that we must believe that K. has been up to this point indulging in a daydream. His speech is interrupted by the noisy antics of the scrubwoman and her law-student friend; and it should be noted that this disorderly couple, in attitude and deportment, plainly rehearses the disorder that K. occasioned in Fräulein Bürstner's room. The attendant uproar is the explosion of his case; a remembrance or symbol of his crime suffices to block and nullify his advance. "K.'s first impulse was to rush across the room. He was sure that everyone else would also be anxious to have order restored and the couple at least removed, but in the first rows before him the men stood fast, no one moved and no one let him through. On the contrary, people blocked his way. . . . K. wasn't actually thinking about the couple any longer. It seemed to him that his freedom was being restricted, that the arrest was becoming all too real, and he recklessly jumped down from the podium" (Chap. 2, p. 62).

But the Court is only performing its duty, physically enforcing the arrest by confining K. in a consideration—here visual—of his guilt. Until he is ripe for death K. inveighs against the manifest unfairness of the proceedings—quite rightly, for the rigor of the examination exceeds that which can be humanly endured. But this critique is tangential; in no way does it mitigate "the guilt that attracts the Court"—and so the trial goes on. And, as if in corroboration of the hopelessness of his endeavors, his staging of the assembly—the factional strife, the cowering judge—disintegrates, i.e., K. is compelled to lose even his optical illusions. "Under their beards, however—that was the real discovery that K. made—there shone on their coat collars medals of various sizes and colors. All had these medals, as far as he could see. All were on the same side, these ostensible parties of the right and left; and as he suddenly turned around he saw the same medal on the examining magistrate's collar, who, his hands folded in his lap, was calmly looking down at the scene on the floor" (Chap. 2, p. 62). Although severely shaken, K. still tries to make an honorable retreat. He elbows his way through the room, shouting virulent condemnations of the Court as he goes. But the judge, assuming for the first time full magisterial dignity, is waiting for him at the door: "One moment please . . . I merely want to call your attention to the fact—it is conceivable that you are not yet aware of it—that you have deprived yourself today of all the advantages which a defendant customarily derives from his hearing" (Chap. 2, p. 63). Aside from his perhaps intentionally ridiculous question, these are the first words the judge has uttered—and, in truth, how well, how ominously he is able to speak! What seemed at first an opportunity, then an insidious practical joke, becomes at the last a defeat not to be taken lightly. The judge's concluding remarks contribute a basic beat to the rhythm of *The Trial*. K.'s adventures are not simply pointless—as a fillip to his despair they invariably end with the suggestion that dealings of great consequence have been mismanaged, that all must be resumed and, if possible, made good. Accordingly, in the first lines of the following chapter, K. indicates that he feels obliged to return to the dusty, muggy attic, even though he departed from the last session with the cry: "'You can keep your hearings!'" even though no new hearing has been scheduled. Nothing has changed. As with the people he meets, so in the things he does, K. is arrested in examination and never comes to a conclusion.

It has been recognized that K. learns nothing from his experiences. Still, we might ask, what is there to be learned? Despite the courtroom debacle, K. has no choice but to persevere in the hope of discrediting the Court. He reasons, with an obvious claim to our sympathies, that no one can be required to undergo an examination that cannot be passed. And, for the most part, his helpers and advisors are sufficiently humane, or sufficiently attuned to K.'s businessman's logic, to support him in this hope, which is, perforce, an error. Neither the lawyer Huld nor the painter Titorelli exhorts K. to go into himself. Instead they outline schemes whereby the case can be handled mechanically through exploitation of the Court's defects—with influence, flattery, bribery, etc. But K. realizes that what they really mean by "handling" is the infinite prolongation he has dreaded since the morning of his arrest, that they are too much his own creatures to know anything of value. It is only in the cathedral adventure that K. appears to meet a man who rises above his own level, who gives every sign of knowing precisely what K. must do to have done with his trial. Again, perhaps to an even greater extent than in the hearing room, K. encounters a scene of boundless promise. There is the overtly religious setting, the fact that an irregular sermon has been prepared for his own individual benefit, and, above all, the presence itself of the commanding, reassuring prison chaplain. For the very concept of a chaplain implies mercy and spiritual guidance. And it soon begins to appear that K.'s priest is eminently worthy of his vocation: he seems positively seized with the righteous mission of retrieving K. from the labyrinth of his doubts, suspicions, and impracticable plans. In an attempt to find an everyday explanation for the extraordinary (his only means of maintaining his sanity thus far in the proceedings) K. expresses his surprise that the chaplain has been waiting for him at the cathedral. "'Never mind about that!' the priest said. . . . 'You are thought to be guilty. Your case may never advance beyond the lower courts'" (Chap. 9, p. 252). K. speaks of the resources still at his disposal. "'You search too much for outside help,' the priest said disapprovingly, 'and especially from women. Don't you realize that that isn't the true help?'" (Chap. 9, p. 253). K. complains of the corruption of the Court, the lasciviousness of the judges. "Then the priest screamed down at K.: 'Can't you see two steps ahead of you?' There was anger in the cry, though at the same time it sounded like the thoughtless and involuntary scream of a person who sees someone falling and is himself terrified" (Chap. 9, p. 254). This severity stands out in relief from all the falsely comforting rationalizations that K. has devised and solicited; he is at once impressed and encouraged. The chaplain, however, has ruled out K.'s only conceivable defense, the humanistic critique of *The Trial:* " 'But I am not guilty,' K. said. 'It is a mistake. How can any man be guilty? After all, we are all simply men here, one as much as the other.' 'That is true,' the priest said, 'but that is what the guilty always say'" (Chap. 9, p. 253). Even yet, K. retains the belief that he is about to be given "decisive and practical advice, not on how the trial might be influenced, but rather on how to break out of the trial, evade it, and live outside of it" (Chap. 9, p. 254). Surely, as K. quite plausibly thinks to himself, if such a possibility exists, the chaplain would be the only court official with the kindness to disclose it.

But the chaplain either cannot or will not be so kind. Instead he offers a parable distended with an opaque commentary that knows no end of scholastic involution. (Or so we might call it, though it is more likely that Kafka was employing a talmudic model, something along the lines of the disquisition into the egg the hen laid on the Sabbath.) Once again the hero's downfall is engineered by an intrusion of the examination; for the physical arrest of the courtroom Kafka substitutes an arrest of mind. Of course, the parable itself augurs a definitive solution since the predicament of the man from the country is clearly K.'s own, and yet no solution is forthcoming: the chaplain simply explains it away. There has been a great deal of critical discussion about this singularly unhelpful commentary, a fact which Kafka allows the chaplain to anticipate: " 'You mustn't pay too much attention to the commentaries. They are often simply an expression of despair that the writing is immutable'" (Chap. 9, p. 260). But, perhaps in deference to the secrets of the cloth, the commentators have, for the most part, failed to see the commentary for what it is—a game of mystification. It has gone virtually unnoticed that the chaplain declines to indicate the relevance of the parable to K.'s condition. Far from explaining what the man from the country might have done to *move*, to advance beyond the gate into the "Law" (which is what K. himself ought to do to make progress in his trial), the chaplain fastens K.'s attention on the "doorkeeper" —the object of the fears that have paralyzed K. and kept him under arrest. There is no need to go over in detail the contradictory arguments in which he involves both K. and himself: the doorkeeper is in his every sentence, the man in few, the meaning of the Law (the reason for its inaccessibility) in none. Again it might be said that with this commentary the chaplain reveals himself to be another of K.'s creatures, an extension of K.'s ignorance of the Law—the ignorance which K. rightly deems responsible for his inability to write his *apologia*. K.'s priest cannot be a priest, cannot lighten K.'s burden with inspirational references to the great, tormented but saved, religious apologists, because in the world of *The Trial* there are no first principles to give direction, purpose, and limit to the examined life. All that he can do is participate in the process of K.'s exhaustion: "K. was too tired to reckon with all the implications of the story, such trains of thought were new to him . . . the simple story had become monstrous, he wanted to shake himself free of it . . ." (Chap. 9, p. 264). There is no begrudging the commentators their interpretations of the commentary; it should, however, be recognized that Kafka's contribution to "the metaphysics of the door" (Buber's phrase) is above all an artistic act, since in making us follow this tedious argument he does not explain, but rather forces us to share, the experience of arrest. We expect a revelation, and are immersed in an interminable, bibleless Talmud. It is, admittedly, a trick: precisely the sort of trick that reality continually plays upon those who have lost sight of "first principles." In the gloom of his thoughts about his affidavit, in the darkness of the cathedral, K.'s incapacitation becomes a representation of the human condition.

Kafka's eschewal of events that would advance his hero's story is, then, yet another aspect of his evocation of reality. We need not ourselves have suffered the extremity of K.'s distress to find life essentially plotless. We can only turn to fiction if we wish to splash about in a steady stream of significant happenings—and to a rather puerile brand of fiction at that. For, to speak with Ortega, the novel is (or should be) a "sluggish genre," [4] fitted to the slow, meticulous analysis and exhibition of the stuff of human experience. The masters of the form have, in fact, necessarily re-veled in the presentation of existence in slow motion, but Kafka presents an arrest. What this difference amounts to comes clear in Erich Auerbach's remarks on one of the great traditional realists, Flaubert:

> [In *Madame Bovary*] Nothing happens, but that nothing has become a heavy, oppressive, threatening something. . . . [Flaubert] organizes into compact and unequivocal discourse the confused impressions of discomfort which arise in Emma at the sight of the room, the meal, her husband . . . he seldom narrates events which carry the action quickly forward; in a series of pure pictures—pictures transforming the nothingness of listless and uniform days into an oppressive condition of repugnance, boredom, false hopes, paralyzing disappointments, and piteous fears—a gray and random human destiny moves toward its end.[5]

In *The Trial*, by contrast, a great deal *does* happen, which, however, leads to nothing—precisely because K. is under arrest, i.e., because his "hopes, disappointments, fears" do not merely color "pictures" of the outside world but are instead acted and bodied out with such insistence as to block his perception of the outside world. Or, more simply, his feelings and thoughts phys-ically constitute his new world. Strangely enough, however, we can find our way around in it. Although point of view thus un-leashed threatens the extravagances of expressionism, K.'s world, while confusing, does not bear the expressionistic aspect of inchoate images, jumbled outcries, and bizarrely shifting scenery. There is an ordering principle that works upon K.'s vision, and it is the same one that Flaubert applies to Emma Bovary's much

[4] Ortega y Gasset, *ibid.*, p. 60.
[5] Erich Auerbach, *Mimesis.* Anchor Books, Doubleday, New York, 1957, p. 431.

tamer sort of "confused impressions of discomfort": *language*. In the manner of a graphic recording device, Kafka's prose both registers and transforms into pattern the slightest beats of K.'s frightfully erratic pulse. The results are at once accurate and easily scanned. And, in this sense, language is the ultimate enforcer of the plot of arrest: the transcription of K.'s frantic pacing establishes the walls of his cell.

I have already had occasion to speak of the rhythm of *The Trial*. It is a rhythm not of motion, but of attempts at (or wishes for) motion. And as such it is a matter of individual sentences rather than completed events. Thus to understand how it is, for instance, that all three of Titorelli's acquittal proposals almost, but not quite, vanish into thin air, we can only return again and again to Titorelli's assurances, the exceptions he takes to them, his exceptions to his exceptions, and so on. K. hopes, becomes disappointed, tires, and—as always—files for future reference (hopes again). But there is nothing chaotic about these currents of emotion; on the contrary, they assume in Titorelli's remarks the form of a well-defined, if inevitably dizzying, whirlpool. We have, consequently, no difficulty in becoming immersed in *The Trial*, though, for the same reason, we cannot easily get out except by determining exactly how the language sets us so regularly spinning. Kafka allows the painter an illuminating comment on the process. " 'Aren't you struck by the fact that I almost speak like a jurist? It is the uninterrupted contact with the gentlemen of the Court that has made me that way' " (Chap. 7, p. 182). The fact is that everyone in the book (including K., naturally) talks "like a jurist"; i.e., Kafka edits whatever is thought and said with a view toward displaying his hero's infinite torment in a finite, and so comprehensible, frame. The frame is, as we have seen, unmistakably circular; "stream of consciousness," confined to the logic of K.'s examination, churns in the orderly circles of a whirlpool. Of course, it is K.'s world and Kafka makes every effort to conceal his presence in it. Nevertheless, the editor can be recognized, especially by virtue of his understandable love of concessive conjunctions, words which promise to continue, but actually curve or reverse the course of thought. K.'s recital of Lawyer Huld's "prog-

/ 209

ress reports" provides perhaps the most sustained and concentrated stretch of such trial talk. The rhythm is indicated at the
outset; "Now and again he gave K. a few empty admonishments.
Speeches as useless as they were boring, for which K. had no intention of paying a single penny in the final bill. When the lawyer
believed he had humbled K. to a sufficient extent, he usually
again began to cheer him up a little" (Chap. 7, p. 138). What
follows is roughly the final tenth of these "admonishments,"
which K. calls "empty" but obviously cannot put out of his mind:

> The affidavit, as mentioned, had not yet been handed in,
> but there wasn't any great hurry about that. Of much greater
> importance were the introductory discussions with the officials
> involved in the case, and these had already taken place, although,
> it should openly be confessed, with varying degrees of success.
> For the time being it would be better not to go into the details,
> since K. could only be unfavorably affected by them, and made
> either all too confident or all too anxious, but this much could
> be said, that some had expressed very favorable views and had
> shown themselves to be willing to help in every way, while
> others had spoken less favorably, but by no means entirely de-
> nied their assistance. The results had been, accordingly, in
> general quite gratifying, though nothing of importance could be
> gathered from them, since all preliminary proceedings began in
> about the same way and, beyond question, only the further
> developments would reveal the value of these preliminary
> proceedings. In any case, as yet nothing was lost. . . . If K.,
> quite exhausted from all this talk, occasionally made remarks to
> the effect that, even in consideration of all the difficulties, the
> case was progressing very slowly, he received the reply that the
> case was progressing not at all slowly, though, to be sure, they
> would by now have been much further along if K. had had the
> sense to consult a lawyer earlier. But he had neglected to do so,
> and this omission would occasion still further difficulties, and
> not just temporal ones either. (Chap. 7, pp. 149–50)

The changes of direction, hinging on "though," "while," "by no
means," "in any case," "to be sure," and the like, are here so pronounced as to be comic: we are amused and so can resist, at least
partially, the hypnotic periodicity of the lawyer's old, unending

song. But K. is denied the distance of laughter; attending to such words as the ciphers of his fate, he invariably succumbs to the spell. The only respite comes during banking hours, though even the talk of the noninvolved, the businessmen, takes on a suspiciously "juristic" tone when K. is the listener. There are, of course, important differences. As the assistant manager pirates away one of K.'s best clients, he employs a commercial variant of the Court's tactics: ". . . [the assistant manager] brought the manufacturer into obvious embarrassment with a telling retort, then, however, immediately rescued him from his discomfort by taking exception to his own remark, and finally invited him into his office where they could together conclude the transaction" (Chap. 7, p. 158). "Conclude the transaction": truly stunning words in the context of *The Trial*. Quite intentionally Kafka here echoes Huld's song and *ends* it, placing his hero's misery in linguistic relief.

Such is the rhythm of the examination that goes on wherever K. goes, in the courtroom, in Huld's bedchamber, in Titorelli's studio, in the cathedral. A rather different rhythm, however, obtains in the attempted answers of the accused, one which is apparent in K.'s thoughts on his affidavit (see page 194) but perhaps even more distinct in the barks and bleats of the man whom five years of trial have reduced to Huld's dog and Leni's sheep—the one-time Herr (Merchant) Block. " 'Aside from Huld,' the merchant said hesitantly and in a tone as if he were confessing something dishonorable, 'I have some other lawyers.' . . . 'It isn't allowed. Least of all is one allowed to hire in addition to a so-called official lawyer the "unofficial lawyers." And that's just what I have done, I have aside from Huld five unofficial lawyers. . . . Right now I am in the process of hiring a sixth. . . . I need them all. . . . Above all I don't want to lose my case, that goes without saying. As a result, I can't afford to overlook any means of help. Even though in any given instance the help promised seems quite negligible, even then I can't do without it' " (Chap. 8, p. 208). The image indicated here is that of a desk calculator that has been posed the problem of 1 divided by 0: it will shake itself to pieces spewing out ribbons of hopelessly inadequate 9's, unless someone has the kindness to unplug it and reset the controls. Whatever Block can do is, if measured against what he must do, "quite negligible"; so, sharing K.'s practical bent of mind, he naturally does whatever he can. "That goes without saying," and yet Kafka gives Block the words to say it, allows the moans and screams of despair to become articulate. Faced with the absurd problem of *The Trial*—life into examination—both the merchant and K. think and chatter a bit queerly, at times even frantically, but they never babble. So it is that the plot of arrest can be presented with inescapable immediacy: with Kafka's unobtrusive support K., though incapacitated, remains lucid.

The Milieu of Distraction

A new world is discovered by K.'s distress, but it is made to fit quite snugly into the old. Throughout the novel, with the possible exception of the nightmarish "Whipper" chapter, Kafka adheres to our notions of time and space to the point of pedantry, denying us the diversion of the wondrous, or even the attractive. Thus K.'s trial becomes an exasperatingly everyday affair; his adventures bog down in the mud of the streets. And doubtless, as has often been said, the adventures are the more "real" for all the mud, K.'s hell—like Dante's—is the more terrifying for all its earthly familiarity. Kafka does not, however, follow Dante's practice of importing empirical reality by means of deliberate, pertinent similes. He operates rather with K.'s first-hand observations, which are as random as the movements of his eyes. Though there is, consequently, never any question about what he sees, we often wonder why he sees it—why, that is, his uniformly dreary impressions of the commonplaces of city life are recorded with a labored, cinematic felicity. The fact that he perpetually complains of foul weather, chokes on soot and dust, may help to convince us of the normality of his existence, but it does not, in any obvious way, define his trial. And yet, to see nothing that delights the eye is itself a torment, one which is, I think, intimately bound up with K.'s unhappy condition. For, as he might have learned on the morning of the arrest, he no longer has anything to gain from opening his eyes: he has as we know become in a very real sense "otherworldly," and so, to his dismay, the sight of the world sickens him. He looks out the window and is enraged that nothing he sees can help him with his case. And, of course, as the rigors of his examination plunge him ever deeper into a state of nervous exhaustion, the daily matter of his life becomes an increasingly irritating distraction. Objects and sounds lose all discretion and command his attention with an impudent assault on his sensibilities. K. muses: "Didn't it all seem to be an official torture, authorized by the Court and meant to connect with and accompany his trial?" (Chap. 7, p. 161).

Accordingly, on a promenade of a balmy Sunday morning, K. suffers from exposure and shock, so dense with minutiae of annoyance is Juliusstrasse, the seat of K.'s lower Court.

> . . . (the windows) were piled high with bedding, above which the disheveled head of a woman would appear for a moment. People were shouting to one another across the street; one such shout occasioned a great deal of laughter right on top of where K. was standing. . . . A fruit hawker, who was crying his wares to the windows above, had, moving along as distractedly as K., almost knocked him to the ground with his cart. At that moment a gramophone which had doubtless been worn out in service in a better part of town began to play—murderously. . . . On his way up the steps he disturbed a great many children who were playing and who gave him nasty looks as he stepped through their ranks. "If I ever come here again," he said to himself, "I'll have to bring candy to win them over or else a stick to beat them with." Just before he reached the first floor he actually had to wait for a marble to complete its course, two small boys with the lined, snarling faces of full-grown toughs held him by his trousers. . . . (Chap. 2, p. 49)

Daylight uncovers ugliness, speech becomes shouting, music "murderous" noise, people are so many moving obstacles. This is more than a matter of estrangement: K. finds his whole being actually challenged and flayed by the outside world. He is, in fact, often afflicted with dizziness and nausea, forced to take on the Court with something of a hangover (his late-night festivities

/ 213

are themselves, of course, suppressed since the logic of *The Trial* cannot grant K. an instant of comfort, emotional or physical), and to follow the chaplain's casuistry with a severe head cold. So the examination, the metaphysical problem K.'s landlady rightly calls "a scholarly matter," is translated into visceral responses. And from the bank we are given regular reports of K.'s growing inability to keep his mind on his work, to speak with, or even listen to, his clients. But the extremity of his involuntary retreat from reality is, I think, reached on the morning of the cathedral visit when K. is confronted with the Italian businessman whom he has been assigned to lead around the city:

> When they had all sat down and begun a brief, introductory conversation, K. noticed with great discomfort that his understanding of the Italian man was a piecemeal affair at best. When the latter spoke quite calmly he understood him completely; such moments were, however, rare exceptions, most of the time the words literally streamed out of his mouth and he kept shaking his head as if in delight at the rapidity of the flow. (Chap. 9, p. 240)

Of course, as mentioned, K. has a bad cold and the Italian does insist on speaking an unfamiliar dialect. Even so, one must be at a considerable remove from the common human pursuits to so visualize an innocent chatterer. As a distraction, as something eluding control and evaluation, life abounds in the grotesque.

By the time K. goes to visit Titorelli the streets have become, if possible, still more trying.

> It was an even poorer neighborhood, the houses even darker, the alleys full of filth which slowly oozed through the melting snow . . . a hole had opened up at the base of the wall, out of which there was gushing—just as K. approached—a repulsive, yellow, smoking fluid, from which a few rats fled into the nearby sewer. At the bottom of the steps a little child lay on its stomach in the dirt and bawled, but its shrieks could scarcely be heard above the deafening din that came from a tin-smith's shop at the side of the entry. . . . (Chap. 7, p. 169)

Climbing up the airless, nearly vertical shaft of stairs to Titorelli's room, K. is again assaulted by a group of pesky children, of whose leader K. notes, as if to assure himself of his misery,

The girl, who was slightly hunchbacked and seemed scarcely thirteen years old, shoved him with her elbow and looked up at him from the side. Neither her youth nor her deformity had saved her from total debauchery. (Chap. 7, p. 170)

Once inside the studio K. finds that he is virtually unable to breathe, since the windows are of a functional, nonopening design. Titorelli chuckles over the noisy brats who have followed K. up the stairs and now keep pounding on the door, screaming that K. is too ugly to be painted. Then he makes a remark that ushers in a paradigmatic moment of horror:

... the painter bent down to him and whispered, so as not to be heard outside, into his ear: "Those girls also belong to the Court." "What?" K. asked, jerking his head to the side and staring at the painter. The latter, however, sat down again in his chair and said, half in joke, half in earnest: "After all, everything belongs to the Court." "I've never noticed that," K. said curtly. The painter's general observation had divested his reference to the girls of its unsettling content. Nevertheless, K. stared at the door for a while, behind which the girls were still sitting on the stairs. One of them had stuck a piece of straw through a crack between the boards and was slowly moving it up and down. (Chap. 7, p. 181)

Here, if anywhere, we feel K.'s eyes widening, straining in the hopeless effort to find some clue, some hint as to the significance of the proceedings. This uncanny study of moving straw is the seal of his doom: he now looks with the desperation of a man who, like Block, "cannot afford to overlook anything." K. no longer has any means of distinguishing and discarding the unimportant. There is not a single detail of his vision of unrelieved shabbiness that he dare pass over, for all has been appropriated, and invested with negative meaning, by the Court. And, for this reason, there is no background to *The Trial:* K. must dislodge and examine the smallest building blocks of experience and so the walls collapse upon him. The crush ends only when K. ceases to offer "resistance" on the evening of his willing walk to death:

The water, glittering and trembling in the moonlight, divided on either side of a small island, on which the foliage of trees and bushes rose in thick masses, as if pressed together. Beneath the trees ran gravel paths, now invisible, with convenient benches on which K. had stretched himself at ease many a summer. (Chap. 10, p. 269)

This intrusion of moonlight romanticism does not, admittedly, register a profound appreciation of nature; but, then again, it is an appreciation of the surface: a nonexamining, unreflected response to, or memory of, "ease" in life. Even K.'s city develops comforts, now that the examined life has expired in the verdict of shame.

I am inclined to regard this presentation of a milieu of distraction as one of Kafka's extremely distinctive feats. Of course, recent fiction has produced a spate of alienated heroes; and, as Auerbach writes: ". . . [the modern author] submits, much more than was done in earlier realistic works, to the random contingency of real phenomena. . . ." [6] But no other novel comes to mind where the "phenomena" are so radically disassembled into a series of precise stimuli which are not intended to function as symbols—except perhaps in Goethe's sense of a symbol being emphatically, untranslatably what it is. Further, even the term "alienation" is an inadequate label for K.'s condition, for he is, as we have seen, inordinately involved and in touch with the world around him. Everything he sees somehow belongs to him, is somehow relevant to his existence. Thus, Kafka reinstates man as the measure of all things—in order to rob him of all assurance and orientation. K.'s vision constructs a "totality," not by stylizing or rounding off reality, but rather by discovering and meticulously noting a jaggedness in experience that confirms human insufficiency. This reinstatement is inflicted upon us by Kafka's reliance on what I have called one individual's point of view and projections, the technique which he identified in a famous remark as the "representation of my dream-like inner life." [7] How is it, though, that Kafka's obviously nightmarish "inner life"—exorcised and clarified as it may be in "representation"—seems so utterly convincing? Why do so many of us find K.'s measurements of reality accurate? There are as many answers to these questions

[6] Auerbach, *ibid.*, p. 475.   [7] Tagelbucher, *Ges. Werke*, p. 420.

as there are appreciators of Kafka. Some consider K.'s year of arrest a product of one or another widespread neurosis, a definition of twentieth-century maladjustment; others deem Kafka's hero an unwitting existentialist and speak sadly of his arrest in the absurd; and so on. But with such formulations we abandon literature for "larger" matters—wrongly, as it seems to me, since Kafka employs K. as a witness, not a propagandizer of some pernicious *Weltanschauung*. To avoid K.'s assassins we may announce reservations about the metaphysics of his examination, or list the peculiarities of his psyche, etc. There remains as the guarantee of *The Trial*'s relevance the formal validity of K.'s examined life.